KOLBE

SAINT OF THE IMMACULATA

Imprimatur
✠ Most. Rev. Sean P. O'Malley OFM Cap.
Bishop of Fall River
Massachusetts, USA
March 25, 2001
Solemnity of the Annunciation

The nihil obstat and imprimatur are official declarations that a book or pamphlet is free from doctrinal or moral error. No implication is contained therein that those who granted the nihil obstat or imprimatur agree with the contents or statements expressed.

OUR FRONT COVER: The illustrations of principal events in the life of St. Maximilian are from a Medieval-style tapestry painted by Jennifer Gay Holms. The concept for the painting was that of Friar Joseph Wood, OFM Conv. who wanted to a have a life of St. Maximilian Kolbe, a modern-day St. Francis, which would reflect the ideals of the founder of the Franciscan Order, St. Francis of Assisi. The central part of Jennifer's painting was replaced by a painting by another artist who copied the well-known painting by Bro. Felix Sztyk of Niepokalanow, who knew Fr. Kolbe personally (see his painting on page 71). Used with permission of Marytown.

KOLBE

SAINT OF THE IMMACULATA

Kolbe: Saint of the Immaculata is a book prepared for publication by the Franciscans of the Immaculate [marymediatrix.com], POB 3003, New Bedford, MA, 02741-3003.

Fr. Maximilian after his return to Poland from Japan. He grew a beard while in Japan. The Japanese looked with respect upon a person with a beard.

Editor's Introduction

THE NAME "MAXIMILIAN KOLBE," depending upon where one is coming from, elicits two extreme reactions - from veneration as "the Saint of our difficult century" as Pope John Paul II called him, to accusation of being anti-Semitic or equally bad, heretical in his Mariology. As such he should never have been canonized a Saint by the Catholic Church. (see articles on pages 100-102). Incidentally, those who accuse Kolbe of being a bigot are the very ones who at the same time show how very prejudiced they are against the Catholic Church. Ultimately, whether they are conscious of it or not, the object of their disdain and hatred is the Catholic Church.

If you cannot find a case against the Church directly, then ignore the facts and create a false image of a holy person, whom the Church honors as a saint, and the Church looks hypocritical. We see this in our day in the mass media which are consistently targeting saintly, well-known Catholic leaders, such as St. Kolbe and Popes Bl. Pius IX and Pius XII, accusing them of being bigots.

They cannot deny the fact that the little Franciscan priest did a heroic thing by giving up his life for a fellow prisoner in the concentration camp of Auschwitz. However, Saint Maximilian, priest, Marian devotee, apologist, evangelist and loyal son of the Church doesn't fit very well into a secularist society that has divorced God from everyday life. He cuts across our comfortable, worldly standards - our "culture of death," and is a real threat to the kingdom and prince of this world and those who reject Christ, the Savior and Mary Immaculate.

Saint Maximilian, prisoner number 16670, had first-hand experience of man's rejection of Christ the King of love and God's action of Grace and Mercy in men's lives - all of which led to the holocaust of the Nazi and Communist death camps and now the far greater holocaust of abortion, infanticide and finally involuntary euthanasia. In 1917 he experienced an open declaration of war on the Church by International Freemasonry (see page 31). He pointed to Freemasonry, a religion of secular humanism, as the "head of the serpent." Under what some think is a strictly "fraternal" society, he saw clearly a "religion" that foments revolution in the civil order and indifferentism in the spiritual order. It gives merely lip service to the Christian God and considers all religions of equal value. It is no secret that this secret society has contributed much to the overthrow of many governments in Europe and South America in the last century.

Of even far greater import, it has contributed immensely to the emptying of churches and removing the supernatural from what was once a Christian culture of Europe. According to their worldly "wisdom," God's influence and presence must be kept within the four walls of churches, not to be integrated into every phase and activity of human life. This widespread evil of ignoring God, the Creator and Savior of mankind, is all too present everywhere one looks in our secularized American culture. This is nothing new. The battle lines were clearly drawn at the dawn of creation between the Woman (Mary Immaculate) and her "Seed" the Redeemer, and the Serpent (Satan) and his followers.

The greatest warfare of all, over the eternal destiny of countless souls, demands a total victory of good over evil, of objective truth over lies and half truths, of life over death, of heaven over hell, of Mary Immaculate over the demon of impurity.

However, there is no question of the ultimate triumph. Christ won the victory two thousand years ago on the hill of Calvary. He mediates that victory through His Mother who stood at the foot of the cross offering her Beloved Son to the Eternal Father in perfect conformity with the Father's Will. Thus, she merits to be the Coredemptrix.

To meet head on and convert our spiritually impoverished secular-consumerist society St. Maximilian offered a two-fold counter attack - evangelical poverty and total consecration to Mary Immmaculate. He gave a new twist to evangelical poverty, or non-appropriation as we read in the sixth chapter of the Rule of St. Francis, "The friars are to appropriate nothing for themselves, neither house, nor place, nor anything else." St. Maximilian realized how very important the observance of spiritual poverty, or detachment from creatures and reliance on Divine Providence, was in the reform and renewal of the Franciscans Order (see page 143). Kolbe carried non-appropriation further, in his total consecration to Mary, by being appropriated by Mary, shifting the focus from appropriating things to being appropriated by Mary Immaculate, as her property to be used as she best sees fit, which amounts to nothing short of total consecration.

As a newly ordained priest he wrote to another young Friar:

"Remember that you are always the unconditional, unlimited, irrevocable property and possession of the Immaculate. Whatever you are, whatever you have, or can have, all your actions -pleasant, unpleasant and indifferent - are entirely her possession. May she, therefore, do with all these as it pleases her, and not yourself."

Christ did not condemn the visible world, created by the loving hands of His Father, but the worldliness that would focus one's attention on this world, to the exclusion of man's last ends and the world to come. St. Augustine spoke of two Cities, one of God and the other of man. He was well qualified to speak, having lived a pagan life as a young man. Kolbe's goal was ever focused on eternal life in accordance with God's intended destiny for every man- eternal unlimited happiness, realized only in heaven. Individual secular humanists, Freemasons, and New Agers and other worldly people were the object of Kolbe's pity and evangelization efforts. In identifying with the Crucified Christ through a life of continuous suffering, prayer and sacrifice, Maximilian was ever the priest-victim, never letting an opportunity for winning the conversion of a sinner pass, "especially the Masons" and other enemies of the Church.

The recent Vatican document Declaration Dominus Jesus (The Lord Jesus) on the unique role of Jesus in the salvation of the world, although stating nothing new, was angrily discredited by many, including Catholic theologians, as anti-ecumenical and another example of the so-called "conservative" element in the Church turning back the Church - an "unprogressive" Church - to the days before Vatican Council II.

A commonly held thesis of those who would base their Faith on feeling rather than truth is:

"do not strive to convert others to the Faith. . . one religion is as good as the next." This flies in the face of the solemn words of Our Lord addressed to His disciples just before leaving this earth for His eternal home, "Go and preach the Gospel to all nations, . . ." and "the truth will make you free." As Cardinal Ratzinger commented on September 5, 2000, the day on which the Vatican document was issued, "If everything is relative. . . all religions are no more than useless, theoretical musings."

Taking a long hard look at the Gospels expounded by the Fathers of the Church, and at the lives and writings of its Saints, one cannot avoid facing the fact that man's ultimate goal, willed by God, is heaven which will be realized only by putting on Christ crucified. Man, persuaded by the secular humanists to focus his attention on an earthly paradise, chooses the ultimate loss of eternal happiness and eternal damnation through his inordinate desire and acquisition of the goods of this world. These souls were St. Maximilian's special concern and the object of his love and pity. Is it too much to hope and pray that through Kolbe's example of total consecration and the virtue of spiritual poverty, this 20th century Franciscan will introduce a similar spiritual renewal of society in our day as that which St. Francis of Assisi introduced in the 13th century?

Dedication and Acknowledgment

This book as well as the other five books of the Marian Saints and Shrines is dedicated to Mary Immaculate, Mediatrix of all graces. Were it not for her, where would be found the very subject matter for these books? The person of Mary is responsible for it all: the inspiration that prompted this editor, the subject matter itself, and trust that she who inspired the editor, at the same time, will see to its happy conclusion. For this purpose she supplied many dedicated Marian "hands," both Religious and lay, to help this Brother produce what many consider a contribution in making Mary better known and loved. All was done for Mary, by her inspiration and help. The editor takes no credit. It would be the ultimate in plagiarism. I was merely her instrument, and a poor one at that. She has produced something beautiful for the glory of God and I am intensely grateful to my Mother and Queen for the opportunity.

— Bro. Francis Mary Kalvelage, F.I.

Preface

Dr. Mark Miravalle, S.T.D.

AS A NOTED MODERN day Franciscan theologian, St. Maximilian Maria Kolbe follows a long and prestigious line of Franciscan theologians, such as St. Bonaventure and Bl. John Duns Scotus, who stressed the Primacy of Christ and championed the Immaculate Conception of Mary. He added even further extraordinary insights. He wondered at and prayed over Our Lady's self-identification at Lourdes when she told St. Bernadette: "I am the Immaculate Conception" (March 25, 1858). In pondering and praying over this title, so filled with supernatural mystery, Kolbe had the profound insight of the intimate relationship between the created (Mary) and the uncreated Immaculate Conception (the Holy Spirit). In an age considered the Age of the Holy Spirit, some contemporary authors have referred to him as the "prophet of the Fifth Marian Dogma." Indeed, history bears out that St. Maximilian was an initial promoter for the definition of Our Lady as the Mediatrix of all graces, as is found in a 1923 reference:

> *"On this truth the Militia Immaculata bases its activities. We have recourse to the Immaculata and we are instruments in her hands because she distributes all the graces of conversion and sanctification to the inhabitants of this valley of tears. Furthermore, we clearly profess this truth in our act of consecration to the Virgin Mary because every grace passes through her hands from the Sweetest Heart of the most pure Jesus to us... Let us pray, therefore, that our Holy Mother may expedite the solemn proclamation of this, her privilege..." (Immaculata magazine Jan/Feb 1997).*

With supernatural insights such as these, it is with little wonder that our Totus Tuus pope, John Paul II, has declared St. Maximilian Kolbe to be "the Apostle of a New Marian Era."

In this regard, a solemn papal proclamation of Mary Mediatrix of all graces, at a Conference in Japan in 1940, St. Maximilian wisely calls for "more prayer and less discussion." (Militia Immaculatae, 1999). There was no mistaking St. Maximilian Kolbe's stance regarding Mary as Co-redemptrix and Mediatrix. If Mary were not the Mediatrix of all graces, his whole life's work, Militia Immaculatae, would be pointless. This indicates how important the definition of this long held Marian teaching of the Church was to him. If the Saint were alive today he would, no doubt, be one of its greatest champions. He is, just the same, interceding from the heavenly communion of saints.

This foundational mariological premise of Kolbe concerning the role of Mary as Mediatrix with the Mediator is revealed and developed in the New Testament from her mediation of the Source of all grace at the Annunciation (cf. Lk 1:38), to her mediating of miraculous grace at Cana (cf. Jn. 2:1-10) to her maternal mediation at the foot of the cross, "Woman behold your son… Son, behold your Mother (Jn. 19:26-27). These words of the dying Savior to the Woman at the foot of the cross established Mary as the motherly Co-redemptrix, Mediatrix, and Advocate. At the very moment when the redemptive sacrifice for all humanity was being completed, Jesus speaks these words to the beloved Apostle John, who represents all followers of the Crucified Christ.

When Jesus gives John to Mary and Mary to John, the Mother of Jesus is established as the new spiritual and universal Co-redemptrix and Mediatrix in the order of grace. The role of Mediatrix of graces is at once a gift of sublime dignity to his co-redeeming Mother and at the same time a sanctifying gift for fallen humanity. Pope John Paul II confirms:

> *"With the redeeming death, the maternal mediation of the handmaid of the Lord took on a universal dimension, for the work of redemption embraces all of humanity. Thus there is manifested in a singular way the efficacy of the one and universal mediation of Christ between God and man" (Redemptoris Mater, n. 40).*

In view of her active participation, Christ, the Mediator, grants his Mother the gift of dispensing all graces, the fruit of his redemptive sacrifice and her co-redemptive cooperation. She is the Mediatrix of all graces given to mankind because she was first of all the Co-redemptrix beside her Son. There is no question that this Kolbean mariological position of Mary as Co-redemptrix and Mediatrix is one with the Papal Magisterium. Modern popes have consistently held the truth of Mary's role as Co-redemptrix, Mediatrix, and Advocate as part of the authoritative teachings of the ordinary Magisterium, with particular emphasis on the universal nature of Mary's mediation. Mary's unique participation in the distribution of the graces of Redemption to her spiritual children does not hinder but, rather, fosters an awareness of and receptivity to the universality of grace that comes to the human family from the one Redeemer and Mediator (cf. *Lumen Gentium*, n. 62).

Blessed Pius IX held that God has committed the treasury of all graces for distribution to Mary: "For God has committed to Mary the treasury of all good things, in order that everyone may know that through her are obtained every hope, every grace, and all salvation" (Encyclical Letter, *Ubi Primum*, 1849). Pope Leo XIII provides an abundance of papal pronouncements referring to Mary in her co-redemptive and mediatorial role, as for example: "[Mary is] the treasurer of our peace with God and dispensatrix of heavenly graces," as well as one "through whom He has chosen to be the dispenser of all heavenly graces..." (Encyclical Letters, *Supremi apostolatus*, 1883; *Superiore anno*, 1884).

Pope St. Pius X, moreover, explains that the strict right of the distribution of grace resides with Jesus Christ alone, but that due to her intimate union of suffering with the Redeemer, the task of the distribution of grace has been given to Mary, Mediatrix:

> *"This source [of grace], then, is Jesus Christ... But Mary, as St. Bernard justly remarks, is the "channel" or, if you will, the neck by which the mystical body is joined to the Head (Christ) and by which the Head sends power and strength through to the whole Body: 'For she is the neck of our Head (Jesus) by which He communicates to his Mystical Body all spiritual gifts'" (Ad diem illum, 1904).*

Pope Pius XI continues the rich papal tradition of Our Lady as Co-redemptrix and Mediatrix of all graces by recalling this maternal function in numerous Church teachings:

> *"We have nothing more at heart than to promote more and more the devotion of the Christian people towards the Virgin who is the treasurer of all graces with God... Jesus, 'the one Mediator between God and man' (Tim 2:5), who wished to associate his own Mother with himself as the advocate of sinners, as dispenser and mediatrix of grace..." (Encyclical Letter, Miserentissimus Redemptor, AAS 20, 1928, p. 178).*

Pope Pius XI also indicates that Mary deserves the title Co-redemptrix, stating that "from the nature of His work the Redeemer ought to have associated His Mother with His work. For this reason we invoke her under the title of Coredemptrix" (Papal Allocution to Pilgrims of Vicenza, 30 November 1933). In fact, Pius XI calls Our Lady the "Co-redemptrix" on several occasions and assures us that all God gives us is imparted through the mediation of Mary: "We know that all things are imparted to us from God, the greatest and best, through the hands of the Mother of God" (Encyclical Letter, *Ingravescentibus malis*, AAS 29, 1937, p. 380).

Pope Pius XII made the classic expression of St. Bernard his own: "'It is the will of God that we obtain all favors through Mary, '" and the Pope added, "let everyone hasten to have recourse to Mary" (*Superiore anno*, AAS 32, 1940, p.145). He affirms in another encyclical, "She teaches us all virtues; she gives us her Son and with him all the help we need, for 'God wished us to have everything through Mary'" (*Mediator Dei*, 1947).

The Second Vatican Council makes a great contribution in explaining Mary's mediation in the salvific role of Jesus Christ the one Mediator by dispensing to us,

> *"the gifts of eternal salvation. Mary's function as mother of men in no way obscures or diminishes this unique mediation of Christ, but rather shows its power. But the Blessed Virgin's salutary influence on men ordinates not in any inner necessity but in the disposition of God. It flows forth from the superabundance of the merits of Christ, rests on his mediation, depends entirely on it and draws all its power from it. It does not hinder in any way the immediate union of the faithful with Christ but on the contrary fosters it" (*Lumen Gentium*, n. 62).*

Vatican II also states that the Mother of Jesus is the mother to us in the order of grace because she uniquely cooperated in the saving work of the Redeemer: "[Mary] shared her Son's sufferings as he died on the cross. Thus, in a wholly singular way she cooperated by her obedience, faith, hope, and burning charity in the work of the Savior in restoring supernatural life to souls. For this reason she is mother to us in the order of grace" (*Lumen Gentium*, n. 61).

But it is precisely the pneumatological dimension of our Mother's universal mediation that has been brought to greatest clarity by our beloved St. Maximilian Maria. God the Holy Spirit's specific mission is to "sanctify the Church forever" (cf. Jn 20:22; Rom 15:16; 1 Pet. 1:2). But the Holy Spirit has chosen to perform his divine act of sanctification, which flows from the cross of Christ, only through the mediation of his human but glorified spouse, Mary. The Holy Spirit, a divine person, and Mary, a human person, were given one unified mission from the Father after Calvary. Both were sent to take the ineffable graces from the sacrifice of the Redeemer and to sanctify and transform the face of the earth by generously dispensing the gifts of eternal life to the human family.

St. Louis Marie Grignion de Montfort in his classic, True Devotion to Mary, expounds on the cooperation between the Spirit and the Mediatrix in the distribution of all graces:

> *"To Mary, his faithful spouse, God the Holy Ghost has communicated His unspeakable gifts; and He has chosen her to be the dispenser of all He possesses, in such ways that she distributes to whom she wills, as much as she wills, as she wills and when she wills, all His gifts and graces. The Holy Ghost gives no heavenly gift to men which He does not have pass through her virginal hands. Such has been the will of God, who has willed that we should have everything through Mary" (n. 25).*

But St. Maximilian offers the Church an ever more complete understanding of the sublime unity and role of the Holy Spirit and Mary in the mysterious distribution of the graces of redemption:

> *"The union between the Immaculata and the Holy Spirit is so inexpressible yet so perfect that the Holy Spirit acts only by the Most Blessed Virgin, his Spouse. This is why she is the mediatrix of all graces given by the Holy Spirit. And since every grace is a gift of God the Father through the Son and by the Holy Spirit, it follows that there is no grace that Mary cannot dispose of as her own, which is not given to her for this purpose" (St. Maximilian Kolbe,* Letter to Father Mikolajczyk, *28 July, 1935).*

He uses the example of the inseparable union between the divine nature and human nature in the one divine person, Jesus Christ, to express the ineffable union between the Holy Spirit and Mary:

> *"The Holy Spirit is in Mary after the fashion, one might say, in which the Second Person of the Blessed Trinity, the Word, is in his humanity. There is this difference: In Jesus there are two natures, divine and human, but one single person who is God. Mary's nature and person are totally distinct from the nature and person of the Holy Spirit. Still, their union is so inexpressible, and so perfect that the Holy Spirit acts only by the Immaculata, his spouse" (*Letter to Fr. Salezy Mikolajczyk, *28 July, 1935).*

With the true distinction between the natures and persons of the Holy Spirit and Mary, St. Maximilian does not hesitate to say that Mary is in a certain sense the "incarnation" of the Holy Spirit. This is an effort to convey theologically this most sublime union of the Holy Spirit and the Mediatrix. "The Third Person of the Blessed Trinity never took flesh; still, our human word 'spouse' is far too weak to express the reality of the relationship between the Immaculata and the Holy Spirit" (Conference, 5 February 1941). The divine Sanctifier therefore transforms human souls into temples of God, adoptive children of God and heirs of heaven only through the spousal mediation of Mary, Mediatrix of all graces. This supernatural activity is based on their ineffable and providential union.

It is because of such monumental insights into the mystery of the Mother of Jesus that Pope Paul VI, in his homily at St. Maximilian's beatification, spoke of Kolbe as "among the great saints and clairvoyant minds that have understood, venerated and sung the mystery of Mary" (*Beatification Mass*).

It is my hope that through the inspiration and insight of St. Maximilian Kolbe as profoundly captured in this excellent work, the final privilege of Mary will be furthered so that we will soon see Mary Coredemptrix, Mediatrix, and Advocate defined as an article of our Catholic Faith, which in turn will hasten the ultimate triumph of the Immaculate Heart of Mary promised at Fatima.

Although endowed with a supernatural infusion of charity which eventually crowned his life with martyrdom, St. Maximilian also manifested extraordinary courage and boldness, which led him

Fr. Bede Hess, the Minister General of the Conventual Franciscans (to the right of Fr. Kolbe) said that if St. Francis was alive today he would feel most comfortable at the City of the Immaculate, where the Franciscan Rule was lived so faithfully.

into directly combat with Freemasonry. How prophetic he was! How subtly and insidiously has Masonry effected major changes in society through the mass media, monetary and political power. This subversive secret society has caused spiritual paralysis, moral compromise, and furthered secular-humanism, which has dominated the western world in modern times. That is why St. Maximilian singled out Freemasonry from the very beginnings of the Militia Immaculatae (Oct. 16, 1917) as the principal enemy of the Church and Christianity (see page 32) to battle with our rosaries, our Marian consecrations and our lives, if necessary. Masonry, the very "head" of the Serpent, therefore is to be crushed by the foot of the Immaculata in her historic and ultimate triumph.

The prophetic call to "aim higher" should inspire us to an ever greater understanding and subsequent "awe" before the mystery of the Immaculata Coredemptrix, she who is the Ark of the Covenant between divinity and humanity, the facilitator and advocate between humanity and divinity, the Father's greatest and most glorious masterpiece, and the maternal remedy for a Church and world in present historic crisis. May this rich anthology inspire us all to an ever greater love and proclamation of truth concerning the Immaculata, leading to the new civilization of love, an era of Eucharistic and Marian peace.

Dr. Mark Miravalle, S.T.D., Professor of Theology and Mariology at the Franciscan University of Steubenville, author of many books on Marian subjects, is the President of the International Catholic Movement Vox Populi Mariae Mediatrici.

Spiritual Militancy: Love in Action

Fr. James McCurry, OFM Conv.

"WHAT'S IN A NAME?" asked Shakespeare. The world-wide M.I. movement has asked itself the same question. In North America it is known as the Knights of the Immaculata, in England and Australia the Crusade of Mary Immaculate, in the Philippines and India as the Militia of the Immaculata. In other English-speaking areas of the world it is known as the Militia of Mary Immaculate. A new Franciscan Order (The Franciscans of the Immaculate), speak of the M.I. as the Missio Immaculatae Mediatrix (M.I.M.). All of these titles translate or adapt the original Latin title of the Marian evangelization movement founded by St. Maximilian Kolbe in 1917 as the Militia Immaculatae. Regardless of the variety of titles, the very name of the M I. signifies the movement's two essential characteristics: (1) it is militant and (2) it is Marian. The name bespeaks a spiritual "Marian militancy" which St. Maximilian saw capable of transforming the world.

Militant vs. Militarist

The words of St. Maximilian himself offer a very revealing insight into "spiritual militancy." Words such as Knight, Militia, Battle, sound bellicose, for they are associated with warfare - not necessarily a war fought with the help of rifles, bombs, rockets, tanks etc., but still, a real and true battle. But what is its tactic? Prayer above all and before all, is the effective weapon in the battle for the freedom and happiness of souls. Why? To attain a supernatural goal only supernatural means will be ultimately effective. Heaven - the divinization, so to speak, of souls - is something supernatural in the fullest sense of the word. Therefore, with natural means this cannot be attained. Here supernatural means are needed, namely, divine grace. This grace is obtained through humility and confident prayer. Grace, and only grace, enlightens the intellect and strengthens the will, and it alone is the cause of conversion, which is the liberating of the soul from the fetters of the Evil One.

In St. Maximilian's view, spiritual militancy is grounded in prayer, operates through grace and aims at the liberation and happiness of souls. The saint did not confuse militancy with militarism. "Militant" implies a zealous and selfless devotion to a cause. "Militarist" implies a self-serving exaltation of war. Those who follow the ideals of St. Maximilian pray for the grace to be militants not militarists - devoted with militant zeal to the cause of evangelization.

This Kolbean ideal of winning the whole world for Christ is derived from the Scriptures. In the Scriptures, selfless militancy for Christ has a distinctive Marian dimension. Both Genesis 3:15 and Revelation 12 employ militant terminology to describe God's plan for the ultimate victory of Christ, and both associate a "Woman" with Christ, who is Love Incarnate.

Militancy in Scripture

From the first book of the Scriptures to the last, the battle lines between good and evil are clearly drawn. The Immaculate Virgin is not only an integral part of the battle, but indispensable in attaining victory. St. Maximilian wanted to establish the M.I. as a whole company of militants collaborating with Mary in the spread of God's love. In 1938 he wrote:

"In America in the clearing of fields and forests, controlled fires are sometimes set; in the spiritual battle we ought to set fire to our faults with the fire of divine love. Then everything will he consumed with fire. As to the fire of divine love, it is stoked by sacrifice. Only sacrifice is that tree which is to be turned into a holocaust on the altar of God's love. Yes, sacrifice is a necessary condition of love. Without sacrifice there is no progress in the divine life. Without sacrifice our love dies out. . . ."

The triumph of Christ's love in the world must begin in each of our hearts before we can spread it elsewhere. St. Maximilian would propose a spirituality of an interior "holocaust" in order to burn away sin and imperfections to let love triumph. Since Mary Immaculate was the first human heart in which Christ's love triumphed, she would serve as spiritual leader and catalyst in our interior love-holocaust of conversion and sanctification.

The act of "Total Consecration to Mary" advocated by St. Maximilian is the concrete expression of our intention to let Mary accomplish the work that God has given her, beginning with the interior holocaust of our own hearts. The spirituality of Marian militancy is rooted in the humble, self-sacrificing holocaust of love that "Total Consecration to Mary" represents. The fruit of this spirituality is love in action. St. Maximilian describes these militant lovers in these words:

"Let us look at the image of a true Knight of the Immaculate. He (or she) does not restrict his heart to himself alone, nor merely to his family, friends, neighbors, co-citizens, but embraces the whole world, each and every human being, because they are all without exception, our brothers and sisters who have been purchased by the blood of Jesus. The militant desires for everyone the light of faith, happiness, forgiveness of sins, and a heart afire with God's love. His dream is the happiness of all humanity in God through the Immaculate." *A condensation of a talk given by Fr. James McCurry. OFM Conv*

All pitched in with the addressing and shipping of the Knight magazine, which had a circulation of near a million in the late thirties.

Contents

From his earliest years, Raymond (his baptismal name), the future St. Maximilian, had a devotion to the national Madonna, Our Lady of Czestochowa. The Polish nation was consecrated to her and they looked upon her as their Queen. Many were the times that she came to their aid as a nation and individually during times of crisis. Opposite page, Kolbe as a young priest.

PART V: His Impact on Society

PART VI: The Papacy on the Saint

PART VII: Appendix

The young priest, Fr. Kolbe

PART I: BIOGRAPHY

The Block of Death at Auschwitz where Fr. Maximilian and nine other prisoners were sentenced to starve to death in a subterranean cell. Right: Prisoner 16670, Fr. Maximilian Kolbe, priest and victim.

The whole concentration camp was lined up on the parade ground that unbearably hot summer day to hear the frightening news that a prisoner had escaped. Ten of them would be condemned to a slow agonizing death.

A Martyr's Death

The Editor

A PRISONER HAD ESCAPED from the concentration camp of Auschwitz — "This should never be allowed to happen!" It was an affront to the meticulously efficient Nazi S.S. officers. To make sure that it would never happen again, ten men would be condemned to die in a subterranean cell bunker by starvation and dehydration, no food or liquid until they died — an agonizing, slow death which could take over two weeks. Added to the physical torture was the mental agony and indignity of being stripped naked and crammed into a space that would not even allow all ten condemned men to lie down at the same time on the cold cement floor. The only furniture in the dark bunker was a bucket used to relieve one's physical needs. All the prisoners in the camp were aware of this inhuman punishment, which the S.S. used to discourage other prisoners from escaping.

The whole prison camp was assembled on the drill field that hot summer day in July. The prisoners, standing at attention for three hours before the brutal S.S. officer, Colonel Fritsch, were exhausted. At 9:00 in the evening, all was quiet except for the occasional barking of tracking dogs, indicating that the escapee had not been found. Suspense added to the unmitigated terror of the prisoners. They had plenty of time to think. Imaginations ran wild with the thought of the torturous death awaiting some of them if the prisoner was not found. When the order was given to break ranks to distribute the meager evening ration, everyone ate except Block 14, the section of the camp from which the prisoner was missing.

Fritsch, the second in command of the camp, with feet planted firmly apart, savored the ultimate power he had of determining whether a man would live or die. In the deathly silence that enveloped the terrified prisoners, he barked out, "The prisoner has not been caught, but to show you how merciful the German Reich is, twenty…" He paused and looked around the lineup of men. "Fifteen… No… I have decided only ten men will die this time." His steely eyes showed not the least compassion. "But the next time twenty men will die… since you did not keep a closer watch over the prisoner that ran away."

The poor, disheartened prisoners were then forced to see their evening meal dumped in a nearby canal. They were then dismissed. Tormented by hunger, and sick with fear, sleep was impossible. They realized the hostages for execution would be selected from their ranks. Motivated by self-interest, everyone was for himself. "My God, let it not be me but someone else."

Of all those standing in the ranks of Block 14, Fr. Maximilian Kolbe alone looked serene and composed. What was the little Franciscan priest thinking? The next day would reveal that, unlike the rest, the last person he was thinking of was himself. His calm appearance reflected his deep, prayerful peace of soul, and his trust that God, his Father, had not abandoned them — what a contrast to the vacant, haunted stares of those around him, many of whom no longer had hope! That evening the men in Block 14 slept little. Those who woke up periodically screamed in terror. Some sat on their bunks, staring vacantly into space. Others walked up and down, while Fr. Kolbe led those who wished to join him in prayers for courage. Still others prayed that the prisoner would be caught.

The following day, after the morning roll call, all the blocks were sent to work as usual, with the exception of Block 14. They remained all day long at attention with the blistering hot rays of the sun beating down on their shaven heads. Their faces became swollen, their vision blurred and spots danced before their eyes. Since nothing was given them to slake their thirst, they became dehydrated and weak. Many passed out. Those who fainted were clubbed and prodded with rifles, and if that failed to revive them, they were simply dragged feet first and piled at the rear of the ranks. It is amazing that Fr. Maximilian, sickly and frail as he was, despaired of by twenty doctors who attended him in his short life, did not collapse. No doubt, he was being sustained by his heavenly Queen.

By 3:00 in the after noon, so many prisoners had fallen, weakened by the previous day's work and no meal, that the

Commandant, not wishing to spare prisoners from the agony of selection, ordered a break, and soup was brought from the kitchen. That evening, when the rest of the prisoners returned from their work assignments and saw the pitiful men of block 14, all they could do for their comrades was to show them sympathy through their pitying looks.

After the evening roll call, Colonel Fritsch, accompanied by Palitsch, the recording officer, and a group of well-armed guards approached the men of Block 14. The deep, penetrating silence accentuated the tension which was near breaking point. The men of Block 14 were lined up in ten rows of sixty each. After Fritsch had made his selection in the first row, Palitsch ordered that row,

"Five steps forward, march."

With a passage opened between the first two rows, the selection continued, Fritsch staring coldly and cruelly into the eyes of each man until his boots halted on the dusty square.

"Open your mouth! Show me your teeth! Stick out your tongue!" When Fritsch pointed to a man, Palitsch wrote down the victim's number and he was dragged roughly out of the ranks. What the Commandant's arbitrary motive for mouth examination was, no one knew. The sadistic Fritsch had a flare for the dramatic. All kinds of thoughts ran through the prisoners' minds. Their whole concentration was on avoiding the slightest movement that might draw attention to themselves.

"Long live Poland!" was the defiant shout of one man selected. "It is for you that I give my life."

"So long friends… we'll meet again up there, and that's where real justice will be handed out to these pigs."

When Fritsch pointed out one of the men, tears trickled down the prisoner's hollow cheeks as he cried out,

"Oh… my wife… my poor children… I will never see them again."

One of the S.S. men translated the Polish. Fritsch ignored the pleas of the helpless victim. Suddenly there was a commotion in the ranks. The unexpected, the unbelievable happened. A small, frail prisoner had broken ranks and stepped forward without permission. So stunned were the guards at this infringement of the usual protocol that Fritsch himself had to reach for his pistol.

"What is it? Who is it?" prisoners whispered amid the confusion.

"It's Father Kolbe."

"What, the Franciscan?"

"Halt!" gasped Fritsch. "What do you want?"

Fr. Maximilian looked serenely into the face of Fritsch as the guards moved in. The prisoner removed his cap and said in so low a voice that only those nearby could hear him,

"Please, Herr Commandant, I would like to take the place of that man." He pointed to the man picked for death and said, "I would like to die in his place."

The speechless Commandant turned to Palitsch and demanded,

"Who is this man? What is it all about?"

Before the German interpreter could answer, Kolbe replied in fluent German, "I am a Catholic priest and I want to take his place. He has a wife and family."

"Are you crazy?" snapped Fritsch.

"I would like to die in his place," the priest repeated. "I'm old, and sick... I can barely work. I'm of no use to anyone anymore. This man is young and strong, and he has a wife and family... I have no one ... "

Fr. Maximilian knew human nature well. He had to make it easier for Fritsch to accept his offer and at the same time save face. Fritsch, in stunned amazement, continued to stare at prisoner 16670. He was totally unprepared and speechless. Here he was, a high-ranking officer in the elite S.S., conversing with a prisoner. The reversal of roles, for it was Fr. Kolbe who was in command of the situation, unnerved Fritsch. The executioner wasn't, at that point, thinking for himself and the suggestion of Kolbe invoked an unwritten law of the Nazi: Cripples and weaklings were not productive members of society and thus must be liquidated (As the saying goes, history repeats itself. It is very much with us today in our culture of death).

Finally, his eyes fell before the tranquil, innocent eyes of the priest, and anxious to end his embarrassment, he turned to Palitsch, and said, "ACCEPTED."

Those who witnessed the encounter that pitted the emaciated little Polish priest in tattered prison garb and the burly, arrogant Nazi S.S. officer in his impeccable, well-tailored uniform, will never forget that day when the inherent human dignity of man, made in the image and likeness of God, was upheld over inhumanity and lack of respect for human life. Fr. Antonio Ricciardi, OFM Conv., the general postulator of Fr. Kolbe's cause for canonization, summed up the scene well in his book Saint Maximilian:

> *"As they stood there for what seemed an eternity, the total contrast between the two was something those eyewitnesses will never forget. Basically, it was the contrast between the man who rejected God and the man who dared to love Him totally."*

Sgt. Francis Gajowniczek's number was stricken from the list of the condemned. At Auschwitz, a human being was nothing more than a number. Gajowniczek, husband and father, covered his face with his hands and rejoined the ranks, while prisoner 16670 was added to the list and pushed to one side to join the other prisoners condemned to death.*

The selection finished, those remaining heaved a sigh of relief. The next order by Palitsch, "Take off your shoes!" was the usual ritual before execution. Another order, "March," and the barefoot prisoners, clothed in just their shirts, walked slowly to the block of death. Father Maximilian was taking up the rear, helping another victim who was ready to collapse — a man for others to the last. That evening, as the sun set in a fiery ball, witnesses agreed that they had never seen such a magnificent sunset. The priest who, as a boy, was offered the red crown of martyrdom, was about to consummate his last "Mass" in the liturgical red of the martyrs.

---

* In the book *Kolbe and the Kommandant*, it is related that when word of Kolbe's heroic death came to the attention of the head of the concentration camp, Commandant Rudolph Hoess, he inquired of his adjutant, Fritsch, how it happened that Fritsch had made a martyr of one of the prisoners. When he heard the name Maximilian Kolbe, he immediately recognized it as the Franciscan priest who founded the Polish City of the Immaculate. When Fritsch told his superior how Kolbe offered his life for another condemned prisoner whom he spared, Hoess replied, "You fool, you should have taken both the priest and the other man too." When he was told that the body of Kolbe was cremated along with the rest, Hoess, a former Catholic, smirked, "A Saint without relics!" (see related chapter on page 149).

The sacrificial death of Father Kolbe, who once said, "Only love is creative," made a great impression on the minds of the other prisoners, since there was so little love of neighbor in that living hell. No one would think of sharing his meager ration of bread with another prisoner, as Kolbe frequently did, let alone give his life up for a total stranger. "Greater love than this no man has, than to give his life for his friend." One of the witnesses states unequivocally that, "the sacrifice of Father Maximilian saved the lives of many of the inmates," for the S.S. officers, "touched, in spite of themselves, didn't mistreat or kill as many." Former prisoners of Auschwitz readily agree that from that time on the hardships in the camp were somewhat mitigated.

The last indignity for Kolbe and his companions was, like Christ in His Passion, to be stripped naked. This humiliating crushing of the last visage of humanity seemed to add yet another diabolic twist to their deaths. When the ten condemned of Block 14 arrived at the dark, dank "hole" where they were to die, there were already twenty prisoners who lay in torment in the next cell. The thick walls could not stifle their screams, moans, and curses. As the heavy door slammed shut on the condemned, some began to sob. One of the heartless S.S. jailers sneered, "You will dry up like tulips."

The Nazi jailers soon realized, however, that this time things would be different — the difference between night and day. Whereas, in the past, howling and curses reverberated from the starvation bunkers like a scene of the damned in hell, this time the condemned prisoners did not curse and tear at each other, but sang and prayed. Soon the condemned in the other cells joined in the singing of hymns to Our Lady. What had formerly been a place of torment and bedlam became a place of divine worship. As if in choir, they answered one another from cell to cell with prayers and hymns. The major cause for the difference? This time a priest, a holy priest, was with them to share their immolation, to counsel, encourage, and administer the Sacrament of Reconciliation.

We have seen how Kolbe, when he was asked who he was, replied, "a Catholic priest." This short identification says it all. Father Maximilian lived his priesthood and would die the good shepherd, ministering to the spiritual needs of his fellow victims. Few recognize that it was this, above all, that must have prompted

Fr. Maximilian removed his cap and looked serenely into the face of Fritsch, as the guards moved in, and said in a low voice, "Please, Herr Commandant, I would like to take the place of that man." The scene has been immortalized by Polish artist and fellow prisoner, Miechislaus Koscielniak.

Kolbe to make the supreme sacrifice. He could not allow these men to die without the ministering of a priest. The details surrounding his death were providentially supplied by a Polish prisoner, Borgowiec, who was assigned the grizzly task of removing the bodies of those who had died during the night. He reported that even the jailers were amazed at the prayerful atmosphere and remarked, "never have we seen anything like this."

Each morning, when Borgowiec entered the cell to remove the corpses, he found Father Kolbe praying, either standing in the center of the death chamber or kneeling. The S.S. officers who watched the Polish orderly as he went about his business would bellow out orders to the condemned. During the first days they were so absorbed in prayer that they were unaware of the S.S. guards' presence. When conscious of the guards, some wept and begged for a little water to relieve their maddening thirst. Father Maximilian, on the other hand, was quiet and asked for nothing.

He prayed, above all for the souls of these enemies of mankind and all that is decent and good, for they above all needed prayers.

When he looked with compassionate eyes and serene countenance at the executioners, they could not stand his gaze and demanded, "Turn your eyes away. Do not look at us that way!" As they left the cell they would mutter to themselves, "We have never seen a man like him." Thus hatred was conquered by love, evil by sheer goodness, and death by one who freely gave up his life so another might live, witnessing to the inherent value and dignity of each human being — but above all to that eternal destiny and life for which each person was created and redeemed.

On the eve of the Assumption, August 14, 1941, there were only four survivors, of whom Fr. Kolbe was the only one conscious. The cell was needed for other victims. Seated in a corner, seeing the executioner approach with a syringe containing the poison that would kill him, with prayers on his lips, he lifted up his left arm to killer Boch, a common criminal. Borgowiec could stand it no more and fled. When he returned he found Father Maximilian's body propped up against the wall. His eyes were open and he had a serene expression on his face. What was remarkable there was a certain radiance of glory, reflecting the Immaculate, from whom, no doubt, he was receiving the reward she had promised her knight while he was in Japan, when she gave him the assurance of his eternal salvation.

Saint Maximilian Mary Kolbe is best known as the hero of Auschwitz who voluntarily gave up his life so that another man might live. The story of such an unheard of heroic act has captured the imagination and admiration of all who have heard or read about it — but there is much more. How many understand that such heroism was only possible through the Woman whom Kolbe loved without limits, she who has been designated (although it has not yet been formally defined as dogma) the Mediatrix of all Graces? Conceived Immaculate in view of the redemptive Sacrifice of her Divine Son, she stood at the foot of the Cross of Jesus, and she stood beside Kolbe throughout his eventful life of heroic sacrifice. This is the story of a modern day Saint who, paraphrasing the great Apostle of the Gentiles, said, "I can do all things in Him who strengthens me through the Immaculate." ❑

Early Years — Promise of Two Crowns

THE FUTURE FRANCISCAN Saint, Maximilian Kolbe, was born and baptized and given the name of Raymond on January 8, 1894, in the little village of Zdunska Wola. He was the second of three surviving sons of Julius and Marianna Dabrowska Kolbe. Two boys, Valentine and Anthony, died in early childhood. Francis, the oldest son, was named after the Saint of Assisi, since both parents were secular Franciscans. They took seriously their vocation as followers of the Poverello and lived frugally. Any extra revenue that came their way through their hard work and long hours at the weaver's looms was not spent on luxuries but was used to help the less fortunate. Though the Kolbes never suffered from want of the essentials, they had to work hard to make ends meet, at a time when there was great poverty throughout Europe.

Julius and Marianna took seriously their responsibilities as parents. By their exemplary lives, they taught their children the importance of religion and the value of the domestic virtues that made for a peaceful and happy home life. They were a family that prayed together, and God was literally the center of their domestic church. As Catholics, they appreciated the infinite value of the Mass, and attended Mass as a family. Their parish in Pabianice had Eucharistic adoration each Sunday, organized by the Third Order of St. Francis. Members of the fraternity each took turns to fill in the adoration hours. Julius organized and kept track of the hours covered by the men adorers.

The personalities of Julius and Marianna complemented each other quite well. Marianna was a year older than Julius and conscientious to a fault in fulfilling her maternal obligations. She demanded much of her sons, and when they didn't measure up to her high expectations, she blamed herself, even accusing herself of being negligent. She was serious and industrious, but had no

Marianna Kolbe, his mother.

trouble in making friends as she was honest and could be trusted. She was ever ready to help others in their needs. She home schooled her children in the elementary subjects of reading, writing, and arithmetic.

At that time, Polish families taught their children Polish on their own in the home, as it was forbidden by the governments in the occupied territories. Julius saw to it that his children not only learned their mother tongue, but also to love their fatherland, its past glorious history and culture. He was of a more easygoing nature than Marianna and made friends readily. In raising his sons, he allowed them greater freedom as a means of instilling in them personal responsibility and the opportunity to profit by their mistakes. It is clear from this that he was like most Poles who had a high regard for freedom and the inherent dignity of man. He, along with Marianna, shared the responsibility of teaching their children the Faith — an uncompromising Faith that required personal discipline and sacrifice.

The three sons, Francis, Raymond and Joseph, were friendly, responsible, and generous, and were taught the value of obedience at an early age. Under the close supervision of Marianna, who was the disciplinarian of the home, they had their share of spankings. Mischievous Raymond, full of life and pranks, accepted punishment with a sense of justice, aware that it was motivated by deep parental love. When he was discovered in some wrongdoing, he would stretch out over a bench to facilitate what was "coming to him." However, that did not stop him from getting into trouble again and again — a typical boy with a "short memory." They each had decidedly different personalities. Francis was the most outgoing of the three and tended to be somewhat frivolous. The youngest son, Joseph, had a quiet and serious nature like his mother, and with his less venturesome personality he got into less trouble than his older brothers. Raymond was a happy balance between the two extremes. All three were religious, but Raymond was, from his earliest years, the most prayerful.

The economic situation in the part of Poland under Russian rule where the Kolbe family lived was anything but good. The industrious parents ran a small variety store to supplement the meager money they made in their "home industry" of weaving. Due to a depression and a disastrous war with Japan in the early years of the 20th century, the economy in Russia was so bad that many people were close to starving. There were also strikes that added to the unemployment of many of the Kolbes' creditors. Under these disastrous circumstances, Julius and Marianna were willing to forego payments for a time. However, as one friend of the Kolbes' put it, "There were neighbors who took advantage of their charity and patience." As a result of the many defaults in the payments due the Kolbes', they went bankrupt and lost their business.

Coupled with the Industrial Revolution and all its attendant injustices was the fact that, for well over a hundred years, Poland was an enslaved country. During the 19th century, it didn't even appear on the maps of Europe. Three powerful nations bordering it — Russia, Austria and Prussia — had swallowed up Poland, partitioning it in 1772, in 1791, and a third time in 1793. This occurred without any military resistance for a number of reasons. At the close of the 17th century, Poland was one of the last countries to emerge from the feudal system. Made up as it was of independent principalities, with a weak and at times corrupt central government and without natural boundaries for protection except for the mountainous to the south, it was easy prey for the newly emerging larger national states. The sad chapter of the partitioning of Poland and its domination by foreign powers was in sharp contrast to its glorious past. Nonetheless, the Poles tenaciously hung on to their culture, language, and above all their Catholic Faith. All this had its impact on the young Raymond Kolbe who was to bring great glory to Poland in the 20th century.

The Poles had been tested constantly in their thousand years of Christianity and were not about to give in to any tyranny imposed on them. The nation was in a very strategic place in the center of Europe, between the East and West. Every armed invasion of Europe from the east had to pass through Poland. The invading armies were, for the most part, non-Christian, in fact anti-Christian. Thus the Poles, in engaging the Moslem Turks or the pagan Tartars, were not only motivated by love of country, but were fighting to preserve their Faith and that of Christian Europe. In the Middle Ages, Poland repulsed ninety-three Tartar invasions. Militarily, the Poles excelled in their maneuverable cavalry of mounted knights, ideal for repulsing enemy invaders on the broad plains of Poland.

In the late Middle Ages, as society in Western Europe become more and more secular, the underpinning of religious values and the influence of the Church on knighthood were lessened. The Spanish writer Cervantes lamented the corruption of Christian knighthood. In his literary classic, Don Quixote, he lampooned a knighthood which no longer stood for the defense of the down- trodden, exemplified by noble, manly virtues. It had become a parody of the real thing.

In Poland, however, it had lost none of its luster. Perhaps this was due to the fact that the Church's influence, especially the Marian devotion of the Poles, was still inspiring chivalry and heroic exploits of her knights in the defense of freedom. Poland in its prime was "a power to be reckoned with" and often the defender of the defenseless. It welcomed the unwelcome from other countries of Europe, such as the Jews (Poland before the Second World War had the largest Jewish population in Europe). During its thousand years as a Christian nation, Poland had always been on the side of justice and a champion of legitimate personal freedom for all men regardless of social rank or circumstances. Poland avoided the many bloody fratricidal religious wars following the Reformation, because it followed the principles of sound political philosophy based on the Gospel and Catholic social teachings.

One of its most famous sons was the international lawyer, Paulus Vladimiri (1372 – 1435). He was an "international man," studying law in Padua, Italy, and philosophy and theology at the University of Prague. He was elected twice to the prestigious office of president of the then famous University of Kracow.

This Christian jurist was the first scholar who championed opposition to genocide in any manner or form. This practice, so opposed to the natural law, divine law and love of neighbor, which he named the "Prussian heresy," is still with us today. Several Italian jurists and scholars at the Council of Constance used arguments formulated by Vladimiri to condemn the brutal practice of forced conversions of pagans to Christianity by the Teutonic Knights. His theories, based on the Gospels and the principles inherited from the ancient Romans and Greeks, were the basis of international law and politics during the 16th and 17th centuries. Although his doctrine and theories were written over 500 years ago, they are strikingly similar to the words of the Second Vatican Council, in the Pastoral Constitution on the Church in the Modern World.

The young boy, Raymond Kolbe

Besides living in a Catholic culture which was aligned with the western part of Europe and ever loyal and submissive to the Church of Rome, young Raymond Kolbe learned from his parents the noble exploits of Poland's national heroes. His father, Julius, zealous patriot that he was, loved to relate how the great General Zolkiewski, at the cost of his life, repulsed the well organized, disciplined armies of Islam during their march into the interior of Poland, preventing them from taking over Europe. Julius would read historic novels by famous Polish writers such as Sienkiewicz* to his sons, which related the many incursions onto Polish soil of greedy, tyrannical neighbors and how they were repulsed by the Polish cavalry. Of particular inspiration were the exploits of the brave and devout Polish King John III Sobieski who, though vastly outnumbered, lifted the siege of Vienna by the Turks in 1687 and thus saved Christian Europe from Islamic domination.

After overrunning the enemy camp, Sobieski sent the captured Green Banner of the Prophet to the Holy Father with the words, "I came, I saw, God conquered!" The threat of the Mohammedan scimitar that hung over Christian Europe for centuries was broken.

* Besides the trilogy, *With Fire and Sword*, *The Deluge* and *Pan Michael*, he authored the famous novel Quo Vadis which has been made into a movie several times.

Sobieski, like other Polish heroes, was a deeply religious man. On his way to Vienna, he stopped at the national shrine of Our Lady of Czestochowa, where he vowed before the miraculous Icon that he would not sheath his sword until the Turks were defeated. He gave his men the battle cry, "In the name of Mary; Lord God help!"

Due to their deep Catholic roots, the Poles ever turned to Mary in good times as well as bad. During the years of suppression, it was their shared love and devotion to Mary that united the Poles from Austria, Prussia and Russia at the foot of the altar of the Black Madonna. Despite all of their efforts, the three neighboring countries failed to suppress the Polish language and culture. The center of Polish nationalism was and is the shrine of Our Lady of Czestochowa. She was more than a spiritual mother revered by all Catholics. In Poland she was so integrated into their culture and so loved by the Polish nation that she was officially recognized as the Queen of Poland. It was she who heard their prayers when all else failed.

It is related that during the height of the many invasions, aptly called the deluge, Our Lady appeared above the walls of the fortress monastery of Czestochowa. The last stronghold in Poland was under siege by an army of Protestant Swedes. The small force of soldiers and monks could not hold out any longer when the Holy Virgin, with the Child Jesus in her arms, appeared above the battlements in the midst of a supernatural light. The enemy fled in panic. In gratitude, King John Casimir officially consecrated Poland to Mary. Ever after, the Polish nation remembered her and publicly acknowledged their utter dependence on Our Lady, Queen of Poland.

In every home throughout the land, there was a quiet corner with its own shrine to the Queen of Heaven and of Poland, where the family gathered to pray the Rosary. From the time that he was a small child, Raymond's parents by word and example taught him to love the Mother of God. Her intervention and the heroic exploits of her patriots fired the imagination of Raymond, giving him an unshakeable confidence that some day Poland would again be a sovereign nation. In his patriotic zeal, and encouraged by his father, he would paint the Polish eagle on the fences of Pabianice. During this time, Julius himself was involved with underground groups planning to break the yoke of the countries suppressing Poland. He was arrested and jailed for a short period.

With such a background as this, is it not understandable that young Raymond dreamed of some day joining the military to help liberate Poland from foreign domination? The idealistic lad had before him national heroes who didn't hesitate to make the supreme sacrifice of their lives for the Faith and their beloved country. These leaders considered themselves as Generals under the supreme command of the Queen of Heaven and Poland.

His devotion to Mary, united with a lively, independent nature, did not prevent him from getting into the usual trouble of boys his age. He could try the patience of his mother who was something of a perfectionist in raising her children. Once she remarked in exasperation, "Raymond, what's ever going to become of you?" She then didn't give it a second thought. Not so Raymond; after this incident there was a noticeable change in the boy's behavior. His mother became worried at the boy's mysterious change. He was more quiet and docile and seemed more serious. Upon questioning, Raymond was reluctant at first to tell her his "secret." This indomitable lady and mother was not to be easily put off in getting at the root of what she saw as a serious problem. Reminding the boy of his obligation of obedience to her as his parent, she finally succeeded.

In tears, the boy told her how much her reproach had bothered him. He had sadly turned to the Blessed Mother in their home shrine and asked her the same question, "Mother of God, what will become of me?" He fled to their parish church and begged Mary, "What will become of me?" The Blessed Virgin took compassion on the miserable boy and appeared to him. With a tender, motherly expression, she held in each hand a crown; one white, the other red. She asked Raymond which one he would choose; the white signified purity, the red martyrdom. The impetuous youth, like another great Saint of our times, St. Thérèse of the Child Jesus, who chose all, answered, "I choose both." He chose well, for Mary smiled and then disappeared. The course of his life was set by no less a person than the Mother of God. He would remain chaste, the white crown, and he would be a martyr, the red crown. From that time on he would frequently talk to his mother about martyrdom.

On one of their annual pilgrimages to the shrine of Our Lady of Czestochowa, the Kolbes promised to make any sacrifice so that their oldest son, Francis, might become a priest. As to Raymond, with his organizational talent and mathematical skill, it was decided that he would stay home to help his mother with the family business. It was not an easy decision to make, but there was little choice because, at the time, the parents felt they could not afford to send both boys to school. Raymond, above average in intelligence, would have been happy to accompany his brother to the business school in Pabianice, but his parents, particularly Mama, had decided "what was best." Raymond never questioned, much less pressed his parents to include him in their plans for formal education.

Fortunately a local pharmacist, Mr. Kotowski, took a personal interest in Raymond. One day when his mother sent him to the pharmacy for some medicine for one of the women she was nursing (she was a midwife on the side), he gave the pharmacist the formula of the medication in faultless Latin without missing a syllable. Kotowski was duly impressed and asked him where he had picked up his Latin. He proudly answered that "Father Jakowski teaches us Latin!" Raymond, of course, was an altar boy, and in those days one had to master the Latin responses at Mass.

Upon further probing, the pharmacist learned that the boy's brother was going to school, but the Kolbes couldn't afford to send both. What a pity! Such a promising boy! Kotowski was one of those Polish patriots who was looking to the future. This youth and others, he reasoned, would be the hope of a resurrected Poland — but to lead Poland to glory, these leaders would need formal education. He helped Raymond with private tutoring which opened further education to him. ❑

> ***The more powerful and courageous a soul becomes with the help of God's grace, the greater the cross God places on its shoulders, so that it might mirror as closely as possible the image of the Crucified in its own life.*** St. Maximilian

Which of Two Knighthoods? A Choice Is Made

THE KEEN disappointment that Raymond had felt in not being able to go to school was reflected later in a letter his mother wrote a friend, "He came back home as though he had wings, and at once related the marvelous good fortune." With the tutoring, Raymond was able to catch up with his brother in his studies and succeeded admirably in passing all his examinations. His parents, seeing the determination of their son in mastering his studies, decided to make an even greater effort to send both boys to school — no small sacrifice considering the depressed economy and the help Raymond had been giving his mother. This was but the first of many sacrifices the devoted parents were asked to make for the boys' vocations.

In 1907, during a parish mission in Pabianice conducted by a Conventual Franciscan, Father Peregrin Haczela, the priest made an exciting announcement. His order was opening a high school seminary in Lwow, and they were looking for worthy young men to dedicate their lives to the service of God and Mary Immaculate. The fact that the Franciscan Order had a long history of Marian devotion going back to its founder, St. Francis of Assisi, and had many saints and theologians who had championed the dogma of the Immaculate Conception, appealed to both Francis and Raymond and prompted them to ask the priest to add their names. Besides having parents who were Third Order Franciscans, the boys themselves gave great promise. They were prayerful. They loved the Madonna and they were respectful — indicating a loving, disciplined home life.

The boys excitedly asked their parents for permission to enter the seminary. Marianna was happy that Francis was taking a major step towards the priesthood. She had been praying that her first boy would become a priest — but now Raymond as well? After much prayer for discernment as to God's will, and with the understanding support of Julius, Mama too gave her consent. Since the Franciscan seminary was at Lwow, in the Austrian part of occupied Poland, their journey had an added bit of adventure. Papa took his sons as far as Kracow. There, they crossed the well-guarded border at Miechow, hidden in a hay wagon for they hadn't bothered getting visas, which would have made the border crossing even more difficult. They arrived in the historic city of Lwow at the beginning of the school year in 1907. How exciting it was for the Kolbe brothers to be in the city immortalized by the historic novels of Henry Sienkiewicz.

Raymond didn't let the noble exploits of the past or daydreaming of the future glory of Poland distract him from his studies. We have the testimony of one of his schoolmates who said of Raymond that he was the most talented in his class, excelling in mathematics and science. However, he never become so engrossed in his studies that he lost sight of his great ambition of one day making his contribution toward the uniting and liberating of Poland. He intended to be a great strategist some day. This was no idle, impractical, farfetched dream. Kolbe was a realist. He once set up, at the cost of much time and effort, a cardboard layout of the city of Lwow, demonstrating an elaborate system of fortifications which would make the city impregnable. Like everything else he planned throughout his life, there was a solid, reasonable basis for the hope of success. Although he was misunderstood at times as an unrealistic dreamer, his "dreams" had an uncanny record of being realized.

Later, when he was a student in Rome, he amazed his fellow students with plans for a spacecraft driven by jets and rockets which would escape the earth's gravitational field and take men to the moon and other planets. One of his professors, seeing the feasibility of his remarkable, well thought-out plan, encouraged him to apply at the Roman patent office for a copyright on his spaceship.

With a quick, creative mind and persevering efforts, he grasped the problems involved in any particular case and solutions soon followed. As one of his seminary professors said of him, "He had a rare natural genius." Later, as a Franciscan, he tapped into the infinite power of God through his vow of obedience and an unlimited trust in Our Lady's direction and help. His exceptional talents carried him just so far; unconditional love and dedication carried him the rest of the way in whatever he did.

Raymond prayed before this painting of the Immaculate Conception, promising to fight for her.

Above the altar in the minor seminary chapel in Lwow, there was a painting of the Immaculate Conception before which Raymond was accustomed to pray. On one of these occasions, prostrate before her image, he received a special grace that was to influence his whole life. In an ecstasy of love, he promised to fight for Our Lady and to ever praise and honor her. He had not the least inkling how this was to be accomplished. In giving a generous soul such as Raymond's a special mission, God always tests that person's sincerity and perseverance. Raymond Kolbe was no exception. After three years, the routine and regularity of life in the seminary, which at first was a joy, and the newness a challenge, became tiring and painfully monotonous.

As the fateful day approached in which he had to decide whether to ask for admission to the Franciscan novitiate or to leave, all sorts of doubts arose, robbing him of his peace of soul. As the saying goes, "The devil likes to fish in muddy waters." The archenemy of the Woman in the Book of Genesis was to kick up much confusion. Could Raymond, sixteen years old, with a lively and independent nature, commit himself to a strict community life for the rest of his days? When the Blessed Mother asked him to fight for her, was it not in a military career for the liberation of Poland? Would he not best serve the Queen of Poland by using his God-given talents as a strategist or an engineer?

The professor of mathematics at the minor seminary, who surely must have been challenged at times by his student who excelled in the subject, expressed his opinion this way: "It is a pity that this young man, so richly gifted, should become a priest." Surely the young sixteen year-old, Raymond, must have recalled his father's stirring stories of past Polish military heroes who fought under Our Lady's banner to preserve the Faith and protect the fatherland from foreign invaders.

He took a long, hard look at the religious life he had chosen and decided he had made a mistake. He would give up the idea of studying for the priesthood and entering the Franciscan Order. All that remained was to inform his superior of his decision and he could leave the next day. He even talked his brother, Francis, into joining him in seeing the Father Provincial to break the disappointing news to him that they didn't have a calling to the religious life. Again, Providence intervened and Raymond readily saw Our Lady's gentle hand nudging him in the right direction.

On their way to break the news of their decision to their superior, Raymond and Francis were called to the parlor — a visitor was there to see them. There they found their mother glowing with exciting news. Their youngest brother, Joseph, had decided to follow Raymond and Francis in entering the Franciscan Order. That was not all. She and Julius had also decided to follow a life-long desire (actually it was mostly her idea) of dedicating their lives in the service of religion. The father had already gone to Kracow to the house of the Franciscans, and she was joining the Benedictine Sisters in Lwow. "Now," she announced triumphantly and with great satisfaction, "the whole family belongs to God!"

One can readily imagine the effect this surprise announcement had on Raymond at the precise moment he intended to leave the seminary. How could he now go through with what he was later to see as a temptation of the devil? He needed no more time to decide. He literally ran to Father Provincial's room, asking him to be received in the novitiate. He would never forget that providential visit by his natural mother, and his heavenly

Mother's intervention, which had caused this attack of the enemy to crumble. In September, 1910, he and his brother were invested in the Franciscan habit and he was given the name of Maximilian, a young Roman soldier martyred for the Faith. The other Maximilian, our hero of the 20th century, would later be added to the calendar of saints as a Martyr of Charity.

Though he regained a measure of peace, it wasn't long before he was plagued by another spiritual cross. Shortly after entering the novitiate, he suffered from an attack of scruples. Everything had to be done to perfection, and when he failed, which was inevitable, he

Fr. Bronislaus — Kolbe's Unique Fellow Novice

The patience of fellow novice, Friar Bronislaus Stryczny, who had to listen to Friar Maximilian's many scruples, was richly rewarded in 1971 when he went to Rome and witnessed the beatification of his friend. Friar Barney, as he was affectionately known in this country, didn't live quite long enough to witness his friend's canonization. In life, however, he shared many intimate confidences with St. Maximilian. As a newly ordained priest, he was the first person in Poland to join the M.I., founded by the Saint in 1917, and was zealous in getting new members. Physically they were much different - Maximilian was small and frail, Bronislaus was a big hulk of a man with the strength of a bull. It was in the spiritual realm that they were of one mind and heart. In Friar Bronislaus's own words, "After receiving ordination to the priesthood, we were to remember one another at Mass to the end of our lives. After the death of one of us, the other was to keep this promise until we met in Heaven. Our conversations were often on the further development of our spiritual lives." Both were noted for their holiness within the Franciscan Order and for their love of Our Lady and devotion to the Eucharistic Lord.

Father Barney also shared with Fr. Kolbe the indignities and cruelty of a Nazi Concentration camp. Though they were in different concentration camps miles apart, Fr. Barney, while in Dachau, learned of his friend's heroic death and the circumstances surrounding it through a spiritual revelation on the day of August 14, 1941. After Dachau was liberated, he heard the news of St. Kolbe's death, which confirmed his revelation. He eventually came to the United States and was a member of the Marytown community for several years. He died while passing through Santa Maria, California, on August 14, 1974.

believed he sinned where there was no sin. The scrupulous person blows up the inadvertent imperfection into a serious sin. Thus the scrupulous person can be a headache to any confessor, whom they constantly insist on seeing. The solution is humility, exercised through blind obedience. The Novice Master of Friar Maximilian had him submit his state of soul to a fellow novice, Friar Bronislaus Stryczny, as often as he had a temptation to be scrupulous. His obedience won out and this experience was later to help him to be understanding and patient in directing others to overcome scruples.

The priests who screened candidates for the novitiate had no doubts in accepting Friar Maximilian. He was conscientious in carrying out the duties assigned him and he practiced virtue with simplicity, not drawing the least attention to himself. With his quick and versatile mind he excelled in his studies. Studious and popular with his fellow students because of his friendly and enthusiastic nature, he was a good community person. He thus was a real asset to the novitiate, where there is much interaction between the young men and good example is so important for the progress of all the novices. The year of the novitiate passed rapidly, and after his profession of simple vows of poverty, chastity and obedience on September 5, 1911, Friar Maximilian remained in Kracow for another year to finish his studies in the humanities. During this period his father was also stationed in Kracow. In the novice's free time, father and son were able to enjoy each other's company as they explored the historic city, so rich in Polish culture, scholarship and art.

In the fall of 1912, Friar Maximilian was told by his superior that he and six other friars had been chosen to go to Rome to study for degrees in philosophy and theology at the International Seraphic College and the famous Gregorian University. It was a privilege not all the seminarians were given — only the brightest and most hopeful. Surprisingly, he was not excited to receive this honor and the opportunity to go to the center of his Catholic Faith to study. With mixed feelings, he declined the honor, giving as a reason that his health would not hold up in Rome. This was eventually confirmed when he came down with consumption in his last years in Rome. This reason which he gave the Father Provincial, however, was not the main reason for having his name removed from the list. The real reason was to come out later in correspondence with his mother.

Among young men in their late teens and early twenties, it is common to have some good- natured kidding. In his case, this kidding may have been motivated by the envy of fellow friars who had not been chosen to go to Rome. Be that as it may, Maximilian was told and was convinced, and no one could convince him otherwise, that the women in Rome "accosted young men in the middle of the street and constantly harassed them." That he took this kidding very seriously is indicated in the last letter he wrote his mother before departing for Rome:

> *"I ask you, mother, to pray for me in a very special way... I understand that some women accost even religious, and yet it will indeed be necessary to go out in order to attend classes."*

From the time that he had been offered the white crown of purity and the red one of martyrdom, and had chosen both, he had jealously kept his promise to the Blessed Virgin. Now he felt that one was being threatened by a serious occasion of sinning against the vow of chastity. After prayer and further reflection, however, Friar Maximilian realized that he had made his decision too hastily. Wasn't he doing his own will over the prudent judgment of his superiors? Certainly they were not deliberately sending him into an occasion of sin. Where was his conviction that God speaks infallibly through lawful authority? Where was his trust that the Virgin of

The Seraphic College, near the Roman Forum, opposite the Palatine hill on the Via San Teodoro, where Friar Maximilian studied for the priesthood. It was here that he established his life's work, the *Militia Immaculatae*.

virgins would surely protect and preserve his purity, if he would but turn to her? Friar Maximilian had the humility of admitting he had been too hasty and wrong. He went to the Provincial, declaring, "Father, do with me as you wish."

The immediate response of his superior was, "Well, son, you will go to Rome."

On October 28, 1912, Friar Maximilian left Poland for the Eternal City of Rome, where he remained for the next seven years. In his first letter to his mother, dated November 21, he writes reassuringly,

> *"Things are not so terrible as I thought when I last wrote you. Would the Italian women really have nothing better to do than to accost us? Besides, we always go out in groups."*

The malicious slander concerning Italian women — that they were waiting to pounce on the innocent friar — was finally laid to rest. He was later to recognize that, again, what at first seemed a virtue — high regard for the virtue of purity — was but another ploy of the devil. In later years, recalling this incident, Father Kolbe asked the rhetorical questions:

> *"In truth, what would have happened if Father Provincial had decided according to my reasoning? Would there have been such a place as the 'City of the Immaculate'? Would we have had the good fortune of working to make known the glories of the Immaculate? Is not then the glory of obedience, blind submission to the will of the Lord?"*

Throughout his life he would practice this virtue of obedience to a heroic degree. Endowed with great reasoning powers, Kolbe had no difficulty in recognizing the supremacy of faith over his own reason, reconciling authority with freedom of conscience.

The high regard that the Franciscan superiors had for Friar Maximilian, in sending him to Rome for his philosophy and theology, was well founded. Less than three years after his arrival in Rome in the fall of 1912, he received a doctorate in philosophy, summa cum laude, at the Gregorian University. He was twenty-one years old but, with a boyish, round face, he looked like a seventeen year-old. He received a doctorate in theology at the international Seraphic College of his Order four years later in July of 1919. A year before, on April 28, 1918, Fr. Maximilian was ordained a priest at the church of Sant' Andrea della Valle. He celebrated his first Mass in the Church of Sant' Andrea della Fratte at the altar erected on the spot where the Blessed Mother appeared to and converted the Jewish agnostic, Alphonse Ratisbonne, in 1842. A year after his ordination, in July of 1919, he returned to Poland. These are the bare facts and dates of Friar Maximilian's academic progress during his seven years in Rome.

All his confreres agreed that Friar Maximilian displayed extraordinary talents in his studies. He often was found far ahead of his class and even of his professors, particularly in the areas of science and mathematics. He would ask his most eminent professors probing questions — not to embarrass them (which happened at times), but ever in the quest of truth and his insatiable desire to get at the bottom of any particular question or problem. Fr. Bondini, one of his professors, humbly had to admit, "This boy asks me questions I cannot answer."

Another professor, Fr. Leon Cicchito, remarked, "While walking with me, he would not give me a moment's rest but plied me with endless questions," and laughingly added, "a real bore." Seriously he would go on to say, "He was the most gifted youth with whom I had been in contact during the years I was vice rector. He had a rare natural genius."

In spite of all, he never paraded his academic achievements, nor bullied others verbally through his superior intellectual gifts. He was ever available to help his classmates and, as one student remarked, "He had a way of explaining things that made it easier to understand." As far as the degrees he had from prestigious colleges in Rome, years later, when one of his brothers was cleaning his office, he accidentally came across the two doctorate degrees. The brother brought his discovery to the attention of his superior, suggesting that they should be framed and hung in his office. Showing embarrassment at what he had intended to remain hidden, Fr. Kolbe told the brother to put them back where he had found them. ❑

> *The source of peace is resignation to the will of God: to do what is in our power and leave the rest to the care of Divine Providence - have the confidence of a child toward its best mother.*
>
> — St. Maximilian Kolbe

Fra. Maximilian with six other Franciscan Friars consecrate themselves to Mary Immaculate on the evening of October 16, 1918, and initiate a new International Marian movement, the *Militia Immaculatae*. This is one of four murals depicting the Life of St. Maximilian, found in the adoration chapel of Marytown, Libertyville, Illinois.

A Strategy for Conquering the World

CONTRARY TO THE general attitude of the intelligentsia of our day, who practically deify higher education and do not hesitate to parade their degrees before the world, there was none of this in the humble Franciscan — a worthy son of the "Little Poor Man" of Assisi. All education to him was but a means to an end — the salvation of immortal souls — not an end in itself. His degrees in philosophy and theology were to be used as tools for evangelizing. With impeccable logic, using the Socratic method of questioning, he would take on street preachers and total strangers in public discussions. Ever respectful and with sharp mind, he would never allow his opponent to better him.

In this regard, one of his close friends related an amusing incident shortly after Kolbe had received his doctorate in philosophy. One day in the streets of Rome, he met a man who was vehemently denouncing the Pope and the Church. Kolbe was ever on the alert to defend the Church he loved. As the young seminarian was bettering his opponent, the gentleman cried out to Kolbe, who at the time was in his early twenties, but looked like he was in his teens, "I know all this, young man! I am a doctor of philosophy."

The young friar shot back, "And I also." With a look of amazement, the socialist abruptly changed his tone. Since he could not win by this bullying tactic, he next had to try dialoging with a respected fellow philosopher. With much patience and respect, the friar drove his opponent to the wall. Father Pal, Kolbe's friend who related the incident, remarked, "At the end of the discussion the unbeliever remained silent and seemed to meditate deeply."

As a future priest and scholar, the importance of formal education in the sciences, especially philosophy and theology, was of utmost importance. It was in the science of the saints, however, that the future Saint excelled. Holiness of life and good example are contagious. While in formation, Kolbe was fortunate in knowing two saintly friars. One was Fr. Venance Katarzyniec, who died at an early age in the odor of sanctity. Friar Maximilian had the opportunity of observing and living with Fr. Venance in the same friary. This young, talented priest, who was noted for his strict observance of the Rule and his outstanding humility, was one of the very few priests of the Order who supported Kolbe's early efforts of furthering the M.I. The other priest was the Rector of the Franciscan International Seminary, Fr. Stephen Ignudi, an eminent religious, a great ascetic, and a promoter of a more primitive observance of the Franciscan Rule.

It was this Father Rector who gave the young seminarian some Lourdes water for an abscessed thumb which the doctors intended to amputate. He related to Friar Maximilian how his mother had applied a compress of Lourdes water to a putrefying leg the doctors intended to remove. The Father Rector, at the time a boy of twelve, had been miraculously cured. The doctor, who was originally a skeptic, was convinced that a divine intervention had taken place. He converted and had a church built at his own expense.

After Kolbe applied the Lourdes water to his thumb, he related the whole episode in a letter to his mother and concluded,

> *"When the doctor learned that I had some water from Lourdes he readily agreed that I use it. What happened? The next day at the hospital, the surgeon told me that an operation was not strictly necessary. After several dressings, I was cured. Glory to God and thanks to the Immaculata!"*

What he did not mention to his mother, to avoid her worrying, was that had he lost his thumb, he would likely never be ordained a priest. He was later to "repay" Our Lady of Lourdes, so to speak, by his great theological insights in regard to the name by which she chose to identify herself to St. Bernadette: **"I am the Immaculate Conception."**

While in Rome, Friar Maximilian was painfully aware that the Church was badly in need of renewal. The Franciscan Order, which he loved, was in particular need. How frequently zealous young men entered the Order and, in a short period of time, lost their initial zeal for the salvation of souls and personal holiness, settling into a "comfortable," mediocre observance of the Rule or leaving the Order. In this regard he wrote later on, "These words were impressed upon my mind: 'refuse to compromise, or it will destroy the Order.'" In a letter from Rome to his younger brother, Joseph, who had also entered the Conventual Franciscans and took the name of Alphonse, we read of his concern,

> *"The most deadly poison of our times is indifference. Its victims are found not only among worldly people, but in our own ranks as well… And this happens, although the praise of God should know no limits. We finite creatures cannot ever give Him the boundless glory He deserves. Let us strive therefore to praise Him to the greatest extent of our powers… All that exists has value to the extent that it is related to Him, the Creator of the universe, the Savior of men. If our actions are directed to this God as our final good, He will give us His wisdom and prudence without limit. What a gift! That, dear brother, is the only way to realize our capacity of giving God the greatest glory.*
>
> *"Life begins to make sense when we recognize and acknowledge God's infinite goodness and our absolute dependence on Him. Our response will be praise and total love expressed in obedience."*

From these basic concepts, Fr. Maximilian developed a synthesis of an amazingly fruitful apostolate along with continuous spiritual growth that ended in his heroic death and canonization.

To fully understand and appreciate the Saint, we must see him organizing and founding his life's work — his *Militia Immaculatae*, the vehicle of all his future conquests for Our Lady. The event which triggered an immediate need for such a movement of renewal and evangelization occurred in Rome in 1917. It was during the bicentenary of Freemasonry, and the Freemasons were making Rome the theater of their sacrilegious demonstrations. In their hatred of the Church, they marched right up to the doors of St. Peter's, where the Pope was a voluntary prisoner. Boldly they displayed their banners: "Satan must reign in the Vatican. The Pope will be his slave." At the same time, they were distributing pamphlets attacking the Church and the Holy Father. The military blood of the young friar boiled. His reaction? To his confreres Kolbe threw out this challenge:

> *"In the face of such attacks of the enemies of the Church of God, are we to remain inactive? Is that all we can do — complain and cry? No! Every one of us has a holy obligation to personally hurl back the assaults of the foe."*

Friar Maximilian analyzed the situation thus:

> *"These men without God find themselves in a tragic situation. Such implacable hatred for the Church and the ambassadors of Christ on earth is not in the power of individual persons, but of a systematic activity stemming in the final analysis from Freemasonry. In particular, it aims to destroy the Catholic religion. Their deceits have been spread throughout the world, in different disguises. But with the same goal — religious indifference and weakening of moral forces, according to their basic principle — 'We will conquer the Catholic Church not by argumentation, but rather with moral corruption.'"*

Was not Maximilian Kolbe's assessment of the real enemy of the Church, Freemasonry, right on target? Is not their goal today,

Father Kolbe with the seminarians in 1933

though not as openly declared, a secularist, humanist, anti-supernatural society and culture? Is it not being realized all around us today, with God and the open practice of religion excluded from the public and personal lives of the average American? To see this, we have only to look at the pervasive anti-life, anti-family, anti-God rulings of the highest court in the land, the Supreme Court (see page 33 and Appendix, for more on Kolbe and Freemasonry).

In that same year, on January 20, 1917, Father Stephen Ignudi, the Rector of the seminary, gave a talk to the students about the conversion of a Jewish agnostic, Alphonse Ratisbonne. This rabidly anti-Catholic Jew, from a prominent banking family in France, had been heaping ridicule and blasphemy on the Church. When a Catholic acquaintance dared him to wear the Miraculous Medal and recite a *Memorare*, Alphonse accepted. Our Blessed Mother appeared to him in a blinding light in the church of Sant' Andrea della Fratte and he was instantly converted. One moment he had been attacking the Church, and in the next, he couldn't wait to be baptized. He ultimately went on to be ordained a priest and work for the conversion of his fellow Jews. Friar Maximilian reasoned that if Mary could conquer the heart of Alphonse through his wearing of the Miraculous Medal honoring her Immaculate Conception, this medal would be an ideal means for conquering other souls.

Although he was enthusiastic and eager to start his special Marian apostolate, he did not rush into it without preparation. During a ten-month period, he worked out a precise strategy for his future army. The militants of Mary would be totally consecrated to win all souls present and to the very end of time. The loss of a single soul was a great misfortune to Kolbe and so he would add a note of urgency, "…as soon as possible, as soon as possible."

The promise of victory in this total warfare between the serpent and the Woman is found in the first Book of the Bible: "I will put enmity between you [Satan] and the Woman, between your seed and hers [Jesus]. You will lie in wait for her heel and she will crush your head." (Genesis 3:15) He would add a corollary to fit our modern age:

> *"Modern times are dominated by Satan and will be more so in the future. The conflict with hell cannot be engaged by men,*

even the most clever. The Immaculata alone has from God the promise of victory over Satan."

To make sure that the inspiration Friar Maximilian had in founding the *Militia Immaculatae* was from the Warrior Queen in her battles against the ancient serpent, he had an infallible test — holy obedience and the cross. Every advance he made in the progress of establishing the M.I. was stamped by obedience. First, he asked the opinion of the regular community confessor. "Having been reassured in the name of holy obedience, I decided to start working." Friar Jerome Biasi and Fr. Joseph Pal, fellow classmates, were the first to whom he confided his plan to start a program to checkmate the prince of the world. In the Saint's own words: "However, I set the condition that they would first have to ask for permission of their spiritual directors, so that we might be sure of the will of God." As he recruited more collaborators, all was done under the direction and obedience of the Rector, Fr. Stephen Ignudi— again we see his fixed idea and invincible weapon of holy obedience.

On the evening of October 17, 1917, Friar Maximilian held the first meeting of the original seven members: Fr. Joseph Pal, of the Romanian province, the only priest member (d.1947); Friar Anthony Glowinski, deacon of the Romanian Province (d.1918); Friar Jerome Biasi, of the Paduan province (d.1929); Friar Quiricus Pignalberi (d.1982), of the Roman province; Friar Anthony Mansi (d.1918) and Friar Henry Granata (d.1964), both of the Neapolitan province. Fr. Kolbe wrote later a detailed account at the order of his superior:

> *"This meeting took place in the evening secretly behind the closed doors of an inner cell. Before us was a statuette of the Immaculata between two lighted blessed candles… we obtained the Holy Father's blessing through Archbishop Dominic Jacquet…"*

That initial meeting was the last for almost a year. One difficulty after another arose — so much so that no one dared to speak of it, even among the friars who were familiar with Friar Maximilian's plans for the Marian movement which he called the "Militia of Mary Immaculate," or M.I. (from the Latin *Militia Immaculatae*).

The Program of the Militia Immaculatae

The program of the M.I. is as simple and as vast as the Church's mission. Its ultimate goal is the conquest of the whole world and each individual soul, to the end of time, for the Sacred Heart of Jesus, through Mary Immaculate. Each member is to give himself entirely to Mary Immaculate - to be used as tools in her Immaculate hands for the salvation and sanctification of all souls, especially those who are bitter enemies of the Church. The original prayer of Father Maximilian singled out the Masons, but the authorized prayer of the M.I. today has the broader meaning, "enemies of the Church," which includes Communists and all other anti-religious groups.

How New Recruits Were to Be Enrolled

One could be enrolled in the Militia and share in all its spiritual benefits by having one's name inscribed in the official register, making an act of total consecration (as composed by Fr. Maximilian), wearing the Miraculous Medal (thus honoring Mary in her great prerogative of the Immaculate Conception), and by reciting, at least daily, the following prayer: "O Mary conceived without sin, pray for us who have recourse to you, especially for the enemies of the Church, and for those recommended to you." Organized action and particular projects are encouraged. In Fr. Maximilian's own words: "Every means (provided it be apt and licit) natural and supernatural, whether from within or without the area of our activity should be utilized." Basically, it is not an organization so much as a movement. Again, in Father Maximilian's words: "The Militia... is not a particular organization having for its scope the formation of a special category of people. It is a movement that must enthuse souls, snatch them from Satan, and, won for the cause of the Immaculate, incite them to the apostolate of realizing the reign of Jesus Christ."

Whoever is punctual at the first instant will be punctual the whole day. Whoever lingers for even a few seconds in rising does not receive from God those graces that he would have received, were he faithful to the first punctuality of the day.

— St. Maximilian Kolbe

At the same time, Mary was quietly marshalling her forces to do battle against the great scourge of the 20th century, International Communism. The M.I. was founded just four days after the final apparition of Our Lady at Fatima and the Miracle of the Sun witnessed by 70,000 people. Our Lady of Fatima had her battle plans and weapons (consecration to her Immaculate Heart, penitence and the Rosary) ready to checkmate the Communist takeover of Russia, which occurred just a few weeks later.

At Fatima, she asked that Russia and the world be consecrated to her Immaculate Heart, promising the conversion of atheistic Russia, the ultimate triumph of her Immaculate Heart and world peace. Toward the end of his life, Father Maximilian made a similar prediction, at a time when Communist Russia was a real threat to world peace, spreading its errors throughout the world. In February of 1937, in the course of an M.I. conference in Rome, he made this declaration:

> *"The day is not far off, nor a mere dream, when the statue of the Immaculata will be enthroned by her Knights in the very heart of Moscow."*

As mentioned above, the second sign, besides obedience, indicating that what he was doing was in full accord with the will of God, was suffering or the Cross. No great enterprise or saint is immune to the Cross. Ultimately, everything of eternal value is done under the inspiration and example of the Suffering Servant (Jesus) and his Sorrowful Mother. One day, during the summer break, while playing football, the young friar began coughing up blood and had to lay down. He was eventually confined to bed. Continual hemorrhaging and spasms continued for two weeks before he was allowed to get up from his sick bed. While finishing his studies with honors, he had a grave relapse and began coughing and hemorrhaging again. He kept the suffering and his illness so well hidden that even his best friends and superiors were not aware of the gravity of his illness.

Nor was physical suffering the only kind he endured. One of the original seven founders tried to convince the others that their movement was non-sensical. The saintly founder could not even defend himself. No doubt because of his ill health, the Father General had forbidden him to be concerned about the *Militia*

Immaculatae (Whoever imagined that obedience is ever easy?). For almost a year, Maximilian had to admit that, "The only activity of the M.I. consisted in praying and distributing the miraculous medals."

Intent upon obedience, and that his work continue indefinitely, Father Maximilian sought the special approbation of Rome. In 1922, the Militia was canonically established as a Pious Union. Four years later, Pope Pius XI elevated the M.I. to the status of a Primary Union, with the privilege of aggregating to itself affiliated unions erected elsewhere in the world. Father Maximilian's dream of world conquest under the banner of her who crushes the head of the serpent was being realized.

It was after his return to Poland that the M.I. really took off, but not without much more suffering, contradiction and misunderstanding. The first major setback of the many he would encounter during his life came in 1920. Chronic tuberculosis, which he had contracted in Rome during his student days, flared up anew, and he was confined to a sanatorium for two years. All activity stopped. This was to be a time of intense interior struggle with no visible results. The young Franciscan priest experienced firsthand the fact of human unworthiness and proof of the infinite difference between divine and human methods. With good reason could he say, "The Immaculate Virgin will maintain her victory over the devil." He said this to make it clear that the victory was hers.

When Father Kolbe was recalled to Poland in the summer of 1919, his superiors may not have realized fully how precarious his health was. Because the need was so great for professors in the seminary in Kracow, he was assigned to teach history, philosophy and Sacred Scripture — a heavy load for even a healthy person. The young priest never complained and they found him full of energy, for Fr. Maximilian threw himself wholeheartedly into whatever obedience was asked of him. However, with his lungs in such poor condition, he eventually couldn't be heard by the class and was assigned to hearing confessions. The long hours in the confessional tired him even more. Still, he found time to promote love and understanding of the Blessed Mother and gather new recruits for his *Militia Immaculatae* among the seminarians. ❑

Freemasonry Goals Achieved in Secular Culture

How Supreme Court Judges Who Were Masons Were Instrumental In Changing the USA into a Secularist State

In the early forties the United States was involved in two conflicts. While World War II was uppermost in people's minds and lives, a more subtle, insidious warfare, directed by Satan himself, was taking place for the souls of future generations of Americans. The United States, originally a Christian Nation, was slowly being changed into a secularist State by anti-Christian and anti-Catholic Supreme Court Justices, most of whom at the time were Masons. Understandably, these Justices were appointed by two Presidents who were themselves high-ranking Masons - Roosevelt and Truman.

From the very beginning of the nation the Masons understood the great power the Supreme Court could have in promoting their evil doctrine. Thus you had Masons represented on Supreme Court from the start, but it wasn't until 1941 that, under Roosevelt, Masons numbered in the majority. They continued to dominate the court for the next thirty years. At one point the ratio was eight Masons to one non-Mason (1949-1956). During these years of Masonic dominance, the Court repeatedly leaned on the "wall" of separation between Church and State clause of the 1947 Everson ruling to put down Christianity and Catholicism in particular.

Our legal system is not based on an unchanging natural law, much less divine law. Rather, it is based on the legal doctrine of *stare decisis*, which holds that a principle of law established by one judicial decision is accepted as an authoritative precedent for resolving future cases. The high court's interpretation of the religion clause in the Constitution rendered in the early forties was the basis for all future decisions regarding separation of Church and State, which resulted in the exclusion of religion from all public life.

Reflecting the philosophy of secular humanism as espoused by the Lodges, some of the consequences of this exclusion of religion from the everyday life of Americans were: outlawing released time for children to attend religion classes within public school buildings, atheism and secular humanism being declared religions protected by law, prohibition of prayer in public schools, banning the singing of Christmas carols in public schools, and so forth. Is it any wonder then that home schooling and religion-oriented private schools are flourishing?

And finally we had the Roe vs. Wade decision in which a woman's "right" to abortion was established and even promoted, opening the floodgates to the culture of death. All of this points to the fact that the Masonic justices in the 40's, 50's, and 60's played their roles well in shaping a culture that, while not openly attacking religion and God, more insidiously ignores Him as entirely divorced from the ordinary lives of men - ignoring Him, along with His code of morals. Today the Masons need not stack the Supreme Court with the "brethren" of the cult. They have succeeded well in turning our beloved country into a spiritual wasteland. Kolbe was 100% right in seeing Freemasonry as the head of the Serpent. Against such pernicious evil only spiritual weapons will prevail - the first and foremost weapon being prayer and sacrifice. Let us pray and be aware of the true enemy, and be the heel of the foot of the Immaculate One to crush the head of the Serpent. (see appendix, page 225 for further elaboration on Freemasonry) - B.F.M.

Has Freemasonry Mellowed?

It has been said that in the English-speaking nations the Masons are not as virulently anti-Catholic as the Continental Masonic Lodges. This may be the case, but right next door to the United States in Mexico, where the Masons have dominated the government since 1929, they have shown anything but a benign face to Catholicism. The leading, or rather the only political power in Mexico for better than 71 years, was the Institutional Revolutionary Party, or the PRI, made up of many leaders who are Masons. They had the support of the United States government over the years, even during the bloody persecution leveled against the Church in the twenties. There is no question that Masons inside the U.S. borders supported their brothers of the lodge south of the border.

However, in the National Election this last summer, to the surprise of everyone, the popular National Action Party candidate, a Catholic businessman named Vicente Fox, was elected. After the long PRI reign which one writer labeled "the perfect dictatorship," the election of Fox gives support to the belief of most Mexicans that Cardinal Posadas Ocampo of Guadalajara was assassinated. It is no coincidence that just a few days before his assassination, the Cardinal had warned his fellow men, "the principles and traditional philosophy of the Freemasons makes it clear that they don't act in our favor." He had the courage to suggest that Mexico's next presidential elections "would be an appropriate occasion [for] change." As one columnist wisely remarked,

"Ironically, the Cardinal may well have initiated his own death warrant."

A few months after the Cardinal was murdered the Freemasons held a World Congress in Mexico City. In his inaugural address the Mexican Grand Master, Salvador Ordas Montes De Oca, attacked the interference of the clergy in politics. High ranking Revolutionary Party members were present arrayed in the usual Masonic aprons and insignia, showing without the least pretense the close association between the two. If our mass media does not reveal the close connection between Masonry and the Mexican Government it is because the Masons themselves are guilty of the very accusations they make against the Church. Judge for yourself:

At the July 1992 celebration in Mexico City of the reunification of Mexican Freemasonry, President Salinas' own personal representative praised the Masons "for having introduced the state's basic institutions into our judicial lives and giving them shape." At the same celebration, the Grand Master Francisco Valle Guzman condemned the Catholic Church as "the most powerful and ruthless enemy of science, progress, civilization, fraternity, and love. Any reconciliation between us is impossible." He added that it was the Masons' historic duty to be the "gravediggers for the old clerical-colonial society."

The motives for the assassination of the popular prelate seems clear enough - not only hatred for the Church he represented, but also because he was speaking out too boldly. He had to be silenced. How to cover up the real reason for the assassination? Supposedly it was mistaken identity-the gunmen thought they were killing a rival drug lord. But there are several holes in the claim of mistaken identity.

While at the airport with his driver to pick up the Papal Nuncio, the tall, clerically clad Cardinal, wearing a large pectoral cross, was shot down within three feet of the gunmen. The drug lord was shorter and chunkier and was invariably accompanied by two or three bodyguards, and didn't wear clerical clothes or anything that looked like a pectoral cross. Mistaken identity?

Moreover, the first special prosecutor in the case was cut down outside his home in 1995. The present government prosecutor ruled out any hypotheses other than the mistaken identity one. As Goebbels once said, "Tell a lie enough times and people will believe you." If the evidence is true, and there is no good reason to doubt it, it wouldn't be the first of many assassinations engineered by Masons in modern times, nor would they hesitate to lie to cover up the crime. — BFM

Developing Battle Plans

TWO OF THE M.I. seminarians who caught his fiery zeal for souls were to be great collaborators in the future development of the Knights of the Immaculate. One of them, his younger brother, Friar Alphonsus, was to be a valuable assistant until his untimely death in 1930. Less than six months before, he had been appointed superior of the City of the Immaculate and editor of The Knight. The other friar, Samuel Rosenbager, eventually became superior of the mission Kolbe established in Japan, and was instrumental in establishing the Japanese province of the Conventual Franciscans after World War II.

The enthusiasm generated among the other seminarians prompted Fr. Maximilian to extend his apostolate to students at the University of Kracow, and to soldiers in nearby barracks. All this was not done without the Cross, ever present throughout his life. All great enterprises in the long history of the Church are purchased by much suffering, physical and mental, persecution from with out and misunderstanding and envy from within.

After a year in Kracow, in August of 1920, Fr. Maximilian, broken in health, had to go to a sanatorium in Zakopane, in the Tatra Mountains, for treatment on tuberculosis. He remained there till April 29, 1921. His breathing was heavy, and though he suffered much from headaches, high temperature and repeated hemorrhages, and the sanatorium directors were hostile to anything Catholic, he carried on a fruitful apostolate among the patients. One house for University students had a particular attraction to Fr. Maximilian. Most of the students there were non-practicing Catholics, puffed up by a little knowledge and academic degrees. With a supply of bullets, as he called the Miraculous Medals, he took advantage of a daily walk to visit these lost sheep.

His youthfulness was somewhat disarming to the young patients, who soon fell under the irresistible charm of the smiling, friendly young priest. They also found him quite challenging intellectually and open to conversation, which helped to pass the time. Soon, some of the students who were open to the truth and to Kolbe's irrefutable logic, invited him to give a series of lectures on apologetics (on the existence of God and the divinity of Christ). The erudite and masterful philosopher soon caused quite a stir when four notorious free thinkers converted.

One of the patients, a Jewish medical student, was moved by these conferences, and realizing he was dying, sought out Fr. Maximilian to be baptized. The priest prepared him for death, then hung a Miraculous Medal around his neck. The dying man joyfully waited "Sister Death" and the promise of entrance into Heaven. One thing worried him. He feared the arrival of his formidable Jewish mother. Kolbe reassured him that his other Jewish Mother, Mary Immaculate, would see to it that he would have already left this world for Heaven. Upon her arrival, seeing the Miraculous Medal around the neck of her dead son, she tore it off his neck, shrieking, "You have killed my son." The director forbade the hunter of souls entrance to that building. He obviously underestimated Kolbe, who was not readily intimidated. He told the director that as everyone else was allowed entrance during visiting hours, there was no reason why he couldn't visit as well.

When Kolbe had somewhat recovered, he was sent to Nieszaw for further convalescence, then back to the friary at Kracow. His superiors knew the doctors' verdict that he was incurable with a contagious disease, and that he didn't have more than a few months to live. Thus, the community's joy at his return was somewhat clouded. He quickly picked up where he had left off. Kolbe lost no time in asking his superior for permission to publish a periodical, which would spread devotion to Our Lady and encourage the growth of the M.I. One can imagine the effect this news had when it got around to the community — a periodical to be edited by one who, in all probability, would not live long enough to see its continuation? How was he to finance such a project, since the Polish province of the Conventual Franciscans was extremely poor? He would bankrupt the province. Who was to write the articles?

Who was to type them?

"Be reasonable Max, you are suffering from tuberculosis; you will ruin the Province." Father Maximilian listened patiently, but in his zeal he remained unmoved and resolute in his plans. All he needed was the necessary permission. After that, it was in the hands of the Immaculate. Unexpectedly, permission was granted, under the condition that Father Maximilian would himself raise the necessary funds. He lost no time in getting out the first issue of the magazine, numbering 5,000, which he named The Knight of the Immaculate. Now he took the magazine into the streets to distribute it himself among the people. He did not care whether they paid or not; distribution was his chief aim. The format of the sixteen-page Knight was simple. He wrote the articles. It had no cover, but the front page informed everybody: "We do not guarantee regular editions of this publication. We are too poor, but we are not too proud to accept financial assistance."

It is not surprising that Fr. Maximilian, more often than not, came back to the friary with very little money in his pocket. He was happy in the knowledge that he was furthering devotion to Our Lady through the Knight — but there was still the balance of a debt to pay for the first printing. Where was he to find help? He went directly to the altar dedicated to the Seven Dolors of Our Lady, celebrated for its miracles, in the Church of the Conventual Franciscans in Kracow. He told her about his problem. On the altar, there was a picture of the Madonna, fittingly called the "Beloved Benefactress." As he started to leave after finishing the prayer, he noticed an envelope on the altar. It was addressed: "To you, O Mother Immaculate." He opened it and found the exact amount necessary to pay the printing bill. The superior allowed him to use it to pay the printer. For the most part, however, his confreres gave him little encouragement. In fact, the opposite was true.

The following passage, written while he was in Kracow, reveals much of what he suffered there. It reads like a passage from St. Paul, the apostle to the Gentiles:

> *"We will do very much more if we are plunged into interior and exterior darkness, filled with sorrow, weakness, exhaustion, without consolation, persecuted at every step, surrounded by*

continual failures, abandoned, ridiculed, scoffed at, as was Jesus on the Cross; provided that we want by all means to draw all men to God, through the Immaculata."

He added, "above all let us desire and desire without limits."

After changing printers five times, the young publisher decided to do the printing himself. He learned that the Sisters of Our Lady of Mercy (the same order to which the recently canonized Saint Faustina belonged) wanted to get rid of an "ancient" press they had. Visiting the friary at the time was an American priest, Fr. Lawrence Cyman, who would eventually become the Provincial Minister of St. Anthony Province of the Conventual Franciscans in the United States. During community recreation, some of the friars decided to amuse the visitor at the expense of the "dreamer," Fr. Kolbe.

They criticized his review, its content and format. One mockingly laughed that Fr. Maximilian planned to conquer the whole world through the printed word and didn't have enough money to buy an old, obsolete press. Throughout the humiliating experience, Fr. Kolbe kept silent, though he was undoubtedly cut deeply. The American priest was not pleased with this type of warped humor. Moreover, he appreciated the vision of Kolbe, using the printed word to extend God's kingdom — something of a novelty at the time in Poland.

"My dear Fathers, instead of making fun of him, would it not be better to help him pay for the machine?" In the silence that followed, Fr. Lawrence turned to Fr. Kolbe, who was now more confused than ever, and said, "As a start, I wish to make a small donation." He eventually wrote a check for a hundred dollars — at that time a small fortune. Thus began a religious printing establishment which would eventually amaze the world. After this episode, even the Father Provincial lent Fr. Kolbe money to pay for the remainder of the printing press.

As the publication became better known and grew in quality, new subscriptions poured in. The staff consisted of only two brothers and Fr. Kolbe. The press had to be manually operated. To prepare five thousand copies of sixteen pages took them about ten days. Often their hands were bloodied. When more and better printing equipment arrived, there simply was not enough room for it all in the friary in Kracow. Moreover, the noisy printing machines were not conducive to the peace and quiet to which the elderly friars were accustomed. It was also a distraction to the student friars in their seminary. In spite of many difficulties and the gloomy outlook of the friars, Our Lord blessed the work. People began to show lively interest in the paper. Encouraging as this was, it brought three main difficulties: The venture required larger premises than were available in the monastery at Kracow; the expanding circulation demanded more capital; and the problem of labor became really urgent. A solution was soon forthcoming.

Just three years before, the Province had reopened a large friary in Grodno, in the northern part of Poland, which was practically empty. The Father Provincial decided to relocate Fr. Kolbe's printing plant there. He arrived at Grodno on October 20, 1922. By July 1927, the printing shop in Grodno was putting out regularly two monthly magazines: The Knight with a circulation of 60,000 copies; and The Seraphic Flame, a Third Order publication with a circulation of 8,000. At the same time, the number of pages of The Knight gradually increased from sixteen to twenty-four, and later to thirty-two.

Since Kolbe was no longer the director of the *Militia Immaculatae*, the saintly Fr. Melchior Fordon, a wise and prudent leader, was appointed to the task by Kolbe's superiors. It was a good choice as he was soon won over to the value of the ideals of the Saint. He was well thought of by the friars in the province and was a very necessary support at a time when some within the order bitterly opposed Fr. Kolbe. He worked well with Kolbe and remained the director of the M.I. until his death in 1927, when "he joined the heavenly reinforcements," as Kolbe would put it.

By the late twenties, there were seventeen brothers in Kolbe's community at Grodno. It was said of Kolbe that he was a regular "slave driver," but that was not even remotely the case. No one was forced to put in extra hours or to do arduous tasks against their will. Kolbe led by example rather than fear or human respect. He asked no more than what he did himself, sickly as he was. Heroism flowed from his total gift of self, to be used by the Immaculate as she saw fit for the salvation and sanctification of souls. His zeal was catching. How else could one explain the many young men he attracted to the order? Many came under the condition that they be able to work under him. His fixed ideal — the Immaculate Virgin — united the members of his community around the feet of Mary, where they experienced peace and joy through a total commitment.

The truth is that when these dedicated brothers asked Fr. Maximilian for permission to put in extra hours, and give up some valuable rest, so they could increase the production of the magazines, he attempted to dissuade them. He would not give his permission, but told them to write his major superior for the blessing of obedience, which ultimately came through. Even as the production of the magazine was soaring, Fr. Kolbe's health was declining. On September 18, 1926, he was forced to return to the sanatorium a second time, and leave the direction of the print shop and editorship of The Knight in the hands of his capable younger brother, Fr. Alphonsus. The sickly Fr. Maximilian was forbidden by his superior to even think about the Knight magazine until he recovered.

On one occasion, when Fr. Alphonsus wanted to check with him on a problem he didn't feel capable of resolving, Fr. Maximilian wouldn't even talk about it until Father Alphonsus got a release from an obedience which forbade him to be involved in the magazine. On another occasion, Father Alphonsus relates how, in visiting his brother at Zakopane, Fr. Maximilian in a weak voice told him, "Alphonsus, help me to hold my head up higher, put my watch and my glasses near the statue of Our Lady Immaculate." Fr. Alphonsus didn't understand the meaning of his brother's strange request.

Father Maximilian lifted his head with a great effort and said the following act of consecration to Our Lady:

> *"With this watch I offer you, Immaculate Mary, all my time in order to have not one moment as my own, but to give you every second as your exclusive property. These glasses symbolize my eyes with which I look at you continually. I offer myself entirely to you to do with me as you wish."*

By April of 1927, after a partial recovery, Father Maximilian returned to the friary in Grodno. He was consoled to see the increase in circulation of The Knight and resumed his work on a larger scale than before. With the obvious success of the Knight

The print shop, in the Friary in Grodno, Poland, which expanded so rapidly that Saint Maximilian had to find larger quarters for printing his many periodicals. Bro. Albert is pictured hand feeding paper through an "ancient" press.

Fr. Maximilian (center, with hands on his knees) with a group of his first Brothers at Grodno. His blood brother, Fr. Alphonse, is to Kolbe's left.

magazine, did the Franciscans from the Province change their opinion of Fr. Maximilian? Yes and No! Some realized that the success of Fr. Kolbe was not explained by mere human effort. Divine Providence and Our Lady were blessing his efforts. Nevertheless, the majority were still pessimistic. Father Maximilian's "dreams" were of such magnitude that they hardly seemed possible. Nevertheless, if it was God's will and work, nothing would stop the sickly priest. The Saint firmly believed,

> *"Everything will progress according to Our Lady's wish; the future is secure in the hands of Mary. My only duty is to discover and implement her wishes."*

The increasing output of the magazine — at the end of 1927 it had reached sixty thousand — made it obvious that Grodno was no longer suitable for future development. The friary had become a noisy printing plant. Machines were placed in every available space, even in the corridors, and the smell of printing ink pervaded the house. Naturally, the friars in Grodno, especially the older ones, were not pleased with the noisy rumbling of presses running daily into the night.

Fr. Maximilian had to make the decisive step of finding another location, larger and more centrally located, to better distribute the magazine. The Grodno friary was situated too far from the center of Poland, and, on account of the distance from the railroad station, the post office was unwilling to transport the entire issue at one time. He also had in mind the great expense involved in business traveling. Every penny was to be best used in furthering the glory of Our Lady. His Polish biographer, Dobraczynski, called him, "God's miser." The ideal location would be somewhere near Warsaw, the capital. As usual, he waited patiently on the Immaculata to reveal to him his next move.

It wasn't long before Fr. Maximilian found a tract of land. A local priest, Fr. Ciborowski, visiting the Grodno friary, knew a certain Prince John Drucki-Lubecki, who owned land near Grodno. As he was leaving, Fr. Maximilian asked the priest if the Prince had any other property. To the casual question, the priest replied, "Yes, he has a large tract of land 25 miles from Warsaw."

"Near Warsaw!" — It was all that he was hoping for: the center of Poland and near to one of the principal railroad lines! The "large tract of property" would allow for almost unlimited expansion! The friary would eventually be named Niepokalanow (the City of the Immaculate).

Mary Immaculate would help him to obtain the property even as she inspired him to make the inquiry of the visiting priest. The Knight magazine could reach many more souls in Poland and develop as an international center to send missionaries throughout the world, thus extending the Queenship of Mary. There was no time to lose. He immediately asked this Heaven-sent visitor to assist him in arranging a meeting with the Prince.

An appointment was made through the Prince's administrator, Mr. Srzednicki, for the 13th of June, 1927. Prince Drucki-Lubecki proved to be well disposed to give him the land. The following month, Fr. Maximilian had a statue of the Immaculata placed on the site and petitioned her, "Take into your possession this field and this land, for it is exactly what we want." ❑

Fr. Maximilian was an avid chess player, who enjoyed recreating with his community.

The first "inhabitant" at the "City of the Immaculate" was Mary herself. It was set up in a vacant field, which Prince Drucki-Lubecki donated to the Saint. On his return he asked to be granted a small plot to be buried in their cemetery.

Buildings were continually being constructed to meet the need of an ever expanding apostolate and to house the many vocations who wished to follow in the footsteps of Saint Maximilian Kolbe.

Building a City of Love for Mary

THE PRINCE had one condition that had to be agreed upon before building could commence. He wanted perpetual Masses said for the intention of the donor and his descendants. The demanding condition did not receive the approval of Kolbe's superiors, so it seemed as though the whole transaction was off. Informed of the superiors' decision, the Prince withdrew the offer of the land and requested the removal of the statue.

Father Maximilian insisted that the statue remain as a witness that the Immaculata, at least this time, had failed to keep her promise. The Prince was impressed by Father Maximilian's humility and childlike simplicity: "If ever there was a man who was not proud, it was Father Maximilian." He went on to say, "I became irritated. They [his superiors] wanted the land, which I was disposed to give, but not the obligation of the Masses." Fr. Maximilian didn't give up. He told the Prince that he would be back in three days for a definite decision.

The Prince was in a state of uneasiness those three days until he definitely decided to give the land with no strings attached. It was the beginning of a friendship between the Prince and the humble Franciscan that deepened over the years and prompted Prince Drucki-Lubecki to give the holy priest more property adjacent to the original donation. "God's miser" did well. In exchange for the substantial donation of land, a small plot in the cemetery of the City of the Immaculate contains the earthly remains of Prince Drucki-Lubecki. Nearby is the grave of the only other layman buried there: Francis Gajowniczek, for whom Kolbe gave up his life.

Fr. Maximilian immediately informed his superiors and obtained permission to go ahead with the mammoth transfer of everything from Grodno to the City of the Immaculate. Before the first contingent left Grodno, Fr. Maximilian made it clear that this twentieth century St. Mary of the Angels (the cradle of the Franciscan Order) was to be a model Franciscan friary, as well as the M.I. world-wide missionary center. The chapel and their prayer life would be central in their daily lives. He pointed out that it was Our Lady herself who chose this location for her City.

She would also choose the brothers who would be prepared for the greatest sacrifices, through absolute poverty, unquestioning obedience and hard work. Here, religious life would flourish, even as it did in the initial days of the Order in Assisi. If any of the brothers felt they couldn't live such a heroic life, he suggested that they not go to the new location. The more austere life at the City of the Immaculate was justified by the twelfth chapter of the Rule of St. Francis, which made it clear that a missionary vocation was strictly voluntary and over and above the Franciscan calling. The extra suffering and deprivations of a missionary vocation were something neither St. Francis nor St. Maximilian would impose on the friars. Twenty out of twenty-two members in the community (eighteen brothers and two priests) were the founding friars of the City of the Immaculate. These religious were able to do practically all the work necessary in transferring machinery and building the large friary complex. "God's miser" was making every penny and minute count when it came to doing more and better in expanding the apostolate of the *Militia Immaculatae*.

His brother, Fr. Alphonse, and a few carpenter brothers, began construction of the simple, barracks-like buildings. At the same time, other brothers at Grodno prepared editions of The Knight for a whole year so the printing machines could be dismantled for the transfer. At the time, building materials were not too expensive, if one had the money, which Kolbe did not. Soon, a providential gift of two carloads of timber arrived from a benefactor. Another large donation of plywood enabled the brothers to begin construction of the printing offices and attached buildings. The primary building material was an inexpensive mixture of the dross from carbon coke and cement. All the brothers were of help in its preparation.

Pounding the mixture demanded hard labor, but it could be easily handled, and so the work progressed rapidly.

The interior furnishings were simple and poor — unplaned tables, rough stools. Table utensils were made of tin. When important guests came, bishops and cardinals, they ate out of the same dishes as the community. Fr. Kolbe was not ashamed of this outward expression of Franciscan poverty. He wanted no exceptions to be made that might lead to a relaxation of evangelical poverty — so characteristic of the Poverello of Assisi and his followers.

One may well imagine how this literal interpretation of Franciscan poverty was received by the friars of his province. The virtue of evangelical poverty has ever been a bone of contention among Franciscans and the reason for many reforms within the Order. Like St. Francis, St. Maximilian did not want buildings of durable brick. He considered that such buildings would hold back the brothers, who would not readily want to be transferred to a less comfortable dwelling. Moreover, Kolbe felt that during periods of social revolution the poor dwelling of the friars would be less likely taken over, which proved to be true. His main reason, however, was to go back to the more literal practice of evangelical poverty of the Founder of the Franciscan Order.

By November, 1927, the other friars from Grodno arrived, and with the wholehearted help of benefactors and the local people, the tempo of work escalated. Local farmers, besides helping to feed the poor little brothers, transferred the machines and other supplies to the building site from the train station. Father Maximilian pitched in with the hard work, as well as assuming the role of engineer and supervisor. The foundation of this new undertaking was the Immaculata's statue surmounted on a slender column in what had been an empty field just a few weeks before.

As the living quarters of the friars were being built, Fr. Maximilian and the brothers were offered lodgings in the attic of a neighbor's farmhouse. When the good lady, Mrs. Jaroszewski, noticed that Fr. Maximilian gave up the bed especially prepared for him to one of the younger, healthier brothers, and chose to sleep on wood shavings like the others, she asked him, "How come?" His evasive answer hid the real reason. He replied that he had taken solemn vows but the brother had not. His example of never seeking deferential treatment as founder and superior, despite his poor health, was not missed by his followers. Heroism of this type is never without fruit. Worthy young men applying for admission to the City of the Immaculate were plentiful, but were carefully screened and not coddled. New applicants had to stand up under rigorous testing. One brother recalled his initial exposure to the City of the Immaculate in its early days:

> *"When I arrived there, I asked a farmer, 'Where is the friary?'*
>
> *'There,' he said.*
>
> *'I don't see a friary.'*
>
> *'Look again,' he said. 'See those sheds?'*
>
> *I saw only some low, wooden buildings covered with a rough coat of whitewash.*
>
> *'Is that the friary?' I asked in utter surprise.*
>
> *'It certainly is! Inside they seem very content. Always singing.'*
>
> *It was Father Maximilian himself who welcomed me. He was coming from work and seemed very tired. He looked at me with eyes that were as kind as a mother's and said, 'You must be very tired and hungry. Come, my son.'*
>
> *He gave me something to eat and drink. Then he said, 'If you love the Blessed Virgin, if you belong entirely to her, you will be happy, my son — so happy!' He smiled as he spoke and seemed radiantly happy himself.*
>
> *I thought to myself, 'What he says, he himself lives.' And suddenly I felt very happy myself and have been happy ever since. I found him both a father and a mother."*

The first structures were not only simple, one-story buildings, but were without heat and proper insulation. The wind blew though them and played on the heads of the sleeping brothers. In the mornings, it was necessary to break the ice in the washbasins before they could wash. It was all taken in stride. For were they not privileged to be part of an adventure so novel and unworldly? —to serve under the inspiring example of this modern day St. Francis, who loved with a total, uncompromising love? All of this appealed to idealistic young men.

Through prayer, the observance of heroic obedience, rigorous poverty, and hard work done in an atmosphere of silence and recollection, religious life flourished. By these means, the Knights of the Immaculata would be made worthy of the cause to which they were dedicated. Speed and simplicity had to be the hallmarks. "God's miser" knew that neither money nor time could be wasted in this modern, highly competitive world. If, in the battle for souls, a lackadaisical attitude prevailed, souls would be lost to Satan, as the demonic is on the alert to take advantage of every opportunity. There is an unmistakable urgency in Kolbe's writings and addresses. He repeated often, "As soon as possible, as soon as possible, as soon as possible... The loss of a single soul is a great misfortune." It was vital that haste be made in furthering evangelization through Mary Immaculate.

From the 17th of November on, he was able to offer Mass daily in the chapel, and by December 8th, the Feast of the Immaculate Conception, all was ready. The printing plant and electrical power station had been installed. Permission for the celebration had been received straight from the Primate of Poland. The vigil of the Feast was a great day. There was solemn High Mass, and the Provincial, Father Cornelius Czupryk, preached. This was followed by the blessing of the new foundation and the official dedication of the first City of Mary Immaculate. For Father Maximilian, Niepokalanow was but the first link in a chain of "Marian Cities" which he hoped would eventually unite all countries and peoples in the love and service of their Queen.

By 1930, Niepokalanow was clearly established. There were now dwellings for aspirants, and professed friars. The central building for the administration and printing of The Knight had been erected. The magazine had reached a circulation of 343,000 copies, and membership in the M.I. steadily increased. The conversion of sinners and the sanctification of all under the protection of the Immaculate Mother, the chief aim of the *Militia Immaculatae*, next had to reach all corners of the world. With this in mind, Fr. Maximilian began looking at the world map, focusing his sight on the heavily populated and hardly touched Far East.

Just a few years after establishing the City of the Immaculate, on February 26, 1930, Father Maximilian departed from Poland for the Far East with Brothers Zeno, Hilary, Severyn and Zygmund. China was his first destination — the world his ultimate goal. After a long sea journey, the missionaries finally arrived in Shanghai. As to be expected, Fr. Kolbe sought out the bishop, head of the local church, for permission to set up a friary for the purpose of publishing a Chinese version of the Knight magazine.

At that time, the various missionary orders and congregations were assigned particular provinces in China for evangelizing. Unfortunately, the Conventual Franciscans were assigned a remote province that would make a printing apostolate extremely difficult, if not impossible. The bishop, not thoroughly understanding what Fr. Maximilian intended to do, did not give him permission to establish a printing apostolate. Father Maximilian, however, was not about to be deterred after just one attempt.

With its large population of several hundred millions, China had a great attraction to Fr. Kolbe. Moreover, the missionaries had become acquainted with a Chinese Catholic millionaire, Joseph Lo-Pa-Hong, whose Catholic roots went back three centuries. He was drawn to the poor Franciscans and was willing to give them a house to be turned into a friary. So it was decided that Bros. Severyn and Zygmund would remain behind to explore other possibilities and to learn Chinese, while Fr. Kolbe and his two other companions proceeded on to Japan. ❑

Fr. Maximilian flanked by two Vietnamese priests. Standing: Bro. Zeno, second from the left, far right, Bro. Sevein (John Dagis)

In the Land of the Rising Sun

THE THREE MISSIONARIES arrived in Nagasaki on the afternoon of April 24, 1930, and headed first to the Our Church to give thanks for a safe arrival. In front of the church was a statue of Our Lady Immaculate, as though to welcome them. Father Maximilian took this as a good sign and predicted, "Our future work here will be very fruitful." His prediction came true as the Japanese missions of the Conventual Franciscans did flourish, and are now a province.

At first it seemed that in visiting Bishop Hayasaka, the Polish Missionaries were to experience another rejection. With typical Japanese courtesy the bishop greeted the missionaries, but he wasn't open to the idea of these little known Franciscans setting up a print shop for a magazine. It is true that the bishop was merely being prudent in dealing with the "zealots" of Our Lady who, hardly knowing a word of Japanese, were intent on promoting love and devotion to Mary Immaculate, not only among his Catholic flock but among the pagans as well. It all seemed very unrealistic.

However, when he learned that Father Kolbe had doctorates in both philosophy and theology, he suddenly became quite interested. Bishop Hayasaka at the time just happened to be looking for a professor of theology. Permission for the missionaries to come into his diocese was granted under the condition that Fr. Kolbe would accept a teaching position in his seminary. It was at great sacrifice that Father Kolbe fulfilled his part of the bargain.

In his weakened state from consumption, Father Kolbe commuted to Our to teach at the seminary as he had promised Bishop Hayasaka. At that time, the only transportation was by streetcar. He had to walk to the streetcar stop, change at another stop and get off at Our, where he climbed the steep slope to the seminary. For a man who wasn't well, it was a great burden. Eventually he began to be driven home in a taxi.

The change of climate, food, and water had caused additional problems in his physical health. He suffered from boils and no sooner had one gotten better than another appeared. Sometimes he could not even stand at morning Mass without being supported by the brothers. There were times when it was impossible for him to work. It was then that he suffered and prayed. One Japanese doctor, upon examining him, could not understand how he could keep going, with continual headaches and high fever. Fr. Maximilian lifted up the rosary which he had been praying and said, "This is what makes it possible." During his years in Japan, more than at any previous time, the sanctity of Fr. Kolbe became apparent. It is said that he reached mystical union with the Crucified Christ while in the Land of the Rising Sun. It was here too that he was given the assurance of being saved (see page 78).

Bro. Sergius relates on one occasion how deeply Fr. Maximilian was suffering, both physically and mentally. There was a small window between his room and that of Fr. Kolbe. One night, after ten o'clock, he called Brother Sergius through the window.

> *"When I went to his room he was sitting on his bed, dressed in his habit. He seemed to be in great suffering. He was reciting Our Lady's name over and over. I felt that I was facing something very serious. When I got closer, he said fearfully, 'My child please sit down.' When I obeyed him he took my hand and said, 'I am not too sure whether I can pass through this night or not. My heart is getting weaker and slower. If I have to leave this world please tell the brothers my last words are to never leave the Blessed Mother. If you forget her, there will no longer be a Garden of the Immaculate.' (the Japanese Marian outpost)*
>
> *"I was very sad thinking that Father Kolbe might die that night. I wanted to go and call the other brothers but he did not allow me to do so. Fortunately, as time went on he grew calm. The words he spoke were from the depth of his suffering as he faced impending death. He wanted to encourage us to be perfect instruments of Our Lady... if we tried to do this with all our might our work would progress. Father's words during this suffering were characteristic of the spirit of the Garden of the*

Immaculata. When he regained his composure a little he fell asleep saying, 'Our Lady has not called me yet.' It was midnight when I went back to my own room."

Like Our Blessed Lord, he was continually misunderstood. Several months after arriving in Japan, Father was suddenly ordered to appear before the Internuncio in Tokyo. He felt that there must have been a serious problem for such an order and told the brothers to pray. The Internuncio was very angry. "Why did you start your missionary work without the permission of the Holy See?" he asked. Thus, he questioned Fr. Maximilian's obedience to Church authority. This would have been totally against Father Kolbe's whole nature, and the accusation caused him much pain. He always consulted his superior whenever he started anything new and never acted without their approval. Why, then, this misunderstanding? Permission of the Holy See was indeed necessary and for Father Kolbe to forget or neglect something so serious was unthinkable.

After quietly listening to the Internuncio's words, he explained the whole situation. The Internuncio was impressed by Father's humble attitude and finally gave his blessing. Fr. Maximilian had actually taken care of the procedure of application to the Holy See before he left Poland. It took longer than expected, and the brothers had arrived in Japan before the communication from Rome. Besides such anxiety caused from outside, Father Kolbe later suffered from internal community problems as well. Some of the priests who came from the Polish Province did not understand the spirit of the Garden of the Immaculata, nor did they understand and accept the M.I. spirituality. Father Maximilian interpreted this spirit of devotion to Mary Immaculate in a heroic way — to bear hunger, heat, cold and other sufferings joyfully for Our Lady's sake and, if necessary, to offer one's life. As Father Kolbe expressed it:

"There is one qualification required to be a member of the Garden of the Immaculata. Anyone who does not understand its spirit or is unwilling to make the sacrifices involved should go to another friary. The donations we receive, or any type of gift given to us, are not to make our life easier. We should use these things for the glory of our Lady only. The property and the house we live in as well as subscription money from the readers are a trust kept by us for our Lady's work. Therefore we should never waste them.

If we forget this spirit of sacrifice or disobey intentionally, sooner or later the Garden of the Immaculata will disintegrate."

In spite of these high ideals and the heroic example of Father Kolbe, some priests and brothers returned to Poland without having made a serious effort to follow him.

Along with major suffering during his time in Japan, Fr. Kolbe set the example for his brothers of following the "Little Way" of Spiritual Childhood, as taught by St. Thérèse of the Child Jesus — offering little sacrifices out of Love for Jesus. The hard straw mat on which Fr. Maximilian slept seemed pitifully inadequate for one so sick. One morning, Brother Sergius shook the mattress to try to make it a little softer and more comfortable. Father noticed this and said, "It is alright, please leave it alone. I want to offer a small sacrifice for our Blessed Mother." Brother did not listen to him and repeated the same action. Father Kolbe scolded him, saying, "Why do you not obey me?" Brother, thinking he could do nothing else, stopped for a while, but continued to feel much pity for his patient and started to shake the mattress again. This time, Father Kolbe apparently lost out to Brother's perseverance, for he did not pursue the matter.

For those who had left their homeland of far away Poland, letters from home gave much joy — a joy which could not be readily substituted. On days when there was not a single letter for anyone, they felt very lonesome. On the eve of the Feast of the Seven Sorrows of Our Lady, there was mail from Poland in the refectory. Everyone felt like dancing as they waited for it to be distributed. No doubt Father Kolbe felt the same, but he did not open any of the mail, even after the meal.

"Tomorrow," he said, "is the Feast Day of Our Lady's Seven Sorrows, therefore let us offer a small sacrifice and wait until tomorrow to enjoy these letters." There was no feeling of pressure, no feeling of being ordered. Rather, the postponement of this pleasure was offered with joy. Any small thing, even the continuation of heavy manual labor and lack of sleep, was offered joyfully. Under Father Kolbe's direction, there were no complaints or murmuring. Observing his fraternal concern brought everyone close to him for, as a superior, Father Kolbe did not put himself above anyone. He always placed himself in a lower position than others and always gave the brothers good example.

Due to Fr. Maximilian's fiery zeal and unwavering trust in Divine Providence, and under Our Lady's inspiration, the same miracle of unbelievable progress prevailed in Japan as in the original City of the Immaculate in Poland. When he informed the Bishop of Nagasaki that he intended to print a magazine in May, which was just a month away, the bishop thought it impossible. Yet, on May 24, he sent a telegram to Niepokalanow:

> *"Today we are mailing out the Knight magazine in Japanese; we have a print shop. Praise be to the Immaculata!"*

The next month, Fr. Maximilian traveled to Poland to attend the Provincial Chapter. He returned to Japan in August, and none too soon. His departure to attend the Province's meeting had been interpreted as a sign that he had given up the idea of publishing a magazine. How was it possible for Fr. Maximilian to publish a magazine in Japanese within a month of his arrival when he, nor any of his companions, knew more than a few words of Japanese, written or spoken? He obviously needed translators. The first was a fiery Methodist, Mr. Tagita Koyo, who was a schoolteacher. Fr. Kolbe made such an impression on him that he recruited a friend,

Fr. Maximilian with Buddhist Monks who came to visit him at the Franciscan Friary known as *Mungenzai No Sono* (Garden of the Immaculate). The Japanese, who have a high regard for heroism, were much impressed with Kolbe and his four missionaries.

Mr. Yamaka, as a second translator. The former vehemently defended the Catholic Faith when his Methodist friends attacked it, and eventually became a Catholic. Such was the strong influence of the heroic witness of Kolbe and his brothers.

The typesetting of the magazine posed a big problem at first as the Japanese typesetters were continually on strike, forcing Fr. Maximilian to assign Bro. Severyn Dagis to learn how to typeset the magazine in the four thousand signs of the Japanese alphabet. By November, Fr. Kolbe could say with pride that this issue of the Knight magazine, titled Seibo No Kishi, was the first publication in Japanese typeset by a European. The circulation of the magazine continually increased and it became the largest Catholic publication in Japan, bringing about many conversions to the Faith. By 1933, the Japanese Knight had a circulation of 50,000, most of which were given away.

The first home of the missionaries, a small house near the cathedral, soon became inadequate for the growing apostolate and more spacious quarters had to be found. A piece of property was located close to a cemetery on the steep slopes of Mount Hikosan. Due to the Japanese superstition over burial grounds, the land was reasonably inexpensive.

Just a year after their arrival in Japan, on May 16, 1931, the Franciscans completed the move and named the new location Mugenzai no Sono (Garden of the Immaculata). Construction was done with the cheapest materials available. A few months later, he had a large statue of the Immaculate placed on the highest point of the property, visible to the whole pagan district of Hongonchi in Nagasaki. It was providential that St. Maximilian didn't build his City in the Center of Nagasaki in the Catholic Urami district. This area was completely laid waste by the atomic bomb detonated over it during the last month of World War II. The Garden of the Immaculate was untouched, protected by the mountain that separated it from the center of the explosion.

In 1933, Fr. Kolbe was again called back to Poland for a Provincial Chapter, where he received much support and encouragement. Nonetheless, largely because of his precarious health, he was replaced as superior of the Garden of The Immaculate by his personal friend and former Father Provincial, Fr.

Cornelius Czupryk. The newly elected Father Provincial, Fr. Anselm Kubit, was very concerned that Fr. Kolbe get proper rest and nourishment. Maximilian accepted with joy the decision confirmed by the Chapter. From then on, the founder was the faithful collaborator and obedient subject of Father Cornelius. Besides continuing as professor of theology, Fr. Kolbe was appointed the International Director of the M.I.

It was during this second period in Japan that Fr. Kolbe went to India to establish another City of the Immaculate. While waiting to see the Archbishop of Ernakulam, a rose detached itself from a vase of flowers in front of a statue of St. Thérèse of the Child Jesus and rolled to his feet. He interpreted this as a sign from the Saint of the Little Way, his co-worker in the vineyard of the Lord, of the establishment and success of a City of Mary in India. Hadn't he made a pact with her, while still a student in Rome, to pray for her canonization if she would support his missionary labors? The Archbishop wholeheartedly welcomed his presence and personally drove Father Kolbe to a piece of land with a house and church for his apostolic work. When Kolbe had completed the transaction, the Second World War held up further development. After the war, a new political order, which was unfavorable to evangelization, came into power. However, it finally became a reality on May 10, 1981, in the town of Chotty, Karala, India, where two Maltese Franciscan Friars established a Marian outpost.

Would this have been enough for Fr. Maximilian? Enough, with regard to furthering love and devotion to Mary and the Gospel, was never enough for the Knight of the Immaculate. He wrote to his friars in Poland from Japan:

" We must work not only for Japan; what about China, India, Turkey, the Arab World and the whole of Africa? All peoples must be led to Christ... Let us abandon ourselves into her Immaculate arms: may she do with us as it pleases her. In this we must put no reservations, and in order to do this we must be of one mind and one heart." ❑

This chapter is largely based upon the writings of Bro. Sergius Pesiek, OFM Conv., who served under Fr. Maximilian Kolbe as a missionary in Japan for a number of years. It appeared in serial form in the bulletin Mission of the Immaculata (1991), Marytown, The City of the Immaculate.

Fr. Kolbe aboard ship on his way to the missions. Following the long line of Franciscan missionaries, beginning with St. Francis, St. Maximilian was missionary in mind, heart and action. Below: The friars went out in the streets of Japan to sell the Japanese version of the *Knight* Magazine.

The "City of the Immaculate" in Japan, *Mungenzai No Sono*, situated on the side of a hill, which protected it from the A-bomb blast over the city of Nagasaki. Due to Fr. Maximilian's fiery zeal and unwavering trust in Divine Providence, and under Our Lady's inspiration, the same miracle of unbelievable progress prevailed in Japan as in the original City of the Immaculate in Poland.

The City of the Immaculate and Real Progress

IT WAS WHILE Fr. Maximilian was in Japan that his brother, Fr. Alphonse, died of pneumonia, in December of 1930, during the novena in preparation for the Feast of the Immaculate Conception. As Father Maximilian left Niepokalanow for Japan, he had a presentiment of his brother's death. When he entered Father Alphonse's cell to say goodbye, he found him sleeping. He leaned down, kissed him lightly on the brow, and exclaimed with emotion,

> *"Sleep, my dear brother. There was never a more merited rest in the service of the Immaculata! Farewell... who knows if we will see each other again on earth."*

Father Alphonse was the closest collaborator and first superior of the City of the Immaculata after his brother left for the Far East. Although Fr. Alphonse never fully understood his saintly brother's grandiose plans, he never questioned them. Somehow they were always realized. An example follows:

Due to the criticisms voiced by some of the friars of the province who feared a colossal bankruptcy, Father Cornelius Czupryk, the Father Provincial, visited Niepokalanow to see for himself the seriousness of the problem. If even half of what they said was true, it would impede the future development of the City. The two brothers were so reassuring and optimistic over the future development of the City of the Immaculate that the Father Provincial, turning to Father Maximilian and his brother, said in jest, "Now, you had better prepare to start a seminary as you will need priests."

It wasn't long after Father Czupryk had returned to the provincialate friary in Kracow that Father Alphonse arrived at his office with construction plans for a seminary. Father Maximilian had already personally drawn up detailed plans and was ready to carry them out. Father Cornelius was astounded that his words had been understood so literally. To Father Alphonse, he said angrily, "You are taking my joke too seriously," and dismissed him. A month of apparent calm followed.

Fathers Maximilian and Alphonse were not at all offended by the bitter remark of Father Cornelius. They were at perfect peace. This was not so for the Father Provincial, who had lost his peace of soul. He spent many sleepless nights, perplexed and uncertain of what course of action to take. He loved Niepokalanow and had great respect for the two hard-working brothers. After all, he had given the permission for the founding of the City; and did he not also have on his kneeler a statue of the Immaculata? Turning to her one night after a prolonged prayer, he jotted down the following note to Father Maximilian:

> *"In virtue of obedience, for the glory of God, the honor of the Immaculata and the growth of our Order, I order the foundation of a seminary in our poor friary at Niepokalanow, beginning with the scholastic year 1929-1930."*

When the letter reached Niepokalanow, the July issue of The Knight was about to be printed. Without delay, Father Maximilian hastened to insert the following announcement:

> *"With the scholastic year 1929-1930 a seminary will be opened at Niepokalanow for vocations for those who desire to consecrate themselves to the priestly and missionary ministry of the Franciscan Order."*

A few days later, Father Provincial presented himself at Niepokalanow to revoke the letter previously written. It was too late. The Knight had already been printed and shipped out. Immediately applicants began to pour in, necessitating the construction of a seminary distinct from the house of formation for the brothers. Thus, in 1929, scarcely two years after its foundation, Niepokalanow had two houses of formation, which rapidly developed, making it necessary within two years to establish two distinct novitiates, one for the brothers and another for aspirants to the priesthood. So it was that the progress of the City continued even while Fr. Kolbe was in Japan.

The "Heart" of the City of the Immaculate was the chapel. Saint Maximilian dreamed of one day having Jesus Eucharist exposed in the monstrance, day and night, as there would be enough friars to adore Him uninterruptedly. It was finally accomplished, without exposition, in 1939.

Above: The expanded chapel at the City of the Immaculate when the friary community numbered over 750. There was a harmonious balance between work, (the printing apostolate) and prayer. As chapter 5 of the Franciscan Rule states, "The friars will work diligently, while avoiding idleness, the enemy of the soul, they will not extinguish the spirit of devotion and prayer to which all temporal matters must be subordinated."

In July, 1933, under the watchful eye of the Minister General of the Order, a Chapter was held in Poland to elect a new Father Provincial. Father Maximilian returned from Japan to participate in the chapter. Father Czupryk was replaced by the new Father Provincial, Fr. Anselm Kubit, who was greatly concerned about Father Maximilian's health. It was obvious to everyone that Fr. Kolbe wasn't well. He could not continue to carry alone the burdens of superior, seminary professor, etc. It was simply too much for even a healthy man. His friend and former Provincial, Father Czupryk, volunteered to go to Japan, allowing Father Maximilian to be relieved of many of his responsibilities and regain his health.

After being founder and first superior of friaries both in Poland and Japan, he returned to Japan a subject. Those friars who opposed him felt vindicated: Fr. Maximilian was being justly pulled back for jeopardizing the province financially with his expansion plans. To Fr. Maximilian, however, it mattered little what others thought, so long as he was assured that he was doing the Will of God. With docility, he accepted the decision of the Provincial Assembly as the will of the Immaculate and was at peace.

He had once said to the brothers in a conference:

> *"The essence of the spirit of a member of the City of the Immaculate consists in supernatural and perfect obedience to the Immaculata through the will of superiors. Whoever does not desire to be perfect in this point is not suited for Niepokalanow."*

There was no question that he demanded of his brothers a certain heroism. What he expected of them, however, especially in the practice of the virtue of obedience, was never anything more than what he practiced himself.

"To suffer, labor and die for God alone, for God through the Immaculate as an instrument in her hands, is the ideal worthy of a knight of the Immaculata" (one consecrated to Our Lady). With such a motto, one could expect that religious life at the City was severe. Once, Father Provincial pointed out to him that the life at Niepokalanow was more rigorous than elsewhere in the Order. To this he replied:

> *"If Niepokalanow... were to favor laxity, or still worse, scandal, it would be better that God immediately send fire from Heaven to burn everything."*

The brother candidates were scrupulously trained and screened. The result was a religious community of the highest spiritual caliber.

Despite their hectic activity, Fr. Maximilian and his co-workers spent, in accord with their rule, at least four hours a day in community prayers and meditation. This was not all. The brothers were taught always to regard their work as a prayer. To keep this truth constantly before their minds, they were to speak only when necessary during working hours. In this immense printing establishment, where silence reigned supreme, the brothers moved about rapidly, with no time to waste. Recollection was the norm, and from time to time they turned their eyes to the ever present statue of the Immaculata in each shop. They greeted one another with the name of "Mary."

Their life was strictly community-oriented. Other than priestly ministering of the Sacraments and preaching, there was no distinction between priest and brother, between superior and subject. The only exceptions to the common life were the sick. They could have special meals and all the remedies they needed — no matter how costly. It was the unanimous testimony of those who knew Fr. Maximilian that his love for the sick was without equal. He endured much physical suffering in his forty-seven years, often abandoned and neglected, and so his great tenderness towards the sick was motivated much by his own personal experiences. His main motive was, of course, imitation of Mary and serving Christ in the suffering.

Fr. Maximilian spared neither his precious time, nor expensive medication, in treatment of his sick friars. In the three years just prior to his imprisonment (1936-1939), one of his main concerns was the construction of a hospital for his large community of over 700 members. The hospital was built in a quiet, tree-shaded section of the City, and he frequently went to visit. In his missions of mercy, he was following the example of the Founder of the Franciscan Order, St. Francis, who also had a predilection and special love for the sick. Numerous are the testimonies of Fr. Maximilian's tender care for them. Brother Lawrence tells us how, "Every day he visited the sick brothers… With the seriously ill he was most generous, spending even entire nights at their bedside."

In one case, Father Isidore Kosbial records how Fr. Maximilian kept vigil by the bed of one of his companions in the seminary who was seriously ill, fervently praying for him and making the Sign of the Cross on his forehead. "The following day he was cured and went to school with me."

On another occasion, when a distinguished visitor was being shown around the City by Fr. Maximilian, he turned to his visitor and said, "Now let us go to the department where work is most intense and valuable." To the great surprise of the visitor, they entered the hospital. Father Maximilian explained:

> *"These sick brothers, forced into inactivity, are the most useful to us since with their sufferings, they draw down on us the choicest blessings of God on Niepokalanow and the apostolate."*

In this and in so many other ways, the Saint shows how deeply he entered into the mind and heart of St. Francis. He has been rightly called, "the St. Francis of our times."

One day, a visiting priest stopped before one of the imposing rotary presses in the printing plant and asked Father Maximilian, "If the Poverello (St. Francis) were alive today, what would he say about all these expensive printing machines?"

Father Maximilian responded without a minute's hesitation:

"Why, he would roll up his sleeves like these good brothers and turn the presses at full speed using this modern means of spreading the glory of God and the Immaculata." Father Maximilian believed that the most modern inventions and machinery should be used first and foremost for the Immaculata.

Father Maximilian's initiative of reaching souls was not limited to just the printed word. He constructed a building for a radio station. On the vigil of the Feast of the Immaculate Conception, December 8, 1938, with a short wave transmitter borrowed from the army, the friars were able to make their first broadcast. After a few broadcasts, however, difficulties arose. The opponents of the M.I., mostly Masons, representatives in the government, refused to grant legal authorization to transmit. They feared that the radio broadcasts from Niepokalanow would be even better received than The Little Journal, which elicited much popular support. Father Maximilian didn't give up, but with the Second World War everything was put on hold.

St. Maximilian, painted by Bro. Felix Sztyk, OFM Conv. who personally knew the Saint.

"The principal reason for Niepokalanow is the sanctification of the brothers, our own sanctification. We must never forget this: we must first be Saints ourselves. The specific character of Niepokalanow? It is to convert and to sanctify souls under the protection and by the mediation of the Immaculata. Thus, it does not suffice to say simply: 'to convert and sanctify souls.' We must add: 'by the Immaculata.' Everyone knows that the Virgin is the Mediatrix of all graces. What characterizes us is our absolute belonging to the Immaculata, which is the raison d'être of Niepokalanow and of the *Knight of the Immaculata* magazine."

Niepokalanow as it looked in 1937. More permanent buildings have been added since then.

The rapid and marvelous fruits of the well-organized work carried out in the City of Mary cannot be explained as merely human effort. A humble religious from a poor family, and poor by virtue of his vows, weakened by tuberculosis, had conceived and brought into existence an apostolic work valued in the millions — the sort of undertaking which would seem to be possible only by a great corporation. Without any capital he had founded a City in which life pulsated intensely and hundreds of brothers worked in shifts, the printing machines and motors running day and night.

Here, work was as St. Francis would have it done, in accordance with Chapter Five of his Rule:

> *"Let the brothers to whom the Lord gave the ability to work, labor faithfully and devotedly so that, while avoiding idleness, the enemy of the soul, they will not extinguish the spirit of prayer and devotion to which all temporal matters must be subordinated."*

The friars at the City of the Immaculata were first and foremost Franciscans, and as such, the Rule of St. Francis was their way of life. They strove and succeeded, under Fr. Maximilian's inspiration and direction, in recapturing the simple life and heroic poverty of the first Franciscans gathered around St. Francis at the Portiuncula.

One would think that in the midst of such feverish activity the religious spirit might suffer. The opposite, rather, was true. There was a palpable contrast between quiet and work, silence and the noise of machines. Niepokalanow was a sign of contradiction in which a virtual bee hive of activity was, at the same time, a house of prayer and contemplation. Father Czupryk's impressions of Niepokalanow in 1936 were shared by the Father General of the Order, the American Fr. Bede Hess, who visited it:

> *"I was able to verify with my own eyes how true it was that from Niepokalanow shone forth the truly Franciscan spirit, a fervent devotion to the Immaculata, much zeal, the greatest poverty and the utmost simplicity. Among the brothers there was an intense spirit of charity. Great harmony reigned, and one read on their faces a serene, Franciscan joy."*

The "perfect joy" of Francis — abnegation, abandonment, penance and identification with Christ Crucified — was not shunned, but embraced out of love. According to Maximilian,

> *"Progress is spiritual, or it does not exist. Consequently, even if we had to suspend our work, even if all the members of the Militia abandoned us, even if we had to disperse as the leaves swept by the autumn winds — if in our souls the ideal of Niepokalanow continued to grow, we could very well say, my little children, that we were in full progress.*
>
> *"The principal reason for Niepokalanow is the sanctification of the brothers, our own sanctification. We must never forget this: we must first be Saints ourselves.*
>
> *"But what is the specific character of Niepokalanow? It is to convert and to sanctify souls under the protection and by the mediation of the Immaculata. Thus, it does not suffice to say simply: 'to convert and sanctify souls.' We must add: 'by the Immaculata.' These few words show the one specific difference between Niepokalanow and other friars, orders, etc. Everyone knows that the Virgin is the Mediatrix of all graces. What characterizes us is our absolute belonging to the Immaculata, the raison d'être of Niepokalanow and of The Knight of the Immaculata."*

He would have his followers settle for nothing short of perfect imitation of Mary Immaculate, that they would personify Mary in the most intimate and total way.

> *"Every thought, action and suffering of the Immaculata was a most perfect act of love toward God, toward Jesus. We must, therefore, say this to all souls and to each one in particular, to those who live today on earth and those who will live. Say it with our example, with the living word, the printed word, through the radio, movies, painting, sculpture, etc. Say and do what the Immaculata in concrete circumstances of life and in every vocation had thought, spoken, and done to ignite on earth the most perfect love of her heart toward the most Sacred Heart of Jesus."*

The presence of the hand of God in the work of Father Maximilian, not only in the foundation of Niepokalanow, but in all his missionary work and during the trials of the Second World War, is confirmed by the following testimony of Father Cornelius Czupryk:

> *"The Saint was not guided by human considerations nor by human interests. He used to say: 'We are instruments in the hands of the Immaculata and therefore in the hands of God.' When he was ill, he did not worry about the work being done, but was accustomed to saying that 'Everything would be as Mary, and therefore God, wanted it to be.'"* ❑

Maximilian's Secret Weapon. . .

. . .is a medal of Mary that is really no secret. It just seems as though it is, as it isn't being used and propagated as St. Maximilian would have us use it in bringing souls to Christ.

The Medal of the Immaculate Conception (popularly known as the Miraculous Medal) figured very prominently from the very beginnings of the *Militia Immaculatae* in St. Maximilian's mind and actions. In his own words, "Because. . . .conversion and sanctification are divine graces, the Miraculous Medal will be a first class means for attaining our purpose. For that reason it is a preeminent weapon of the Militia; it is the bullet with which a faithful soldier hits the enemy, that is evil [sin] and thus rescues souls."

The story of the miraculous conversion of the Jew, Alphonse Ratisbonne, related in his seminary days, convinced St. Maximilian of the power of Mary Immaculate working through this sacramental. He personally saw many conversions of non-Catholics, even anti-Catholics, which took place through the medal. Such accounts appear constantly in his extensive correspondence. It seems he never left "the City of the Immaculate" without being well armed with his "bullets." Kolbe, a truly apostolic man, would never consciously let an opportunity go by to win a soul the grace of conversion

In Kolbe's mind the Medals were even more than a great aid in bringing about conversions. Besides being a proof of unwavering trust in Our Lady's powerful role in bringing about a change of heart, members of the Militia were to wear the Medal as a sign of their total consecration to Mary, and to recite daily the invocation circling the image of the Immaculate on the medal, "Oh Mary Conceived without sin, pray for us who have recourse to thee!" To the last sentence he added, "especially the Masons and the enemies of the Church."

The altar in the Church of Sant' Andrea della Fratte, Rome, where the agnostic Jew, Alphonse Ratisbonne, saw the Blessed Virgin, was converted and eventually became a priest. She granted him this grace through his wearing of the Miraculous Medal and reciting the *Memorare*.

The medal honors Mary in her great prerogative of the Immaculate Conception, and also depicts Mary as the Mediatrix of all graces. Her hands are extended and rays came from rings on her fingers. Our Lady explained to St. Catherine that, "these represent graces that I have for my children."

On the opposite side we are reminded by the two Hearts, the Immaculate Heart of Mary and the Sacred Heart of Jesus, that the whole purpose of the *Militia Immaculatae* which he founded in 1917 in Rome is to establish, through the Immaculate Heart of Mary, the reign of the Sacred Heart of Jesus throughout the whole world in every soul living and to the end of time - and that "as soon as possible, as soon as possible!" ❑

Father Kolbe was assigned to a work detachment under a capo (guard) who was a common criminal, bloody Krott. He was a sadist who hated anything that reminded him of God, in particular priests, whom he worked to death. Among the Jews and priests in his detachment, prisoner 16670 elicited a special hatred of Krott. Kolbe's meekness and peaceful resignation under cruel treatment seemed to increase the capo's rage.

Above: The first imprisonment of the friars from Niepokalanow was on September 19th when forty, including Fr. Maximilian, were deported to Germany.

All Roads lead to Calvary and Glory

WHEN FATHER KOLBE was given the obedience to return to Poland for a Province Chapter, it was with heavy heart that he left Japan. Though he had suffered much in the years he spent in the Land of the Rising Sun, he had many fond memories and had received some remarkable graces. These graces were of a mystical nature. One such episode, which he related to his friars, was reminiscent of the Last Supper, when Our Divine Lord revealed to the Apostles His coming Passion and Death and opened His Heart to them.

It was Sunday, January 10, 1937. During supper, Father Maximilian announced that during the community recreation that followed, any of the solemnly professed religious who wished to stay behind with him in the refectory could do so. Fr. Kolbe had something very special to share with those who stayed behind. The slight trembling of his voice accentuated the solemnity of the occasion. One of the brothers recorded the words of Father Maximilian:

> *"My dear brothers, for the present I am still with you. You love me and I love you in return. However, you must realize that I will not be here always. I will die, and you will stay. Before departing from this world, I would like to leave you a remembrance... You call me Father Guardian, and that is what I am... But what am I really? I am your Father, really and truly, even more than your earthly fathers who gave you mortal life. But from me you have received the spiritual life, the divine life, your religious vocation that rises above this temporal life. Is that not so?"*

They all agreed and he listened to their protestations of loyalty with a smile. "Therefore, I am really your Father. Do not call me guardian or director, but simply Father."

There was a moment of silence while Father Maximilian paused, in his deep humility, hesitating to communicate something very dear to his heart. Shyly, he continued, "My children, you are well aware that I will not always be with you. That is why I would like to leave you something in remembrance of me."

"By all means, Father. Tell us!" they exclaimed. Deeply moved, Father went on.

> *"If you knew, my dear brothers, how happy I am! My heart overflows with happiness and peace, as much as one is able to be happy on this earth. In spite of the troubles and anxieties of daily life, somewhere at the bottom of my heart there is always this peace, this joy that cannot be expressed in human words. My brothers, love the Immaculata, love the Immaculata. She will make you happy. Give her your confidence, without limits. Not everyone is privileged to understand the Immaculata; it is given only to those who ask for this grace through prayer. The Immaculata is the Mother of God. Do you understand what it means to say Mother of God? Really, truly Mother of God! Only the Holy Spirit is able to make known His spouse to whomever and however He wills. I would like to tell you one more thing... but I think this is enough."*

At this point, Father Maximilian gazed lovingly at his faithful followers, as though he feared he had already said too much. They earnestly begged him to speak and to keep nothing from them.

> *"I told you, my brothers, that I am very happy and that my soul is flooded with joy. Do you know why? Because Heaven has been promised to me in all certitude. My sons, love the Immaculata, love the Immaculata, as much as you know how and can."*

Tears welled up in his eyes. There followed a momentary silence which no one except Father Maximilian dared to break.

"There it is, brothers. That will be sufficient... "

Their entreaties were touching: "Speak, Father; perhaps we will never have another Last Supper like this one."

After a moment's hesitation, he spoke a few words more: "This happened in Japan."

Some of those present coaxed him in vain to uncover a little more of his secret, but Father Maximilian kept silent, plunged in deep meditation. After a few moments he spoke:

> *"I have disclosed my secret to you in order that it might be a strength and support in the tests that are ahead of you. There will be sufferings, temptations; perhaps you will be haunted by discouragement. Remember then what I have told you and learn to be ready for the greatest sacrifices, ready for all that the Immaculata will ask of you. My sons, do not desire extraordinary things, but simply perform the will of the Immaculata. May her will be done, not ours. You must tell no one what I have just confided to you as long as I live. Say nothing to anyone."*

On another occasion, in February, 1937, Father Maximilian made a prophecy relating to Russia which ties in with the ultimate triumph of Our Lady's Immaculate Heart as prophesied at Fatima: "But in the end My Immaculate Heart will triumph. Russia will be converted and there will be a time of world peace."

On the occasion of the twentieth anniversary of the founding of the *Militia Immaculatae* (October 16, 1917, just a few days after the great Miracle of the Sun at Fatima), Father Maximilian was the main speaker at a conference at the International Center of the M.I. in Rome. In the course of the conference, he predicted, "We do not believe the day to be far off, or a mere dream, when the statue of the Immaculata will be enthroned by her Knights in the very heart of Moscow." Father Quiricus Pignalberi relates a private conversation at the same conference, in which Fr. Maximilian said that,

> *"... a statue of the Immaculate would be set up in the center of Moscow, but first we must pass through a trial of blood. I understood that this would occur in the City of the Immaculata. He mentioned this trial of blood again in Rome a few days later. That was on February 11, a feast of the M.I. This decisive announcement disquieted me, but he insisted that things would go well this way. Moreover, that it was really necessary."*

Though Father Kolbe knew nothing about Fatima and its message of world peace through consecration to the Immaculate Heart, this incident now makes it clear that the two — Fatima and the founding of the M.I. — were related. Atheistic communism would arise in Russia within a month of both events, and both were calculated from Heaven to meet it. The corporate consecration of the world, and Russia in particular, to the Immaculate Heart of Mary has already brought about the end of the repressive Red rule in Russia. The complete conversion of Russia, however, will only be realized through the total consecration of individual souls to Mary Immaculate, as promoted through The *Militia Immaculatae.*

The Saint had insisted to Father Pignalberi that much suffering would be necessary, and this was soon to be realized with the invasion of Poland by the German armies in the fall of 1939. With no natural borders and only cavalry units to defend against the blitzkrieg (lightning war) of the Nazis, Poland's defeat was inevitable. Divisions of tanks and armored vehicles, with dive bombers for air support, rolled across the broad plains toward the center of Poland. Since the City of the Immaculate was only twenty-five miles from strategic Warsaw, it wasn't long before invading army divisions surrounded it. The time of dispersion of the friars, as prophesied by Kolbe, had arrived. He had told the brothers many times that, "The true City of the Immaculata is in your hearts." Now was the time of testing for their vocation and consecration.

On September 5, 1939, Father Maximilian gave his blessing to the departing brothers and predicted that he would not survive the war. He and about fifty brothers remained at Niepokalanow when the vanguard of the German army arrived. They allowed the friars to continue to be of assistance to the refugees and wounded who had arrived ahead of the German armies. In the middle of September, the German soldiers, as to be expected, began pillaging and destroying everything they could lay their hands on — furniture, clothes, files, religious articles, especially crucifixes and statues. The machinery was spared with the intention of eventually sending it intact to Germany. As the product of twelve years of hard labor was being destroyed by the Nazis, there was not a word of resentment from Fr. Kolbe towards the vandals and their irresponsible actions. His response: "The Immaculata has given all. She has taken it all away. She knows how things are."

The material destruction was insignificant compared to the loss of human life throughout Poland. After the Jews, Catholic priests and potential leaders were targeted. At the University in Kracow, practically the whole teaching staff was sent to concentration camps, where many perished. All institutions of higher learning were closed "for all times." Hitler's final solution regarding the Poles was to wipe out one third of the general population. Those on farms, approximately a third, were to remain as serfs under the German "land owners." The remaining third were sent to Germany as slave labor in war-related manufacturing plants.

The first imprisonment of the friars of the City began on September 19th. Forty of the friars were deported to Germany, with only two friars left behind who tended the wounded. They were first jammed into trucks. The second night, near the German border, they were thrown into livestock wagons. To help lift their spirits, Kolbe quipped, "We at least are getting free transportation." Their destination was the holding camp at Amtitz. The brothers and Father Maximilian suffered much from inadequate food rations and cold, as they slept outdoors. As one brother relates,

> *"Every suffering seemed normal and even sweet, because it was accepted with resignation and out of love for the Immaculata. It was enough to look at Father Kolbe to be inspired and feel capable of enduring any suffering with joy."*

The barracks where they were imprisoned became a little Niepokalanow, with community prayer before a statue of the Immaculata shaped out of clay by one of the brothers. Their spiritual Father explained that this was to be their mission on German soil: to pray for their persecutors. So depressing were the conditions that one of the brothers became quite irritated when Fr. Maximilian repeatedly told them that they would soon be set free.

On November 9, they were sent to Ostrzesrow, in Polish territory, through the sympathetic efforts of a new commanding officer at Amtitz who happened to be a Catholic. They received better treatment here and were given a measure of freedom to fulfill their religious practices. On December 8, the Feast of the Immaculate Conception, they were able to receive Holy Communion for the first time in three months. That afternoon, they were ordered to leave the camp and return to their homes. The friars arrived back at the City on December 10, the Feast of Our Lady of Loreto. On the day of their arrival, Fr. Maximilian announced that the chapel was to be restored as soon as possible in order to inaugurate Perpetual Eucharistic Adoration.

He not only showed a fatherly solicitude and gave much encouragement to the friars who remained at Niepokalanow, but kept in contact with the dispersed brothers through many moving letters and bulletins. We have these letters and the responses of the friars in exile, many of whom were on the Gestapo list to be eliminated. The following are a few samples from these letters of Fr. Maximilian:

> *"The soul consecrated to the Immaculata will work always wherever it finds another soul... Let us apply ourselves in missionary action to conquer other hearts for her. Let us pray for the coming of her reign. Let us offer our sufferings for this end... What will the good God not do for the souls who love Him? But if one stays outside of the friary voluntarily how can that soul hope to have this special grace?"*

At this time, there was little action on the Western Front. Even though Poland was under German occupation, life began to resume a more normal course. The buildings at Niepokalanow were turned into a hospital. The friars were pleased to have this opportunity of extending Christian charity and furthering the apostolate of the *Militia Immaculatae*. Harboring Jews at the City reminded Kolbe of the days he spent in the sanatorium at Zakopane and his contact with the Jewish intellectuals there, many of whom had converted to the Catholic Faith. It was thus easy for him to understand and help them in their great suffering. Though he had a Christmas party for the Christians, he did not neglect having a New Year's celebration for the Jewish refugees. He saw to it that there was absolutely no partiality between Christian and Jew. Contrary to what the mass media in this country says, the Polish Christians got along well with their brother Jewish Poles. How else do we explain the fact that little Poland had, by far, the largest Jewish population of any country in Europe? Kolbe looked upon them as worthy Polish citizens and children of the same heavenly Father.

During this period, after a good deal of prayer and much prodding on the part of Fr. Maximilian, the Nazi authorities in Warsaw allowed the publishing of one more edition of the Knight magazine. In his last published article, he wrote,

> *"No one in the world can alter the truth. All that we can do is to seek it, find it and live it... If good consists in the love of God and springs from love, evil is substantially a negation of love... "*

Understandably, such words were contrary to the Nazi ideology, based on hatred and lies. The Nazis regretted having given him permission to print the magazine and all future publication was forbidden. The Nazis made a last attempt to win the support of the influential little priest, who had a German-sounding name, by having him say he was of German extraction. They utterly failed as Kolbe loved his country and vigorously affirmed his Polish nationality.

On February 17, 1941, at 9:45 a.m., two cars with Gestapo license plates drove up to Niepokalanow. As the cars approached, the Brother Porter hastened to phone Father Maximilian. Brother Ivo Achtelik, who was in his office taking dictation when he received the call, relates that the Saint answered with a trembling "Yes," but, immediately controlling himself, added: "Alright, my son. Mary!" He courteously greeted the five Nazi officials. They responded by roughly questioning him. He was taken to Warsaw and placed in the infamous Pawiak prison, the beginning of his assent to his Calvary and death. Within a few days of his arrival, he won the hearts of his fellow inmates through his priestly ministry. Shortly after his arrival, the Nazi head of Kolbe's prison section made an inspection. When he saw Father Kolbe in a religious habit, he was infuriated. The man's hatred was not only for the habit, but above all for the crucifix and the rosary which hung from the Franciscan cord around Kolbe's waist. The S.S. officer seized the crucifix, pulling it violently, and yelled, "And do you believe in this?"

Father Kolbe answered in a calm, strong voice: "Yes, I believe."

According to a fellow inmate:

> *"The German raged in fury. He immediately struck Father Kolbe on the face. Three times he repeated the question; three times he received the same reply, and three times he struck him... Father Kolbe remained totally calm and the only indication of the incident was the livid color on his face... After the section officer left, Father Kolbe started to walk up and down in the cell, praying. We two were more irritated than he was... It was precisely Father Kolbe who sought to calm us saying, 'There is no reason for getting so upset... This is a small thing; everything is for the Immaculata.'"*

During this time, his brothers and the authorities of the Franciscan Order tried in every way to gain his release. In fact, twenty of the brothers offered themselves as hostages in the place of Father Kolbe. Their heroic offering was rejected. In the middle of May, his name was placed on the list of Poles to be sent to Auschwitz. The 320 prisoners in his transport were packed into freight cars that were bolted from the outside. As soon as the train began to move, someone intoned religious and national songs. It was Fr. Kolbe. Despite the crowded, suffocating conditions, and the realization that most of them were heading toward a cruel death, the songs helped them to forget their sad lot. Upon arriving at Auschwitz, the most notorious Nazi concentration camp, they were greeted by the mocking sign above the entrance: "Work makes one free." They were told unceremoniously,

> *"Jews, do not have a right to live more than two weeks. If there are priests, they can live a month; the others three months."*

The following "Credo," found after the camp was liberated, helps us to better understand the depravity and hatred that motivated the S.S. guards:

> *"Prayer books are objects for women, also for those women who wear pants. We hate the smell of incense; this ruins the soul of the German, like the Jew ruins the race.*
>
> *We believe in God, but we do not believe in His representatives. This would be idolatry and paganism.*

We believe in our Fuhrer and our great country. For this and for no other reason do we fight: then when it comes time for us to die, it will not be with the words, 'Mary pray for us.'

We live free and want to die free. Our last breath — Adolph Hitler!"

On the third day after his arrival, Father Kolbe was assigned, along with other priests, to a work detachment under a capo (guard) who was a common criminal: the bloody Krott, who held the power of life and death. Krott was a sadist who had a hatred of anything that reminded him of God, in particular priests, whom he worked to death. Among the Jews and priests in the detachment, prisoner 16670 elicited a special hatred in Krott. Kolbe's meekness and peaceful resignation under cruel treatment seemed to increase the capo's rage. He loaded on the shoulders of the little priest heavy pieces of wood, and then ordered him to run. When Kolbe fell to the ground, the Nazi kicked him in the stomach and face, howling, "You don't want to work, faker! I'll show you what it means to work."

He ordered Kolbe to stretch out on a tree trunk. Uttering words of derision and blasphemy, he had one of the strongest prisoners inflict fifty lashes on the frail priest. When Krott thought he was dead, he threw Kolbe into a mud hole and covered his body with brush wood.

Later, when the group started back to the barracks, they found that he was still alive and carried him back to the camp "hospital."

The following account by a young priest, Father Conrad Szweda, who was a prisoner orderly in the camp hospital, sums up well the typical selflessness and heroism of Father Maximilian, and what made his heroism possible:

> *When I learned that Father Kolbe was in the hospital, I went right away to see how he was. His face was all bruised, his eyes lusterless, and a fever burned his body to the point that his swollen tongue couldn't move and his voice died out in his throat. But in spite of the extreme fever, he wasn't delirious… Because with a high fever one suffers a lot without any liquid, I brought him once a cup of tea, carefully saved, so he could moisten his feverish lips. I could see how parched he was. To my astonishment, he refused to take it. 'I can't,' he said, indicating the other patients. 'They don't have any; let's give it to them.' To console me, he added, "Don't worry, I'll get along somehow. The Immaculata is helping me still… '*
>
> *"I must say too that, in spite of his fevered condition, it was he who comforted me. When after my day's work I came to him, he pressed me to his chest as a mother her child. Sometimes I was deeply depressed and complained that I could not go on. 'But what if God wants you to live and survive this camp?' He asked. He held out Mary to me saying, 'She is the consoler of the afflicted who listens to everyone, helps everyone who calls on her.' I especially found comfort in his urging, 'Take Christ's hand in one of yours and Mary's in the other. Now even if you are in darkness you can go forward with the confidence of a child guided by its parents.' I owe a great deal to his motherly heart."*

Fr. Maximilian would have been touched by this testimony, which compared his own "motherly heart" to that of his heavenly Mother. It is evident that Kolbe, above all others, owed much to the Heart of the Immaculata. Thus, on the vigil of Mary's Assumption into Heaven, her faithful Knight commended his soul into her hands.* His body was burned in the ovens of Auschwitz on her Feast, fulfilling a prediction he had made, that his ashes would be dispersed by the wind. He was beatified as a Confessor by Pope Paul VI on October 17, 1971, sixty-four years to the day after the founding of his world-wide movement — the Knights of the Immaculata. He was canonized by Pope John Paul II as a Martyr of Charity, at a huge gathering in St. Peter's Piazza, on October 10, 1982. ❑

Saint Peter's in Rome was packed for the Beatification of St. Maximilian on October 17, 1971. I to such a large crowd he was canonized eleven years later in St. Peter's Square on October 10, 19

PART II:
INNER DYNAMISM

Fr. Kolbe hard at work in the editorial department in the Japanese "City of the Immaculate." It would seem he could have used a computer or at least a couple of file cabinets.

Fr. Kolbe returns to Zakopane in 1937 for a rest. It was in this mountainous southern part c Poland, during the twenties, that he spent some time in a sanitarium recovering from tuberculosis It was a great opportunity to evangelize the young college students with his mastery of apologetic and his warm, attractive, personal approach. He brought many of them back to the Faith.

St. Maximilian— Master Apologist

By Fr. Maximilian Kolbe

AS WE PASSED Przemysl, and our train was quickly approaching Krakow I noticed some young people sitting by the window. One of them I found out was an artist, a portrait painter, and our conversation soon revealed he was Jewish. We spoke about the purpose of man, and we came to the conclusion that it was in being like God - in other words man's purpose is to serve the glory of God and this constitutes the perfect happiness of human beings. At the next station a well dressed and groomed gentleman entered our compartment with others and sat down directly across from me. He immediately entered into our circle's conversation:

"But can we know that God exists?" he began.

"Why, yes! I would say so."

"In this matter I dare say one can only believe; no one can really prove that God exists.

"Please sir, let me clearly prove it to you."

"No one can convince me!"

"True, if from the beginning you reject all reasoning."

"Not at all."

A lady sitting on the other side of me, entered the conversation "I would also like to hear a clear proof of His existence!"

"Excuse me," I said, turning to the young people sitting near the window, "May I return to the question which we have already discussed, in order to satisfy the wishes of those who have just come in?"

"Please do."

"In the first place, may I ask you sir, what kind of an education do you have?"

"I studied law at the university."

"And philosophy, too?"

"No! After all, what has philosophy to do with faith?"

"Faith must be reasonable and that is why it is properly accompanied by philosophy - particularly concerning the question of the existence of God. And now, let us begin with what it is that we all agree on. It is fitting to begin with that; otherwise we would be building on an uncertain foundation. Do you exist sir?"

"Yes, but I am only a portion of the world"

"Please sir, we will talk about what we are later. For now I simply ask: do you exist?"

"Yes."

"And you, madam?"

"I agree."

"Does anyone here judge otherwise?" All expressed agreement.

"Therefore, our existence is certain.

"Wait-I would not say so."

"And why?"

"Because in general we can know nothing for certain; what some affirm, others deny."

"Therefore, you are not sure that you exist?"

"I am only a portion of the matter which is in the universe."

"I am not concerned with - I repeat - what you are, but whether you actually exist, that is, whether you are something, or nothing."

"Evidently, I am nothing."

"For sure?"

"For sure."

"And do you have a watch?"

"I have," he answered, reaching into his pocket."

"Is it yours?

"Yes."

"For sure?"

"Without a doubt."

"Excuse me, if you have a doubt about it, I would like to put it away in my pocket." All laughed. "Therefore your premise that we can know nothing for certain is false. You clearly have no intention to doubt that the watch belongs to you. Now, do I exist?"

"Yes!"

"And that lady, that gentleman, and in general all of us who are present here?"

"Yes."

"Are you sure? Why do you affirm it?"

"Because my eyes clearly tell me so"

"And those fields and meadows, which we observe through the windows of our moving coach, indeed the whole world and the stars above our heads, do they exist?"

"Yes. In general, I admit that - that everything we see must exist. But after all, we do not see God."

"Please sir, is there a locomotive in front of our train?"

"Certainly."

"For sure?"

"For sure."

"And do you see it?"

"No, but if it were otherwise, our coach would not move forward."

"Therefore you admit that we can not only come to know a certain thing through our immediate sight, but that we can know something from an effect-that our reason can come to the knowledge of a real cause. Is this not true?"

"It is."

"What would you think of a man who would thus argue about your watch: This metal cover has separated itself from a gold mine, by chance melted itself down and purified itself and formed itself into its present shape. The inscription on it was also inscribed by chance. The glass on the cover was also melted and polished by chance. Likewise the delicate wheels and springs in it have made themselves. The other constituents of that watch have formed themselves altogether by accident; afterwards they became linked together in their present order without human thought and without a human hand to give us the proper time. If the owner of the watch would dare assert this in all seriousness, what would you say about him?"

"That he suffers, I dare say, from a mental disorder!"

"Well, now, in nature we have organisms much finer in comparison. Certainly, one has to admire, if in studying anatomy, the complexity of the human eye. How many different parts it has, how delicate they are, and how marvelously they serve together in giving sight. The whole of nature is composed of millions and billions of organisms which live, which develop, which multiply. Therefore, could it be asserted that these marvels of nature are mere accidents? Someone might indeed say: 'This does not happen without a cause.' True, but such a cause has its own causes, and these also have their own causes. Is it not clear that with respect to this series of causes - even if thrust into infinity- that we must accept a First Cause? For all other causes

do not give of themselves any perfection but merely hand down what they themselves received. But our reason is obliged to be concerned with the Source of perfections. There must be some kind of a First Cause, and that is God, our Creator."

"Of course."

I noticed that the face of this gentleman had a kind of amazed expression. He had not previously come to such a conclusion. It may be that he had never before encountered an occasion to think through this truth.

This chapter is a free translation of an article by Fr. Maximilian in Polish that appeared in his publication, the Knight of the Immaculate. ❑

St. Maximilian's Apologetics

Apologetics is defined in the Webster's Dictionary as "a systematic argumentative discourse in defense of the divine origin and authority of Christianity." To Saint Maximilian the science of apologetics was much more than just a defensive approach to the Faith.

Traditionally, Catholic apologetics was not meant to be just a defense of the truths of the Faith. Rather it is more a love of the truths of the Faith with a zeal to spread these truths. Jesus Christ is the Incarnation of Truth. He identifies Himself as the Way, the Truth and the Life. Nothing could be more positive and exciting than sharing this Truth, Jesus, with others. The greatest minds over the centuries were apologists: St. Augustine, St. Thomas Aquinas, St. Bonaventure to mention a few from the past; and in our own times, Cardinal Newman, G.K. Chesterton, Bishop Fulton Sheen and Frank Sheed. The latter used to go to Hyde Park in New York City as a member of the "Catholic Evidence Guild," to present and explain the truths of the Faith to others on a soap box.

Obviously, one must first know the Faith in order to explain it. St. Maximilian, a man of superior intelligence, had a doctorate in Philosophy at age twenty-one and another in theology at twenty-five. However, he never took a superior attitude over his opponent. The manner of presenting the truth is of vital importance. It had to be done in humility and in charity. Bishop Sheen used to say, "Win an argument and lose a convert." Note how courteous our saint is and how he avoids offensive language and confrontation. He allows the truth to speak for itself, yet how persuasive is his reasoning.

Building a Civilization of Love

Fr. James McCurry, OFM Conv.

"OH PLEASE! JUST what we need: one more organization!" So moaned a well-intentioned but overworked parish priest when an ardent member of the *Militia Immaculatae* suggested placing an MI promotion on the parish bulletin board.

The MI is not really an "organization," however. It never was. Basically the MI is a person: Mary Immaculate. St. Maximilian Kolbe founded the MI in 1917 to make the Blessed Virgin Mary more visible in the world. In particular, St. Maximilian wanted the Immaculata's presence to be as real and influential in the lives of simple people today as when she appeared to St. Bernadette at Lourdes and identified herself: "I am the Immaculate Conception."

Why does the Church "need" the MI? Why would a parish "need" the MI? The question can be restated: Why does the Church "need" MARY? The answer is disarmingly simple: because God wills the Church to "need" Mary! God incorporated Mary into his plan for our salvation. He did not have to do this, but he did. That is reality. She would not only bear Christ our Redeemer; she would be the first of Christ's redeemed. Preserving Mary free from Original Sin at the first moment of her Immaculate Conception, God gives his first proof of the power he has over sin, a power that will eventually bring salvation and peace to all of us.

So the Immaculate Conception of Mary is in fact the "mystery" of how God worked out in human history his divine will for you and me to "need" Mary. The Church "needs" Mary in order to verify, prove, authenticate, and show the real, saving Presence of Jesus Christ in the world.

Blessed Pope Pius IX in 1854 looked out from the Vatican at a world increasingly ready to deny Christ's real Presence. The "isms" which plague us today in the twenty first century were already raising their hoary heads. Marxism, materialism, evolutionism, determinism, and process relativism, secularism were not merely academic topics for university students. These "isms" spawned social movements, many of which were rabidly antagonistic to the Catholic Faith. Freemasonry would be recharged by these movements that promised a "perfect world"-without God. Prophetically, Pope Pius IX saw in all of this the seeds for the destructive upheavals that would shake the twentieth century.

What antidote could the Pope give? In 1854 he would proclaim infallibly the Dogma of the Immaculate Conception. This Dogma would affirm two things: Mary's freedom from sin and her fullness of grace; that is, Mary's twofold stance of total reconciliation (conversion) to God, and full maturity in holiness (sanctification).

By incorporating this teaching into the life of the Church, Pope Pius wanted to assert the absolute promise of victory over godlessness that humble believers like Mary can have. Mary's humble stance of conversion and sanctification would become the guide or road map for all the rest of us to follow in our lives of faith and grace.

St. Maximilian Kolbe used the term "blueprint" to describe this role of Mary Immaculate. Vatican II would confirm the reality by saying that our Lady is the "image and first flowering of the Church as she is to be perfected in the world to come." God set her up as a "blueprint" of the perfect society - the kingdom of the humble and lowly - wholly converted and sanctified - who comprise a civilization of love which participates in the divine life of the Father, the Son, and the Holy Spirit.

Fifteen hundred years ago St. Augustine wrote: "Two loves have created two cities: love of self, to the contempt of God, the earthly city; love of God, to the contempt of self, the heavenly City." He knew well the reality, ever ancient and ever new, that the "heavenly" civilization of love would ultimately triumph. Christian tradition has long described that triumphant "reign of love" in terms of the humble image of the Sacred Heart of Jesus.

When St. Maximilian Kolbe was forming plans to found his MI movement, he prayed daily before a large painting of the Sacred

Heart (still preserved at Casa Kolbe, Rome). He belonged to an Order (the Conventual Franciscans) which in 1913 had solemnly renewed its act of consecration to the Sacred Heart; prayerfully he saw the Sacred Heart's triumph of love first realized in the stainless and Immaculate Virgin Mary. With mystical intuition, the saint came to understand that none of the false and godless "isms" of his day would "win" ground wherever the presence of the Immaculate Virgin was secure. Her presence would serve to guarantee an open door to the Sacred Heart's "Civilization of Love." She would open our hearts to His!

But HOW could her presence be made tangible enough, real enough to open the world's heart to Christ? This was St. Maximilian's question in 1917. The answer which God gave him in prayer consisted of two words: *Militia Immaculatae*. He would found a movement to make her presence explicit. This MI movement would be, in the words of its founder, "a global vision of Catholic life under a new form, consisting in its link with the Immaculata, our universal Mediatrix with Jesus."

Simple as we are, we people of God NEED to find a way to win the daily battle against sin. We NEED to find a simple way to grow in an authentic love that never compromises truth. We NEED to find a simple way of "joining" humble Mary in her activism against sin and for grace. The MI movement involves us with Mary; it engages us as sharers and participants in her God-given role of embodying and thereby building a divine civilization of love. This is why the Church (and the world) "needs" the MI. No mere organization, the MI is a communion of people who together live and act as "other Marys"-helping the world to see, understand, and love her as God does.

In the apse behind the main altar of St. Peter's Basilica, Rome, is the great "Chair of St. Peter" suspended amidst the glory of Bernini's artistry. On the marble walls underneath this venerable relic, are inscribed commemorative details about the 1854 papal proclamation of the Dogma of the Immaculate Conception. The juxtaposition of the two bespeaks the reality that this Dogma upholds all that the Church represents.

A monumental statue of St. Francis stands by these marble slabs-not for mere adornment. Commissioned by Christ's own voice to "rebuild my Church," St. Francis of Assisi inspired his followers down through the centuries to become leading promoters of Mary's Immaculate Conception. From this noble line, faithful to St. Francis and to the Chair of Peter, St. Maximilian Kolbe taught us how God wills the mystery of the Immaculata to be "needed" by the world. May the MI enable this mystery to engage you and me, the Church and the world in a consecrated bond to Mary. May we help her, thereby, to fulfill God's plan for the coming of a great Civilization of Love. ❑

It was said that Fr. Maximilian was a regular "slave driver." However, the opposite was true. He asked no more of his Brothers than what he himself did. His zeal and heroism was catching. His infectious joy as seen in so many pictures of the brothers surrounding him.

Is The Martyr of Charity a Heretic?

Fr. Peter Damian Fehlner, F.I.

MOST ORDINARY CATHOLICS on hearing accusations of anti-Semitism leveled against St. Maximilian Mary Kolbe are rightly shocked and, to put it mildly, offended and irked. How, they ask with the instinct of faith - the sensus fidelium - could the Church canonize as a martyr of charity, as patron of this age so troubled by the profanation of charity, anyone even slightly implicated in a material sin of hatred?

The reply, of course, is that the Church did not err in so canonizing him, because she could not. St. Maximilian is neither directly nor indirectly guilty of such prejudice. And to say that Kolbe disagreed with those Jews who do not recognize Jesus, the Son of the Virgin Mary, as their promised Messiah no more makes him guilty of anti-Semitism, than it makes Catholics anti-human or anti-gentile because they do not agree with those gentiles who reject their Savior.

While the accusations of hatred for the Jews on the part of the victim of Auschwitz continue to circulate, a new accusation, equally startling and shocking is beginning to be heard: St. Maximilian was at least a material heretic, whose writings are replete with thoughts contrary to the fundamentals of Catholic faith. Again, the instinctive reaction of the believing Catholic is: how could anyone whose thought patterns are radically anti-dogmatic have been canonized as a martyr? It seems a contradiction in terms, impossible. Do those making such charges mean to suggest that two Popes made a mistake in beatifying as a confessor of the true faith (Paul VI) and in canonizing as a martyr of charity (John Paul II) this Polish Franciscan?

And if they were wrong, how does the claim of papal infallibility in the canonization of saints stand as true? So linking the papacy to the sin of anti-Semitism and the error of Marian "piety", the accusations in this context are also radically anti-papal. The primary intent, however, of the accusations of heresy, like those of anti-Semitism, seems to disjoin sanctity and virtue - and in the end blessedness - from considerations of doctrine and discipline, that is, from the truth proclaimed by St. Paul that there is no salvation apart from the Cross of Jesus: foolishness (read "heresy") to the Greeks (read Gentiles) and a scandal to the Jews, but to those who believe (as St. Peter and the Popes) the wisdom (doctrine) and power (discipline) of God. (cf. I Cor. 1, 23).

Curiously, most of the accusers, when pressed, admit that St. Maximilian's death was truly noble and worthy of emulation. What they will not admit is that there is any link between heroic death (martyrdom) and a life based on doctrinal truth and discipline as found in total consecration to the Immaculate. In their view a dogma-free, authority-free virtue is possible.

Their accusation of Marian heresy and their recognition of the exceptional generosity of St. Maximilian's final gesture prove, for them, the disjunction between charity and dogma, between martyrdom and dogmatic faith and membership in the Church as the pre-condition for canonization. Indeed, according to his accusers, had St. Maximilian committed any other "fault", except anti-Semitism, his fault and his error might well have been touted as the proof of his courage in resisting tyranny within and without the Church.

So runs the thesis in a recent book: Making Saints, by K. Woodword. This is not a new thesis, but the old syncretism and the old modernism set forth in terms calculated to appeal to anyone influenced by today's fashionable thought. But as in the case of accusations of anti-Semitism, so too accusations of heresy against St. Maximilian simply are not true.

Such accusations of heresy were first heard on the eve of the Martyr's canonization in 1982. The National Catholic Reporter of Oct. 3, 1982 published a long center spread article by the English ex-Jesuit priest, Peter Hebblethwaite, making essentially one point. The Polish Pope was beatifying Maximilian for nationalistic, not spiritual and theological, reasons, for while the death of the Blessed was noble, his life should not and indeed could not be imitated, for it represented the worst in unsound, traditional Catholic Marian piety. With this the author intended to imply that the doctrine underlying this piety, total consecration to the Immaculate, is "heretical", and to affirm that the proponent of a system of spirituality based on Marian mediation could not lead one to authentic holiness, but only to bizarre life styles.

Since then voices questioning in principle the traditional Catholic practice of consecration to Mary and through Mary to Christ have become more noticeable, particularly within the last decade as more and more requests for a solemn dogmatic definition of Mary as Coredemptress, Mediatrix and Advocate have been heard.

Critics of traditional Marian consecration argue thus: Mary neither consecrates nor is an object of consecration, because both in the active and passive sense consecration is something exclusive to a divine person. To hold or practice otherwise is to detract, especially at the moment of that sacrifice by which we are sanctified and consecrated to the Father by the Redeemer Son, from the unique mediation of Jesus and the unique sanctifying role of the Holy Spirit.

Many are the considerations which may be adduced to rebut these objections based on Protestant "Christ alone" theories of redemption. One, however, that of Scripture, will suffice to illustrate the mystery of the "joint predestination" of Christ and Mary so basic in Catholic tradition. Christ is consecrated a priest at the moment of His virginal conception by the power of the Holy Spirit and the unique maternal action of Mary. In actively participating in His consecration Mary in no way reduces or obscures the divinity of Jesus.

And at the end of His life, just before dying on the cross, as a kind of conclusion to and completion of His entire redemptive work, Jesus consecrates all for whom He died to His Mother Mary as Mother, and hence through her to Himself. This coredemptive role of Mary on Calvary is the basis of the practice of total consecration to Mary in the Church. Just as her divine maternity in no way detracts from the sovereign divinity of her Son, so neither does her position as Coredemptress, the object of consecration, detract from the sufficiency of Christ's priestly sacrifice as Redeemer.

This argument reflecting the convictions of St. Maximilian is fully in accord with those of St. Louis Grignon de Montfort adduced by some to criticize the Martyr of Charity. True, St. Louis insists on consecration to Jesus through Mary. But the premise of that consecration to Jesus is made explicit in the teaching and practice of the Franciscan Saint: consecration to or "transubstantiation" into Mary.

Very recently, a prominent writer on things Marian, Rene Laurentin, has published in French a very interesting two volumes on the Holy Spirit. In the first volume, entitled (in French) The Holy Spirit, That Unknown, he has included extensive remarks on St. Maximilian, no doubt because the Saint reflected and wrote so much on our Lady and the Holy Spirit. Unfortunately, Laurentin's remarks are intended, not to approve, but to point out how disastrous the Marian maximalism of this Saint is for genuine Catholic theology and mariology.

For Laurentin, who for years has opposed the practice of consecration to and through Mary, the title Spouse of the Holy Spirit given commonly to our Lady is a dangerous one, opening the door to all kinds of trinitarian errors (heresy). To call the Holy Spirit the "uncreated Immaculate Conception" and to describe the union between the "uncreated Immaculate Conception" (Holy Spirit) and the "created Immaculate Conception" (the Virgin Mary, Mother of God) a "quasi-hypostatic union" borders on the rankest of heresy, at the same time detracting from the uniqueness of the Incarnation. Titles such as Coredeemer, according to Laurentin, are properly due only to the Holy Spirit.

In a chapter as short as this we cannot refute in detail the basis for the charge of heresy against St. Maximilian by these authors. But it is possible to state in a few words what is wrong-headed about them. Let us begin with the last point. St. Maximilian never said and never implied that the singular union of love between the Holy Spirit and the Virgin Mary, rooted in the grace of the Immaculate

Conception, was a hypostatic union, or quasi-hypostatic union. He merely observed a few times in passing that this union could be called a quasi-Incarnation, that is, likened to the union between the divine and human natures in the Son of Mary, but also by that very fact unlike, not the same as a hypostatic union. In Jesus, wrote the Saint, two natures are united in the substantial unity of one divine person. Whereas with the Holy Spirit and our Lady two distinct persons and two distinct natures are united in a unique bond of love brought to pass by the grace of the Immaculate Conception. The accusers, then, are evidently prone to misquote and caricature the doctrine of the Saint, which as the Saint expounds it is fully orthodox.

Laurentin is anxious that titles given Mary, such as Coredemptress and Mediatrix do not obscure the role of the Holy Spirit as Coredeemer. What he fails to appreciate is the fact that Mary has never been called Coredeemer, but Coredemptress. She is Coredemptress, the only Coredemptress who therefore makes possible the cooperation of Christians in applying the fruits of the redemptive sacrifice of Jesus, that is to say, "coredeemers". Thus St. Paul speaks of the believer's obligation to fill up with his personal suffering what is lacking to the Church in the passion of Christ (cf. Col 1,24). St. Paul does not mean that the passion of Christ is incomplete or insufficient, but that the distribution of the blessings or graces of that passion is not yet completed.

Where the evidence from Scripture and Tradition for Laurentin's assertions about the Holy Spirit being "coredeemer" is to be found is somewhat shrouded in mystery. The fact is, the Holy Spirit cannot in any proper sense be called a "coredeemer", because he is not incarnate. He has no body of his own like the Son of God and so cannot suffer in the proper sense. But through the suffering of Christians as "coredeemers" the Holy Spirit works in us. So, too, in a still profounder way, the Holy Spirit works through our Lady as Coredemptress, as uniquely sharing Christ's passion with her compassion, as earlier the Holy Spirit worked through her as Virgin Mother.

For Laurentin the title "Spouse of the Holy Spirit" is especially reprehensible. But in propounding such a view the French mariologist is treading on thin ice. It was not St. Maximilian, but

St. Francis and his first followers who popularized the title in the Church. It has long since been accepted and used by the Popes, including the present Vicar of Christ, John Paul II, and by the faithful in general. To attack the title is to attack St. Francis and a long-accepted Marian title in the Church, not exactly a prudent step. We know how Catholic and orthodox the thought and piety of the Seraph of Assisi is. Can we be equally sure of those who criticize a Marian title which reflects the distinctive character of St. Francis' Marian piety?

We may add, this title, Spouse of the Holy Spirit, is the key to grasping how St. Francis came to be perfectly conformed to Christ crucified and fulfilled the Redeemer's request that Francis repair a church about to fall down. Repair here meant not primarily the material and temporal aspects of the Church, but the spiritual, so as make the Church in every aspect, including the temporal, more and more an extension of the Immaculate: without spot or wrinkle (cf. Eph 5, 27), thus verifying the other famous title St. Francis gave our Lady in his "Salute to the Virgin": the Virgin made Church.

Let us now examine in the famous antiphon for the Office of the Passion composed by St. Francis which stands behind Kolbe's Marian doctrine and practice. Our Lady is called Spouse of the Holy Spirit by St. Francis, because she is uniquely united to the Holy Spirit, so perfectly that there is no trace of sin in her, not even original sin. Thus she is consecrated, as he says in his Salute to the Virgin, to the triune God with such holiness that she can be the one chosen to be Mother of God, that is, of the Father's Son, not only at Bethlehem, but on Calvary and at every eucharistic Sacrifice, where she complements the sacrifice by the compassion of her maternal heart.

And thus united to her Son as His Mother and the Mother of the Church, she reveals herself to be the firstborn daughter and handmaid of God the Father, one with him in his will that the eternal Son should be really and truly her Son, virginally conceived and virginally born; and one with the Father in the will that this Son should be obedient even to the death on the Cross. For which reason God the Father has exalted Jesus to glory (cf. Phil 2, 5-10) and for which reason all generations will call her blessed (cf. Lk 1, 48).

Such a vision of reality, the only valid one, far from minimalizing the role of Mary in the plan of salvation, strives to find in it a speculative and practical keystone to holiness, to union with Christ. The logical conclusion of the "mariology" of St. Francis is total consecration to the Immaculate and through her to Christ Crucified. This is the doctrine St. Maximilian propagated and lived. It is this doctrine and practice which prepares one for that perfect charity of giving one's life for - not simply temporal life - but the eternal life of one's neighbor. Like the death of the great High Priest of our confession (cf. I Tim 6, 13), the death of St. Maximilian is Marian, that of a child of Mary.

As Jean Borella has remarked in his book (in French, 1979) on "the subversion of the Christian soul" the central heresy of the twentieth century is the "profanation of charity". In St. Maximilian, this Catholic philosopher avers, we behold the only sufficient remedy: total consecration to the Immaculate Coredemptress. It is no wonder that the "liar and murderer from the beginning" (cf. Jn 8,44) would try to deceive men with a false wisdom, not that of the cross, not that of Mary, which ridicules the wisdom of the cross, the wisdom of Marian consecration.

We can hear in this misguided mariology, in all these accusations of heresy and anti-Semitism what is so tragic in all Marian minimalism and rightly identified by G. K. Chesterton in his poem, A Party Question, as "the little hiss that only comes from hell", the little hiss of the one who "lies in wait for her heel" (Gen 3,15).

Let us recognize with the Church that Mary is the one who alone crushes every heresy in the whole world, above all the denial of true charity in the evils of contraception, abortion, infanticide, euthanasia, and a host of other profanations of charity constituting the "culture of death". At the same time She seeks the conversion of the heretics, their profession of faith and practice of true charity through total consecration to Herself, the key to the "culture of life and the civilization of love" (Pope John Paul II). Let us beg her to give us the strength, above all in the hour of our death, to praise, like St. Maximilian, the goodness of God and the kindness of His Mother and ours. ❑

Left: Fr. Maximilian with the minor seminarians. Right: their professor in consultation with Fr. Maximilian.

Fr. Kolbe with Fr. Cornelius Czupryk (the Fr. Provincial) and Fr. Alphonse, with some of the first students of the newly established seminary at the "City."

Father Maximilian with the minor seminarians of Niepokalanow on an outing in 1937.

PART ONE

Mariology of St. Maximilian Kolbe

Fr. James McCurry, O.F.M. Conv.

WHEN POPE JOHN Paul II canonized the Conventual Franciscan Friar-Priest-Martyr, St. Maximilian Kolbe on October 10, 1982, the Gospel chosen for the liturgy was John 15:12-17. "There is no greater love than this: to lay down one's life for one's friends". This is an appropriate text for celebrating the memory of the Auschwitz inmate who volunteered to die of starvation in place of a condemned fellow prisoner. The "key" to the "no greater love" in our Saint might well lie in his theological - and more specifically, mariological - insights.

The first step in surveying the Saint's thought is to ask what is his starting point. Beginning with his formula of "Consecration to the Immaculate," composed in 1917, through his final meditation on the Immaculate Conception, dictated to his secretary only hours before the Nazis arrested him in February, 1941, St. Maximilian's writings exhibit a singular preoccupation with one all-consuming objective: to "extend as far as possible the blessed kingdom of the most Sacred Heart of Jesus." The dynamic principle governing his thought and action is based on a principle from his background in the physical sciences:

> *Everywhere in the world we notice action and the reaction which is equal but contrary to it; departure and return; going away and coming back; separation and reunion. The separation always looks forward to union, which is creative... First, God creates the universe; that is something like a separation. Creatures, by following the natural law implanted in them by God, reach their perfection, become like him. Intelligent creatures love him in*

a conscious manner; through this love they unite themselves more and more closely with him, and so find their way back to him.[1]

In this synthesis St. Maximilian articulated, through the action-reaction analogy, his conviction that the Kingdom of Christ would be held together by a powerful force: love. In the spiritual order such love, however, would find its fullest realization in the person of Mary Immaculate: "The creature most completely filled with this love, filled with God Himself, was the Immaculata. . . United to the Holy Spirit as His spouse, she is one with God in an incomparably more perfect way than can be predicated of any other creature."[2]

In view of our Saint's zeal to proclaim the Kingdom of Christ's Sacred Heart, which is equatable with a kingdom of love, and which in turn finds its first verification among creatures in the figure of Mary Immaculate - the little Franciscan's emphasis on the Immaculate's role in building this Kingdom becomes clearer. In 1933, while returning from the Orient to Poland, Kolbe summarized the Immaculate's role and his own apostolic objective:

> *We have to win the universe and each individual soul, now and in the future, down to the end of time, for the Immaculata, and by her for the Sacred Heart of Jesus. Further, we must be on the watch so that nobody tears any soul away from its consecration to the Immaculata; we should strive rather that souls may constantly deepen their love for her, that the bond of love between her and these souls may grow ever closer, and these souls may henceforth be one with her, with her alone.*
>
> *This is how the Immaculata is able to live and to act in these souls, and through them. For just as the Immaculata herself belongs to Jesus and to God, so too every soul through her and in her will belong to Jesus and to God in a much more perfect way than would have been possible without her. Such souls will come to love the Sacred Heart of Jesus much better than they have ever done up to now. Like Mary herself, they will come to penetrate into the very depths of love, to understand the cross, the Eucharist much better than before. Through her, divine love will set the*

1 H.M. Manteau-Bonamy, O.P, Immaculate Conception And The Holy Spirit, pp.3-4
2 Ibid., p.4

world on fire and will consume it; then will the "assumption of souls in love" take place. When, oh when, will the divinisation of the world in her and through her come about?[3]

The underlying theological premise that informs all of the speculative and apostolic dimensions of Saint Maximilian's work is the proclamation of the primacy of Christ in this world - a primacy which finds concrete verification in the Immaculate Conception of Mary, who in turn serves as means for drawing creatures into that Kingdom where Christ's love holds primacy. Anyone familiar with the centuries-old "Franciscan School" of theological reflection can immediately see the "seraphic" antecedents of St. Maximilian's thought in this regard. The Martyr of Charity himself acknowledged the Franciscan connection in a letter which he wrote to young friars studying in Rome at his Order's Collegio Serafico:

From the very cradle of our Order seven centuries ago, a golden thread of the cause of the Immaculate has without interruption been developed. It fought for the knowledge of the truth of the Immaculate Conception of the Blessed Virgin Mary. The battle ended with victory. This truth is universally acknowledged and has been proclaimed as a dogma of the Faith. And now, is it the end of the matter? No one interested in building a house will rest satisfied merely in describing the plans for it. But is not the plan necessarily merely a preparation for the actual realization of the building?

Now, then, a second page of our history is opening, namely, we must disseminate this truth into the hearts of all men, those who now live and all who will live until the end of the world, and we must watch over the growth and fruitfulness that leads to sanctification. We must introduce the Immaculate into the hearts of all men that She may erect the throne of Her Son and lead all to the knowledge of Him and inflame them to a love of His Most Sacred Heart.[4]

---

3 Ibid., p.117

4 Maria Was His Middle Name: Day By Day With Blessed Maximilian Kolbe Excerpts From His Writings And Addresses, compiled by Jerzy M. Domanski, Benziger Sisters Publishers 1977, p.194.

This Franciscan backdrop begins to provide an answer to the second question which a survey of Kolbean thought must pose: what are the sources for the Marian Christocentrism which we have already seen as characterizing Kolbe's fundamental perspective? While Friar Maximilian was studying in Rome from 1912 to 1919 and living at his Order's Collegio Serafico, he was exposed to the rich Franciscan tradition which stressed the Primacy of Christ (and its pastoral correlative, devotion to the Sacred Heart of Jesus). At the same time it linked to Christ's primacy a theological and devotional emphasis on the privilege of Mary's Immaculate Conception. One reference should suffice to demonstrate that St. Maximilian is an authentic offshoot of the Franciscan trunk. The reference, penned by the Saint in 1940, is part of the "Schema" for a book which he was preparing on the Immaculate Conception:

> *Among the innumerable possible beings that could express his different perfections, God from all eternity saw one endowed with perfect form, immaculate, with no slightest taint of sin, a creature that would reflect his own divine qualities in the most perfect degree possible for a created nature. He rejoiced in this vision, and from all eternity decided that in time he would call such a creature into existence.*
>
> *When he had created the angels, God willed that they should spontaneously give him a proof that they would always and everywhere accomplish his will. He revealed to them the mystery of the Incarnation and announced that some day he would call into existence a human creature made of body and soul, a creature that he would raise to the dignity of Mother of God....*[5]

Before moving into a deeper consideration of characteristic features in saint Maximilian's mariology, two other very significant influences on Kolbe's Marian Christocentrism should be noted - the national cult of the Virgin, particularly the Czestochowa madonna, so ingrained in Kolbe's Polish background; and the spirituality of the "French School," particularly the dynamics of "Total Consecration to Mary" seen in St. Louis de Montfort.

---

5 Ibid., Manteau-Bonamy, p. 78. The phrase "e annuncio," which Manteau-Bonamy omitted, has been restored.

The Polish Marian cult taught Kolbe to recognize the presence of Mary the Queen in practical human affairs (political, social, cultural, and so forth) as an active dynamic force while the influence of de Montfort refined Kolbe's understanding of the spiritual nature of a person's self-surrender to Jesus through Mary.

Three salient features characterize Kolbean mariology:

1) the Immaculate Conception in its relationship to the Mission of the Spirit.
2) the Immaculate Conception in its relationship to the Mission of the Son.
3) the Immaculate Conception in its relationship to the Trinity.

All three points share a common denominator: they focus on the mystery of the Immaculate Conception as the mystery of Mary's personhood or identity. Several of Kolbe's written meditations repeat the question: "Who are you, O Immaculate Conception?". Mary's disclosure of her name to Bernadette at Lourdes was seen by St. Maximilian as a type of "identity statement," akin to Yahweh's self-disclosure on Mount Horeb:

> *At Lourdes the Immaculate Virgin replied to St. Bernadette who asked her who she was, by saying "I am the Immaculate Conception." By these luminous words she tells us not only that she was immaculate in her conception, but beyond this that she is the Immaculate Conception as such. Something white is one thing; the whiteness of a thing is something else. When God said to Moses "I am the One who is," God was telling him: "What is proper to my essence is that I should always be, by my very nature, of myself, with no other principle of being." The Immaculate Virgin of course, was created by God; she is a creature; she is a conception; still, she is the Immaculate Conception! What depths of mystery lie hidden in those words!*[6]

In our Saint's view, then, the mystery of the Immaculate Conception is the mystery of a person. All of his theological speculations derive from this insight and attempt to unravel the layers of personal relationships -- with God and with creatures - that the person of the Immaculate has. ❑

6 Ibid, p. 72.

In the Divine Economy the Mission of the Holy Spirit and the commission given by God to the Immaculate were inseparable. — *St. Maximilian Kolbe*

PART TWO

Mariology of St. Maximilian Kolbe

ON THE LEVEL of the Immaculate's personal relationship with the Holy Spirit, Kolbe's fertile mind was at work almost until the very hour of his final arrest by the Nazis on the 17th of February 1941. Early that morning he arose, summoned his secretary, and began dictating a new theological insight that appears only this once in all his writings: the identification of the Holy Spirit as "uncreated Immaculate Conception" uniquely bonded to Mary as "created Immaculate Conception." Saint Maximilian's insight here stakes out new territory in delineating the intimate nature of the union between Mary and the Holy Spirit. First note his description of the Holy Spirit:

> *And who is the Holy Spirit? The flowering of the love of the Father and The Son. If the fruit of created love is a created conception, then the fruit of divine Love, that prototype of all created love, is necessarily a divine "conception." The Holy Spirit is, therefore, the "uncreated, eternal conception," the prototype of all conceptions that multiply life throughout the whole universe.*[7]

Next note how his description of Mary Immaculate is totally bound up in this image of the Holy Spirit as "uncreated conception":

> *United to the Holy Spirit as his spouse, she - the Immaculate - is one with God in an incomparably more perfect way than can be predicated of any other creature.*
>
> *What sort of union is this? It is above all an interior union, a union of her essence with the "essence" of the Holy Spirit. The*

7 Ibid, p. 3.

Holy Spirit dwells in her, lives in her. This was true from the first instant of her existence. It was always true; it will always be true. In what does this life of the Spirit in Mary consist? He Himself is uncreated Love in her; the Love of the Father and of the Son, the Love by which God loves Himself, the very love of the Most Holy Trinity. He is a fruitful Love, a "Conception." Among creatures made in God's image the union brought about through married love is the most intimate of all (cf. Mt. 19,6) . In a much more precise, more interior, more essential manner, the Holy Spirit lives in the soul of the Immaculata, in the very depths of her being. He makes her fruitful, from the very first instant of her existence, all during her life, and for all eternity.

This eternal "Immaculate Conception"(which is the Holy Spirit) produces in an immaculate manner divine life itself in the womb (or depths) of Mary's soul, making her the Immaculate Conception, the human Immaculate Conception...

If among human beings the wife takes the name of her husband because she belongs to him, is one with him, becomes equal to him and is, with him, the source of new life, with how much greater reason should the name of the Holy Spirit, who is the Divine Immaculate Conception, be used as the name of her in whom He lives as uncreated Love, the principle of life in the whole supernatural order of grace?[8]

This passage indicates the careful, step-by-step reasoning of the Saint as he attempts to describe two realities in more "personal" language than ever before: A) the second procession within the Trinity (ad intra); B) the Mission of the Spirit outside the Trinity (ad extra). The Martyr of Charity attempts to recast the traditional terminology "conception," and by characterizing the first instance of the Holy Spirit's Mission ad extra as the intimate interpersonal union of the two "conceptions," one divine (the Holy Spirit), and one human (Mary) , both Immaculate.

In earlier conferences on the nature of the bond between Mary and the Holy Spirit, Kolbe lamented the fact that even the phrase "Spouse of the Holy Spirit" seemed inadequate to express the depth of their interpersonal bond:

---

8 Ibid, p. 3.

> *The Third Person of the Blessed Trinity never took flesh; still our human word "spouse" is far too weak to express the reality of the relationship between the Immaculata and the Holy Spirit. We can affirm that she is, in a certain sense, the "incarnation" of the Holy Spirit.*[9]

It is important to note that St. Maximilian qualifies his attribution of the word "incarnation" here by the phrase 'in a certain sense." Elsewhere he speaks of the Holy Spirit as "quasi-incarnatus" in the Immaculate, again using the all-essential qualifier "quasi" as he boldly stretches human language to its limits in attempting to describe an ineffable reality as "personally" as possible. Constantly maintaining that only the Son, not the Holy Spirit, was truly made man in Mary, Kolbe attempts nonetheless to specify the unique personal way in which the Holy Spirit indwells in Mary Immaculate as in a sanctuary or temple which becomes much more than an impersonal shell.

Lest anyone confuse or misinterpret his meaning, our Saint carefully asserts that Mary's intimate union with the Holy Spirit is a union of two persons with two natures, it is not of the same ilk as the Hypostatic Union in which the Second Person of the Trinity assumed a human nature. Kolbe clarifies the distinction:

> *The Holy Spirit is in the Immaculate as the Second Person of the Most Holy Trinity is in Jesus, but with this difference: There are in Jesus two natures, the divine and the human, and one sole person, the divine. The nature and person of the immaculate are distinct from the nature and person of the Holy Spirit.*[10]

Why would Kolbe get into such linguistic gymnastics? Not simply to accentuate the personal intimacy between Mary and the Spirit, though that is certainly part of the picture, as we have just seen. More significantly, Kolbe's overriding Franciscan objective - the divinization of the world in and through the Immaculate - would be illumined by these new insights. Saint Maximilian came to realize that in the Divine Economy the Mission of the Holy Spirit

9 Ibid, p. 50.

10 Massirniliano M. Kolbe, Gli Scritti Di Massimiliano Kolbe, Eroe Di Oswiecim E Beato Della Chiesa, 3 volumes (Firenze, Italy: Citta di Vita 1976-78), vol.1 p.189, translation by author.

and the commission given by God to the Immaculate were inseparable.

The Immaculate would be the tangible terminus which the Divine Person of the Holy Spirit would make his base of operations. As the immediate term of the Mission of the Spirit, Mary Immaculate would become the focus for the spirit's sanctifying/divinizing operation among creatures-- akin to the way in which Jesus' humanity had served as term of the Mission of the Son and consequently focus of the Son's saving work. It is in this light that Kolbe states: "The Holy Spirit acts solely through the Immaculate; consequently she is the Mediatrix of all the graces of the Holy Spirit."[11]

The second salient feature of Kolbean mariology to note is the relationship of the Immaculate Conception to the Mission of the Son. The Scotistic underpinnings of Kolbe's thought are evident in his perspective on her Divine Motherhood and on her Mediation. One of his many texts on the subject should suffice to illustrate this view:

> *Of herself, Mary is nothing, even as all other creatures are; but by God's gift she is the most perfect of creatures, the most perfect image of God's divine being in a purely human creature. She is God's instrument. With full consciousness and total willingness she allows God to govern her; she consents to his will, desires only what He desires, and acts according to his will in the most perfect manner, without failing, without ever turning aside from his will.*
>
> *She makes perfect use of the powers and privileges God has given her, so as to fulfill always and in everything whatever the Lord wants of her, purely for love of God, One and Three. This love of God reaches such a peak that it bears the divine fruits proper to God's own love. Her love for God brings her to such a union with him that she becomes the Mother of God. The Father confides to her his Son; the Son descends into her womb, and the Holy Spirit fashions out of her perfectly pure body the very Body of Jesus.*[12]

11 Ibid.,Scritti vol. 1 p.189.

12 Ibid., Manteau-Bonamy, pp. 133-134.

Mary's Immaculate Conception implies that she is the most perfect of all creatures in view of her future role as Mother of God and in advancing the Mission of the Son. Saint Maximilian wrote of the interconnection between Immaculate Conception and Divine Motherhood: "She was Immaculate because she was to become the Mother of God; she became the Mother of God because she was immaculate."[13] Mary's conception of Jesus Christ is seen by Kolbe in the light of the relationship which she already had with God by reason of her Immaculate Conception: "The Immaculata becomes the Mother of God. The fruit of the love of His trinitarian life and of Mary the Immaculata, is Christ the God-Man."[14]

Her role in the Mission of the Son advances, in Kolbe's view, from motherhood to mediation. Carefully he delineates her mediation (bound up with that of the Holy Spirit) in its relationship to the unique mediation of Christ:

> *Just as the Son from all eternity is like a Mediator between the Father and the Holy Spirit, so, too, Jesus, the Incarnate Son becomes the direct Mediator between the Father and the Holy Spirit, as He is in a sense incarnated in the Immaculata, the Representative and Spiritual Mother of the human race.*[15]

As is evident from these cursory glimpses into our Saint's thought, the relationship of Mary to Christ -- as mother and mediatrix — hinges on her relationship to the Holy Spirit qua Immaculata. From these considerations of the relationship of the Immaculate Conception to the Mission of the Second and Third Divine Persons, the third salient feature of Kolbe's mariology emerges: the relationship of the Immaculate Conception to the Holy Trinity. Kolbe's explicit trinitarian synthesis began taking place during the years of his life as a missionary in Japan, 1930-36, years noted by his biographers as ones of intense mystical experience.

Out of our Saint's mystical intuitions came the gradually refined understanding of Mary Immaculate as "complement" of the

---

13 Ibid., Manteau-Bonamy, p. 53.

14 Ibid., Manteau-Bonamy, p. 125.

15 Ernesto Piacentini, O.F.M. Conv., Panorama Of The Marian Doctrine Of Bl. Maximilian Kolbe, Franciscan Marytown Press, p.35.

Holy Trinity. He did not invent this phrase; it derives from writings of the Fathers of the Church (e.g., the Fifth Century Heysichius of Jerusalem), as Saint Maximilian himself explained in 1935: "The Immaculate is a person so sublime, so close to the Most Holy Trinity that one of the Fathers did not hesitate to call her "complementum Sanctissimae Trinitatis."[16]

The Saint sees the Immaculate as the fullest exemplification of the trinitarian life among creatures:

> *She is steeped in love of the Holy Trinity, becomes from the first moment of Her conception and forever the "fulfillment," the "completion" of the Holy Trinity. In the union of the Holy Spirit with Her, love unites not only two beings, but one that is the entire love of the Trinity, the other the entire love of a creature, and in this union heaven and earth are united -- the height of love is achieved.*[17]

The Immaculate's complementarity with the Trinity, in this Kolbean view, must be seen as referring to the "outer" Trinity, i.e., the Trinity in its operations ad extra, outside Itself. Just as there is a complementarity between the two "outer" Missions (those of the Son and the Spirit), so too, Kolbe points out, there is a complementarity between the created terms of both Missions: Mary Immaculate in her dual role as womb of the Son and spouse/temple of the Spirit. By reason of her engagement in both Missions, the Immaculate is complement to the operations of the Trinity ad extra. As such, she gives to the Father new meaning in his work as Sender ad extra. She gives to the Son ad extra his humanity. She gives to the Spirit ad extra his fecundity. As such a "complement," the Immaculate herself functions as God's instrument, or in the words of St. Francis 'hand maid of the Father," drawing all humanity back to the Father through Christ in intimate collaboration/union with the Holy Spirit. St. Maximilian thus summarizes the whole interpersonal dynamic that this role involves:

---

16 Ibid Scritti, vol.1 pp.188-9. In patristic times the title Complement of the Bl. Trinity was commonly given to the Holy Spirit, as the bond of unity of the Father and Son. After St. Francis and his sons had popularized the title, "Spouse of the Holy Spirit" for Our Lady qua Immaculata, theologians and spiritual writers began to commonly ascribe the title "Complement of the Bl. Trinity," to the Immaculate as well.

17 Ibid., Maria Was His Middle Name, p.44.

But if anyone does not wish to have Mary Immaculate for his Mother, he will not have Christ for his Brother; the Father will not send the Son to him; the Son will not come down into his soul; the Holy Spirit will not make him a member of the mystical body through the gift of His grace; because all God's marvels of grace take place in Mary Immaculate who is full of grace - and in her alone.[18]

Practically speaking, in the life, work and death of St. Maximilian the Immaculate is not only the Complement of the Blessed Trinity at her conception, as Spouse of the Holy Spirit, the eternal Immaculate Conception, she is that Complement at the birth of the Savior as His Mother. She is that Complement as well on Calvary as His Coredemptress, and she continues to be that Complement as the Mother of the Church and Mediatrix of All grace. To her Immaculate Heart as the exemplar of perfect love for Himself and his Father's Will, Jesus consecrated us on the Cross, as he continues to do at every Mass. To that Consecration we must say. "Amen" by consecrating ourselves to her as her possession and property - to share Her charity and compassion on Calvary, at the Mass, in our ministry which is to give our lives for the conversion and sanctification of our neighbor. This is the witness of the Martyrs of charity totally consecrated to the Queen of Martyrs and advocate of sinners.

Having examined the foregoing features of St. Maximilian's mariology, there remains one final practical question: What special significance is there in the Pope canonizing this Saint? The testimonies of survivors of Auschwitz who shared the barracks with him provide some startling clues toward the Church's motive in canonizing the Saint. To a man, these survivors recall less frequently the image of St. Maximilian's final gesture of volunteering to die for another than to recall the frequent scenes of Kolbe giving conferences to his fellow inmates on the mystery of the Immaculate Conception — and the Trinity, the Incarnation, the Mission of the Spirit. Amazingly, the testimonies concur, Kolbe held his audiences spellbound. Kolbe the theologian, Kolbe the evangelist, and Kolbe the martyr were one and the same person — an "integral

18 Ibid., Manteau-Bonamy, p. 126.

theologian." His canonization reflects the Church's recognition that dogma and life can and should be integrated.

On his first Christmas as a priest, in 1918, Kolbe offered his Mass for the intention: "Pro Amore Usque Ad Victimam." His final realization of this victimhood at Auschwitz, however, was grounded in an "Amore" which Kolbe came to understand only through intense and consistent theological reflection on the primacy of Christ and the mystery of she who identified herself simply as the Immaculate Conception. ❑

In the summer of 1927 Father Maximilian found a piece of land for sale near Warsaw that would be ideal for the site of his "City of the Immaculata." He began negotiations, and on August 6th he set up a statue of the Blessed Virgin, blessed it and prayed: "Immaculata, deign to take into your possession this field and this land for it is exactly what we want." She did just that even prompting the owner, Prince Drucki-Lubecki, to donate the land to Fr. Kolbe for the erection of "Niepokalanow."

Key to Eternal Life

Fr. Peter D. Fehlner, F.I.

"Everyone who acknowledges me before men, I also will acknowledge him before my Father in heaven" (Mt 10:32).

ABOVE ALL IT IS the martyr who acknowledges Christ before men. The martyr sets his seal on this that God is true (cf. Jn 3:33). St. Maximilian in acknowledging Jesus before the masters and inmates of Auschwitz set his seal on this that the goodness and love of God revealed in the priestly sacrifice of Jesus on the cross is indeed a dependable guarantee of our hope of life everlasting, even in the worst of circumstances. The saint's death thus saved not only temporal life for one man, but eternal life for innumerable souls by rescuing them from despair.

In acknowledging the martyr before his Father in heaven, Christ sets his seal of approval on the holiness of the martyr. In the case of St. Maximilian that seal of approval, which validates the cause for which he gave up his life, is the *Militia Immaculatae*. This movement he founded, is the secret of his inner life, the source of his courage to confess Christ, to be conformed perfectly to the crucified Savior, to bless and to teach others to bless and not curse God in that place of horror, to die for love of his love who deigned to die for love of our love.

The heart of the MI is total consecration to the Immaculata, that is to incorporate that mystery into one's mind, heart, soul and body, in all one's activities to such an extent as to be solely her possession, her docile instrument for the conversion and sanctification of all for whom the Son of God gave up his life on the cross. St. Maximilian's total consecration to the Immaculata is the key to his life as a Franciscan: perfect conformity to the Crucified, living in obedience, without property and in chastity; perfect identification with Christ the priest as victim for the sins of the world.

To live in this way is to share the love for Jesus of the Immaculata. She is the perfect fruit of a perfect redemption by a perfect Redeemer. We are to magnify the Lord with her and to rejoice in God our Savior. To live in this way is to give one's spirit to the Father like Jesus and through Jesus for the life of one's brethren, for their eternal life. Is it any wonder that the martyrdom of St. Maximilian was consummated on the vigil of the Assumption of the Immaculate Virgin into heaven? The message is clear: to glorify the Immaculate Heart of Mary on earth is the surest and quickest way to follow the straight and narrow path which leads to the gates of heaven.

It is not a new way, for it lies at the heart of salvation the Son of Mary brings us. The MI is but the form reserved for this love of God's Mother and ours in a time of battle when the very goodness of divine love-from womb to tomb-is being violently profaned and denied. In the martyr, Maximilian, the Woman and her Child are once again victorious, and the love of the two hearts, of the King and of his Mother, is vindicated in all who by faith and hope keep his commandments and hold fast to the testimony of Jesus, so forming the rest of her offspring, the brothers and sisters of Jesus (cf. Rv 12:17).

It is Jesus Himself, who from the cross, consecrates, entrusts us to Mary Immaculate: "Son, behold your Mother," that is, to the Woman (foretold in Genesis 3:15 as victorious over her enemies) whom he had just commanded to be our Mother (cf. Jn 19:25-27), and the disciple "took her into his own." Should we not do as our Lord tells us, and after the example of St. Maximilian consecrate ourselves to the Immaculata to be part of her Militia? So to serve is to begin to reign in the kingdom of the Sacred Heart of Jesus. ❑

Fr. Maximilian upon his return to Poland from Japan.

PART III: HE TOUCHED THEIR LIVES

Above: Francis Gajowniczek (left), along with John Dagis, carry in procession the portrait of St. Maximilian. Gajownieczek commissioned Bro. Felix of Niepokalanow to do the painting. Left: The statue of our Lady in front of the Nagasaki Cathedral.

Above: Left to right: Brothers Severyn and Zeno, with Fr. Maximilian, just before they left for Japan. Right: Bro. Severin, the first European to master the extremely difficult typesetting in Japanese.

John Dagis: Marian Apostle and Missionary

He Went to Japan with St. Maximilian

SINCE SAINT Maximilian was canonized so soon after his death, many of his close collaborators, fellow religious, and intimate friends were still alive at the end of the 20th century. One of these, John Dagis, was among the four brothers who accompanied the saint to the orient. While in Nagasaki, he was for a time Fr. Kolbe's personal secretary, and looked upon his former superior as a personal friend and saint. John is an example of how St. Maximilian's holiness and apostolic zeal for the cause of Mary Immaculate rubbed off on others.

He was born at the turn of the century in what was then the Russian-occupied part of Poland. His Lithuanian father and Polish mother died at the time of the Russian revolution when he was but a small boy. He and his brother spent their early childhood, up to their teens, in an orphanage run by sisters, whom he always remembered with great fondness. In the chaotic period of the collapse of the monarchy in Russia and the Bolshevik revolution, John attempted fleeing Russia several times. He eventually succeeded in crossing the boarder into free Poland.

There he attended a Salesian trade school learning the rudiments of printing. He was seriously considering joining them, but in 1926 he changed his mind and decided to join Fr. Kolbe in Grodno. Fr. Maximilian had previously visited the Salesian school, and we don't know if John had made a personal contact with him at that time or had read about the newly established Franciscan community, founded by Fr. Kolbe, in his Knight on the Immaculate magazine. Coming from an unstable childhood, he was greatly attracted to the close and happy Franciscan community and the total dedication of St. Kolbe and his followers. When Kolbe decided to establish another "City of the Immaculate" in the Far East in 1930, he selected four brothers for the mission. John Dagis, who was then known as Brother Severin in the Conventual Franciscan Order, was one of those who accompanied him to Japan.

On their way to Japan Fr. Kolbe stopped in Shanghai, China, leaving John and another brother there, intending to eventually established in that vast country another "City of the Immaculate." Fr. Maximilian had already made a contact with a wealthy Chinese businessman who was willing to help set up the Franciscans in their printing apostolate. But as was common in those days another religious order had been established in that area and looked upon the Franciscans as intruders in "their territory."

Dagis then joined Fr. Kolbe and the other brothers in Japan, experiencing all the hardships (as described in chapter 7of Part I) of those early days as a missionary. When Fr. Kolbe was able to get movable Japanese characters for setting up type in that language, Bro. Severin was probably the first westerner to master the hundreds of characters in the Japanese language for setting articles in the Japanese version of the Knight.

With the approaching involvement of Japan in the Second World War, John almost ended up in prison as a spy, due to his taking pictures that had the Nagasaki harbor in the background. However, by that time in the late thirties, Fr. Kolbe and his brothers were becoming better known and trusted. Nonetheless when war struck, the community did not escape house arrest. By then, however, Bro. Severin had already left Japan for Rome.

When Poland was invaded in 1939, in a moment of patriotic fervor he had decided to leave the Franciscan Order in Japan for a time in order to do his part in contributing to the liberation of Poland. Arriving in Rome, he was granted a dispensation from the three vows as a religious and was free to join the Polish army in exile in England. He served in the army of liberation for over four years, through the bloody engagements in Italy, to the final battles in France, up to the end of the war.

John went through a spiritual crisis at that time due to the betrayal of his country by the three major powers conference in Yalta, in which England and the United States sold off Poland, giving in to Stalin's demand that it be a satellite under Communist

Russia. All he had sacrificed and fought for seemed to be in vain. He was in a state of despair when another soldier contemplating committing suicide, approached him. He talked his friend out of suicide and in the process realized all was not lost, that Our Lady had not deserted her Poland. He regained hope. However, for one reason or another, he never returned to the vowed life as a religious.

He eventually came to the United States where he managed an office cleaning crew. It was in this capacity that he was able to help other Polish displaced persons get a start in their newly adopted land. In 1971 he joined the friars of the Marytown in the United States on their St. Maximilian beatification pilgrimage and ever after was a strong supporter of Marytown and its efforts of promoting the ideals of St. Maximilian Kolbe. He purchased literally thousands of the short biography of St. Maximilian published by Marytown and gave them away - at times on the front steps of the Franciscan church of St. Peter's in the center of the business district in Chicago's loop.

He returned to Japan in 1973 to help further the cause of Bl. Maximilian and, as he put it, to "make propaganda." With this purpose in mind he received permission from the Reader's Digest to have reprints made of the story on St. Maximilian in Japanese from their June 1973 issue. His zeal knew no bounds in furthering the cause of the Immaculata and his former superior.

On occasion John would recall how as a member of Fr. Kolbe's community in Japan, he and the other brothers were invited by the saintly superior to take a fourth vow - to always spread devotion to our Lady. As he pointed out, he had been duly dispensed of his religious vows of poverty, obedience and chastity, but smilingly he added, he had never been dispensed from keeping the vow of furthering at every opportunity devotion to Mary Immaculate. When Patricia Treece was preparing her book on St. Maximilian, *A Man for Others* which had many quotations from people who personally knew the saint, John Dagis was a fertile source (see the accompanying testimonies of John Dagis taken from her book). He died a layman in 1992, yet he lived a poor, simple life, ever exemplifying Franciscan joy.

The little man with the big heart had many charities. Like his mentor, St. Maximilian, he was indeed a "man for others." At his own expense, he sent large quantities of leaflets and Miraculous Medals to Australia, Africa and India. He played the lottery in hopes of winning so that he could further expand his charities.

After he retired, he helped his friend Marie Sochacz. She in turn watched after him, visiting him daily in his last days. It was she, his faithful friend, who informed the friars of his holy death on May 24, 1992. Although he had been urged on many occasions to let the Franciscan Brothers know when he was sick so they could visit him, he declined to inform them, knowing how occupied they were with their duties. He would not think of imposing in any way on anyone. They did, however, attend the wake and funeral of their faithful friend and fellow Knight. Marie had an image of St. Maximilian engraved on his tombstone with a mention of his relationship with a saint. John would have been very pleased with that. ❑

"For years I suffered great doubts over the part I played in contributing to Fr. Kolbe's death. This great day has put an end to my doubts forever."— *Francis Gajowniczek*

Above: Gajowniczek presenting the offertory gifts to Pope Paul VI at the beatification Mass of Bl. Maximilian Kolbe. Right: His wife and two sons, before WW II. Both sons were killed shortly before the war ended.

Francis Gajowniczek — the Grateful Benefactor

THE SPEAKER WAS at ease, with military bearing and steady voice, without the least tremor belying the fact that he was just months away from his ninetieth birthday. It was hard to believe that this elderly, modest man whose life spanned two world wars in which he was personally involved, was a survivor of five years and five months of Hitler's death camps. His story, which he has related hundreds of times, is actually more about a Franciscan priest who offered his life in a sublime act of love to die in his place than it is about him. How Francis Gajowniczek's life was spared from a cruel death by starvation and dehydration in an underground starvation bunker in the concentration camp of Auschwitz is told in another chapter of this book (see page 7).

At first Gajowniczek was bewildered by Father Kolbe's offer to die in place of him. It finally dawned on him that he was not dreaming when Kommandant Fritsch ordered him to return to the ranks of those not chosen to die. Fritsch then sent the frail little prisoner, who identified himself simply as a priest, along with the nine other victims to die in a starvation bunker. Feelings of remorse and despair swept over Gajowniczek when he realized that it was his agonizing cry of despair that he would never see his family again that initiated the drama and dialogue between the priest and the Nazi that would culminate in the heroic death of Fr. Kolbe, the founder of the "City of the Immaculate" and famous throughout Poland. He was thinking: "Why do I deserve to live instead of the priest? Am I not the cause of the death of this priest?" He wept and wouldn't eat until a fellow prisoner scolded him: "Take hold of yourself! Is that priest to die for nothing?"

The former career soldier who served in two World Wars, finally realized that he did have reason to survive the horror and inhumanity of Auschwitz. The fact that he miraculously was able, through divine intervention, to avoid the grim reaper at least a half a dozen times in the death camp took on a special meaning and mission for Francs Gajowniczek.

When the invading Germans overran Poland in 1939, Sergeant Francis Gajowniczek was captured and made a prisoner of war. He escaped and was recaptured but this time he was sent on September 8, 1940 to the concentration camp of Auschwitz. He was the only recorded survivor of the 700 deportees on one of the first transports of Polish prisoners to Auschwitz.* While in the death camp, he narrowly escaped executions at least three times. Several times he had to hide out overnight in the lavatory to escape the Gestapo who were looking for him. Once he contracted typhus, a sure death warrant at Auschwitz, but friends substituted a corpse for him and he once again escaped liquidation. Everyone was anxious to see him survive, as he was a symbol of hope over despair, of human dignity and love as opposed to the Nazi culture of hatred and racism. Fellow prisoners reasoned that Fr. Maximilian's heroic death should never be forgotten, and he would be a concrete reminder for decades to come of Fr. Maximilian's heroic sacrifice.

After surviving four years in Auschwitz, Francis was transferred to a camp in Sachsenhausen, Germany, where he remained till October of 1944. Again he faced death in a death march to Berlin. He was finally liberated on May 3, 1945 in a forest near Berlin by the U.S. Army.

When he returned home he found that his two teenage sons had been killed during the Warsaw uprising. His wife was so distraught by their death so near the end of the war that she never fully recovered, and died of heart failure in 1982.

It wasn't long after the war that Gajowniczek visited Fr. Kolbe's Franciscan confreres in Niepokalanow and told them the story of how their founder and former superior gave up his life for

---

*Most people hearing for the first time the story of how his life was spared when Fr. Kolbe offered to die in his place, have the erroneous belief that Gajowniczek was a Jew. Not so. He and the first prisoners at Auschwitz were all Polish Catholics. It was soon after that the Jews were rounded up and sent to the extermination camp.

him. It was the beginning of his fulfilling a promise he had made to God to make St. Maximilian's heroic sacrifice known whenever possible. In his own words Gajowniczek said, "After Fr. Maximlian's sacrifice for me, it strengthened my spirit. What I do now is my mission for him and his message. And I will do so as long as I live! I was raised a Catholic and I kept my faith in the darkest moments.... religion was my only hope. The sacrifice of Fr. Maximilian strengthened my faith and bound me more closely to the Catholic Church, which had given rise to such heroes." He readily admitted that it never entered his mind that Father Maximilian wouldn't be canonized some day.

St. Maximilian's giving up his life for Gajowniczek was the immediate cause for his being canonized a "Martyr of Charity." This finally dawned on Gajowniczek, and ended once and for all his mental suffering on his role in the death of St. Maximilian. After the canonization ceremony, he summed up his feelings in this way: "For years I suffered great doubts over the part I played in contributing to Fr. Kolbe's death. This great day has put an end to my doubts forever. Today is the happiest day of my life." The trip to Rome and all the excitement was too much for the elderly Francis. While in Rome he developed bronchial pneumonia and again almost died.

It wasn't quite three weeks after his return to Poland that his wife, Helen, died in his arms. Without the care of his devoted, loving wife his health gradually deteriorated. From a healthy, 165 lb. husky man he went down to 100 lbs. At this point the women in his parish arranged for a widow Janina Gajowniczek to take care of him. Her arrival on the scene saved Francis's life, as she took excellent care of him and met every one of his needs with a motherly care. They were eventually happily married. Janina accompanied him the last five years of his life and watched over him.

It seemed as if the devil couldn't wait to see him exit this life for all the good he was doing. He was attacked by a dog, and was poisoned by the medication they gave him. He related that during this time he had an out-of-body experience in which he felt a great peace when he saw Father Kolbe at the end of a bright path. The priest told him he would survive.

In the 50 years after the war, from the time of his first visit to the "City of the Immaculate" to the day of his death, March 13, 1995 he spent himself in never turning down an opportunity of singing the praises of his benefactor, St. Maximilian. He visited almost every country in western Europe speaking on the evils of war and exhorting audiences to avoid falling into the clutches of inhuman totalitarianism.

The first time he came to the United States was in 1976. He returned at least four times on speaking tours. The highlight of Gajowniczek's 1989 visit was a fifteen minute visit with the President of the United States, President George Bush, in the Oval Office of the White House, arranged by Fr. James McCurry, O.F.M. Conv. The President was visibly touched as Mr. Gajowniczek retold for the umpteenth time of how his life was spared by the little Franciscan priest whom the Catholic Church now venerates as St. Maximilian Mary Kolbe.

In the community cemetery of the friary founded by St. Maximilian, there are only two graves of laymen, — one for Prince Drucki-Lubecki, who gave Fr. Maximilian the property upon which his "City of the Immaculate" was built. The other grave is that of Francis Gajowniczek, for whom Fr. Maximilian gave up his life. In the center of the cemetery, among the many crosses over the graves of the friars, is a large crucifix of Him who gave His life for their salvation and who will unite them all, on the last day. ❑

The Boxer's Encounter with a Saint

By Joseph Czarnecki

One of the most visited cells in the concentration camp of Auschwitz is the one in which St. Maximilian met his end just over fifty years ago. Millions of Catholics have visited this cell, including Pope John Paul. The walls are darkened from candles burnt in this cell, but not so completely blackened that a drawing of a boxer is barely visible.

Recently we became aware of the story behind this unusual drawing. The following is excerpted from the chapter "Heroes" from the book, "Lost Traces: The Lost Art of Auschwitz," by Joseph Czarnecki. The paragraphs in italics are the editor's.

I SIMPLY could not imagine what a boxer might have to do with Auschwitz. Then one day I picked up a copy of a recently published autobiography by an Auschwitz prisoner named Tadeusz Sobolewicz, in which the author describes a boxing match that took place in the camp.

Looking into the matter further, I discovered that this boxer's name was Tadeusz Pietrzykowski, and that he now lived in Bielsko-Biala, less than an hour's drive from Auschwitz. I decided to go see him. The boxer in the drawing had a head of clearly drawn curly hair, and I knew that I was on the right track when Pietrzykowski, a short but well built man with close-cropped curly hair, opened the door. . . . "Teddy," as he was known in the boxing world, had begun making a career for himself in the ring and was already the bantamweight champion of Warsaw and Eastern Poland [when the war broke out]. He was a student of the legendary Polish trainer Felix Stamm, whom Pietrzykowski credits with having made a "gentleman" out of him, by teaching him the meaning of Poland's national motto: "God, Honor, Country."

The author then describes how Teddy was able to survive the horrible ordeal of the concentration camp through his boxing skill.

Boxer Tadeusz Sobolewicz (Teddy) as he looked in his prime. Right: Teddy (left) with two other survivors of Auzchwitz. The man on the right, Ted Wojkowski, was in the fatal line up when Kolbe gave up his life for Gajowniieczek.

He goes on to describe how he dealt with the capos who were common criminals put in charge of other prisoners.

"Sometimes there were these capos who used to beat the prisoners in order to impress the SS men. My friends would go up to them and goad them into fighting me, saying, 'Teddy is out of shape.' When I got hold of a guy like that, I would play with him, not knock him out and end the fight. This would give my friends some entertainment, and teach the capo a lesson. Once, I fought with this guy who was a real murderer, I went five rounds with him, and they had to carry him out of the ring. .. . That was a German capo from Mauthausen, and he just couldn't hit me. Interestingly, the Germans didn't take his side; they took mine. They used to call me the White Fog, because nobody could hit me."

Teddy had thirty-seven fights at Auschwitz and won all of them except two matches with a Jewish boxer, Lew Sanders, the Dutch light-middleweight champion. "His wife and children were gassed in Birkenau," Teddy told me. "He was a very good boxer, and in the fight with him I had to make the greatest effort of my life. The fight ended in a draw...." Not all of Teddy's fights were inside the ring. Once, while working on a farming kommando, he saw one of the capos beating a prisoner who was down on all fours. Teddy went up to the head of his kommando and told him that he was a boxer and would like to "train" with the capo who was beating the prisoner. The SS men of both details agreed to Teddy's proposition, thinking to have a bit of fun.

Teddy went up to the capo and asked him why he was beating the prisoner. "Shut your mouth, you dumb Polack. Do you want to get it, too?" he said, coming at Teddy. Teddy dropped him with two punches and answered: "How'd you like to go to the crematorium?"

"I don't know how that fight would have ended," Teddy says. "I was just getting ready to give him a really good beating when the prisoner who was being beaten, a man with wire-rimmed glasses held together with string, stood up and said to me, 'Don't beat your brother, my son!'"

'"Bug off,' I said, thinking to myself. Whose son do you think I am, anyway? And I hit the capo on the jaw a third time." The man with the glasses continued begging him to stop fighting and fell to his knees, grasping his hands, imploring, "Do not fight, my son."

"His face was almost strangely calm," Teddy recalls. "I just didn't know what to say, as if I had no tongue in my mouth. So I just waved my hand, because the break was over and it was time to go back to work."

The man whom Teddy tried to defend was none other than Father Maximilian Kolbe. The two met again, and Kolbe told Teddy to leave to God the job of meting out justice, and also told him about his missionary work in Japan. Teddy gave the priest a piece of bread, and was ready to fight again when he heard that another prisoner had stolen it from him; but again Kolbe would not allow it. When Teddy gave him another piece of bread, Kolbe broke the bread in two, gave half of it to the thief, and said, "He must be hungry, too."

Teddy saw Father Kolbe for the last time in the summer of 1941, when a selection was being made for death by starvation as punishment for the escape of a prisoner. He saw Father Kolbe push his way to the front of the kommando and ask to die in place of another prisoner; and Teddy saw him taken away to Block 11. As fate would have it, it was in Father Kolbe's cell in Block 11 that I found the drawing of Teddy the boxer.

The drawing on the cell in which St. Maximilian died was done by an artist-prisoner who drew it in gratitude to Teddy for favors he had received from the boxer. ❑

Bro. Zeno in Rome for the Beatification of his superior in Japan. He was known throughout Japan for his charitable works and was honored by a shrine and a high government award.

Above: Bishop Januarius Hayasaka, Fr. Maximilian and other Franciscans before the incomplete building of the "City" in Japan.

Bro. Zeno occupied in the many jobs he was involved in at the Japanese Marytown.

Brother Zeno,

Father of the Poor

Bro. Zeno Zebrowski, one of the four missionaries who went with Fr. Kolbe to Japan in 1930, is little known outside of Japan, but in Japan he is a living legend - though he died in 1982. The little Franciscan Brother who is still remembered as a national hero and the "Father of the Poor," received the prestigious "Third Order of the Rising Sun" by the Japanese government for his vast charitable activities. He was lauded at that time, "No foreigner, more than Brother Zeno, has contributed to the welfare of the Japanese people during a period of 40 years."

The Japanese government also conferred on him the Yoshikawa Aliji award, which is normally given to writers, although he never wrote anything remotely resembling a literary work. As one writer put it, "There was perfect poetic justice in it, for it appropriately crowned all the improbable incongruities he accomplished in persuading people to help his hundreds of orphans and thousands of destitute rag-pickers. Zeno's simple beautiful life was his literary work."

In the early 1920's, as a young man in his thirties he lost his mother, whom he loved dearly. Upon returning from one of his adventuresome trips he learned of her sudden death, which caused him much pain and resulted in his examining his heretofore irresponsible lifestyle. He went through a change of heart and joined the Conventual Franciscans in 1925. At that time Father Maximilian was just beginning his press apostolate in Grodno, Poland and was short-handed. The Father Provincial of the Conventual Franciscans sent Bro. Zeno to Fr. Kolbe, hoping that he might be of help in settling down the undisciplined Zeno.

Used to the freedom to do as he pleased, to the restrictive life of a religious in community was almost too much for him. One night Fr. Maximilian noticed a light on in his room well past the hour of retirement. He asked the Brother if there was anything wrong.

"Father, I am going home," he said. "I am neither a housekeeper nor an errand boy."

Kolbe invited him to his room to speak with him. We don't know exactly what transpired in that long conversation but it did change the entire direction of Zeno's life. Three years later he was one of the four Brothers chosen by Fr. Kolbe to accompany him on his first missionary endeavor to Japan. The primitive conditions that he and the other three Brothers experienced there demanded great sacrifice, and endurance. All was made possible through the love of Mary Immaculate and the never failing dedication and example of their leader, Fr. Maximilian. Besides the generosity of Bro. Zeno, there was the added attraction of adventure, but that soon wore off.

Some of his companions became discouraged and returned to Poland. Of the original group which set foot on Japanese soil, Brother Zeno was the only Brother who persevered for fifty-two years. The Italian missionary magazine Mondo e Missione dubbed him "the greatest apostle of Japan in our times" for his apostolic zeal and his many charitable works - a true Franciscan, he preached almost exclusively by example rather than words.

Brother was very close to Fr. Maximilian, who thoroughly understood him. He could be considered Kolbe's right-hand man, as he was ever ready to fulfill any and every obedience his beloved superior asked of him. Sometimes he did so in a very imaginative way, as when they first started printing the Japanese magazine and had no way to trim the large number of copies. No problem for Zeno. He used a saw!!!

He filled a multitude of jobs in the missions, from laundry man to salesman for the Japanese version of the Knight of the Immaculate ("Seibo no Kishi"). Dedicated as he was to the ideals of his superior and friend he was intent in getting the Japanese Knight magazine in as many hands as possible. In order to get names for the first mailing, as was the custom in Japan he would approach total strangers in the streets, in restaurants, on buses and on streetcars and ask them for their calling cards in the few words of Japanese which he was able to master. By the time the first issue was ready for mailing he gave Fr. Maximilian a nice pile of "meishi" (calling cards). The first printing of the magazine was 10,000. By the time of the fifth issue 25,000 copies were printed. Just prior to World War II the circulation climbed to 65,000 - the largest Catholic publication in Japan. By then the versatile Zeno was gaining a reputation for helping the poor and orphans.

The Japanese loved and respected him, so much so that during the Second World War he was the only friar who was permitted to go and come as he pleased. When some questioned the police why this foreign friar was permitted to walk the streets of Nagasaki at will, they answered that "He is more reliable than the Japanese themselves." He would visit war casualties in the hospitals, bringing them milk and spiritual comfort. He even repaired the shoes of returning soldiers.

When August 9, 1945 came with the explosion of the second atomic bomb over the Urakami district of Nagasaki (heavily populated by Catholics) his great love of all men regardless of race or religion and his never faltering initiative combined to meet the tragedy. After the smoke had cleared over the bombed Nagasaki, just over the hill from where the friary of the "Garden of the Immaculate" was located, there was human suffering and misery beyond description. Nagasaki and the whole of Japan became a vast field calling for immense aid. Bro. Zeno began in the center of desolation, the Urakami district, which had been hardest hit in the atomic blast. He brought home to the Friary two small boys, without names, without a past, and without a future. This was the beginning of a large orphanage he had built in Nagasaki. Nor did he confine his charity to just the local children. He sought out the abandoned and homeless living in bombed-out ruins and housed them at first in the Friars' former seminary. His outstanding charity was acknowledged when the Emperor himself visited the orphanage. With tears in his eyes the Emperor praised the Brother and the Catholic Church which had done so much good in alleviating the suffering of the smallest and most helpless of his people.

But this charity could not be done alone. Zeno, true to his calling as a Franciscan, did not hesitate to go on begging tours from one end of Japan to the other. He saw the need and as an instrument in the hands of a compassionate heavenly Mother nothing could stop him, and no one could refuse him. He visited government offices and industrial plants, and stopped American servicemen on the street. He not only received financial help but also got their extra clothing "right off their backs." He had the greatest admiration for the United States servicemen. "Their generosity seemed to be limitless," Bro. Zeno points out, "and we were able thus to extend our aid to many thousands of distressed people."

When his confreres opened new missions in Tokyo and Osaka, Bro. Zeno went with them to see what could be done to help the many poor who were living in shacks of cardboard, crating boards, or in tents in the public parks and under bridges in the most miserable circumstances. In his own words: "When I came to Tokyo I could not stand idle looking at the starving, naked and homeless." With great trust, but with little ability in expressing himself in the difficult Japanese language, his friendly smiling face and gestures expressed well enough what was on his mind. In fact the very fact that he butchered the oriental language worked to his advantage. People smiled as they remembered some of his more obvious errors. Generous offerings began to come in from every side and he learned to say 'Thank you' to the Americans, 'Danke shoen' to the Germans, 'Merci beaucoup' to the French, 'Tante grazie' to Italians, 'Bog zaplac' to Poles and even 'Spasiba' to the Russians -- and, of course, 'Arigato Gozaimasu' to the Japanese. Tokyo, as the capital of Japan, had visitors from all over the world. He concludes, "I channeled many things from the 'haves' to the 'have nots.'"

Thus, Bro. Zeno spent himself gathering the badly needed necessities of life for the poor from all over Japan, and merited the title, "Father of the poor." Later, as Japan began to recover, he gave talks and made appeals to school children as well as university students and large civic groups. More than once he was invited to appear on television to talk about his charitable works. Sometimes he required a Japanese interpreter, because his Japanese was kodomarashi,* but his eyes, shining with tears which ran down his cheeks, spoke most eloquently as he described the needs of the poor.

That he was successful in touching the hearts and opening the pocketbooks of the 'haves' is well attested to in the many charitable institutions established by him. Perhaps the most famous was "Ants Town" in Tokyo, where he inaugurated a self-help program for the many poor beggars of the city of Tokyo. So successful was it that the program was spread to other large cities by Brother. When he first became aware of the Village of the Ants he asked, "Do you want money, food, clothing? What do you need most?" The Japanese replied "We want to be treated like human beings, for our work is not dirty." With the war destroying 99% of Japan's industrial power and 50% of the housing, hundreds of thousands were left homeless and without jobs. Thus it is understandable why, out of sheer necessity, the bataya (rag-pickers) were many. It was Bro. Zeno who introduced the public to the plight of the rag-pickers through the mass media, thus bringing badly needed support.

Near Hiroshima university students helped Zeno during their vacations to construct a home for handicapped children which was called "Zeno Boys' Ranch" in his honor. Subsequently others were built either by him or inspired by his example. Natural disasters frequently hit the various islands that make up Japan, but right on the heels of these disasters was the little black robed Franciscan, with his battered hat, worn shoes and little satchel, bringing help, hope, joy and consolation to the suffering. He rode all the public conveyances of Japan free of charge as he traveled throughout Japan going about his works of Charity.

Books, plays and movies about him and his most famous collaborator, Reiko Kitahara, the madonna of Ants Town, brought them to the attention of millions. She died a holy death praying the "beads" which Bro. Zeno taught her to use, when he first met the twenty-year-old Catholic college student outside of her home in 1950. At that time she was a recent convert to the Faith, and was intrigued at the habited Franciscan. Upon visiting Ants Town with him, her heart was touched in seeing the squalor and poverty in

* "Like a child's babble."

which the children were forced to live. Upon meeting their chief, Mr. Motomu Osawa, she said, "From now on, I will live here among your people. I will take care of the children." Nor did the frail, aristocratic young lady, used to a comfortable life, find it beneath her dignity to pull a cart, picking up cans, dirty bottles, and scrap paper. Mr. Osawa, deeply impressed with Kitahara, eventually entered the Church, followed by the Buddhist writer, Mr. Toru Matsui, who wrote a popular life of Bro. Zeno entitled No Time to Die.

Exhausted but happy, Kitahara identified with the Little Poor Man, St. Francis of Assisi, living in poverty as did Christ and His Holy Mother. But due to the many privations, poor diet, and cold and damp weather, she contracted tuberculosis and died in 1958, before her 30th birthday. Tokyo had never seen a funeral quite like hers. There was the Archbishop of Tokyo, dozens of University instructors, journalists, writers, photographers, politicians etc., but above all the weeping rag-pickers - thousands of them who knew her and loved her deeply. And so the indirect influence of St. Maximilian through his close follower, Bro. Zeno, had its impact on the heroic life of Kitahara, who some day may be raised to the altars.

With all the worldly acclaim and notoriety given to Bro. Zeno, he ever remained the simple, unaffected follower of St. Francis of Assisi and faithful knight of the Immaculate, following in the footsteps of the "Martyr of Charity," St. Maximilian Kolbe. ❑

***Mugenzai no Sono*, The Garden of the Immaculate in Nagasaki, Japan at the time when Father Maximilian left it for the last time.**

PART IV: ST. MAXIMILIAN A 20th CENTURY ST. FRANCIS

Paul VI asks: "Which virtue should chiefly distinguish your [Franciscan] religious life? Whoever knows the Franciscans answers: poverty, a poverty that changes into love, which wants to imitate and love the poor Christ."

Kolbe's "Lady Poverty"

THE TWO OUTSTANDING characteristics of the Poverello (little poor man) of Assisi are found in a preeminent degree in St. Maximilian Kolbe. They are his love of "Lady Poverty," and Our Lady Immaculate - Queen of the Franciscan Order. Throughout the book we touch upon the Marian dimension in the Franciscan charism of St. Maximilian. In this chapter we will see how Kolbe's love of "Lady Poverty" was lived and practiced in the context of the life and rule of St. Francis, which he professed.

When St. Francis first went through a radical conversion, his friends thought he was enamored over a new lady friend. He left them wondering who it was. He simply replied that he had fallen in love, alright. But the Lady he loved to whom he was espoused, was none other than "Lady Poverty." Some perceptive Franciscans believe that Francis had in mind not only the virtue of spiritual poverty, but the Woman, Our Lady, who perfectly exemplified this characteristic mark of the Franciscan Order. St. Francis explained why poverty was so important to him and those who would follow him. It was to imitate "the life of poverty of our most high Lord Jesus Christ and His Most Holy Mother."

In Chapter VI of his Rule of Life, Francis wrote that his brothers should "not appropriate anything to themselves, neither house, nor place, nor anything," but rather they should be "as pilgrims in this world, serving the Lord in poverty and humility, confidently begging alms." To St. Francis the ideal of poverty was nothing less than complete dispossession of everything, as a community and individually, in imitation of the poor Christ and His Holy Mother.

Up to the thirteenth century, no one had made so much of evangelical poverty as had Francis and his early followers. Even to this day Franciscans are associated and identified with the poor. St.

Francis ardently wished to imitate the poor Christ and His Immaculate Mother Mary. He wrote:

"Jesus could have come as the son of a powerful emperor, born in a royal palace, but He did not. He came into the world in an oppressed nation of a poor, though royal artisan's family. . .

"Without poverty and dependence upon the Providence of God one cannot talk of progress, of mounting an offensive." St. Maximilian Kolbe

---

"Throughout His life He possessed nothing. He once said 'The foxes have their holes, the sparrows their nests, but the Son of Man has nowhere to lay His head'. . . .He did not even have His own tomb to be buried in."

Yet, the vow of poverty and its interpretation throughout the over seven-hundred year history of the Franciscan Order has been the cause of countless reforms, divisions, and misunderstandings. What should be a virtue that would unite the followers of St. Francis, sad to say, in fact often divides them. This points up the fact that poverty is a key virtue in the identity of Franciscans, whether it be: First Order (priests and Brothers), Second (Poor Clare Nuns), or Third Order (seculars living in the world according to the Franciscan ideals).

One seldom finds heat generated among Franciscans over the "spirit of poverty," which like the "spirit" of Vatican Council II, has a vast spectrum of interpretations. But when expressed in the concrete observance of a poor life style it is another matter. Out of necessity, Father Kolbe started out dirt poor in his apostolic work, living in a country, Poland, rich in faith but economically depressed, at a time when inflation in Germany and Poland was out of control and followed by the great depression affecting the whole world.

Yet, Saint Maximilian made it clear how much he valued the voluntary Franciscan poverty: "I could have been involved in other religious communities, such as the Jesuits or Dominicans, but the Franciscan concept of poverty was more attractive to me. I am most happy to be a Franciscan and work on the foundation of Franciscan poverty."

The Salute of St. Francis to the Virgin

The *Salute to the Virgin* and his *Salute to the Virtues* are interchangeable. To salute the Virgin is to salute the virtues; and to salute the virtues of wisdom, poverty and charity is to salute the Virgin Mother of Incarnate Wisdom in the poor stable of Bethlehem willing to offer her Child for the sake of sinners.

In the sixth chapter of the Rule of St. Francis, the chapter which constitutes a hymn to poverty, there is a clear allusion to the link between poverty and charity of the Cross in terms of Our Lady, "If a mother cherishes and loves the son that is born to her, how much more deeply one should love and cherish his spiritual brother!" What mother St. Francis had in mind is made explicit for us by St. Clare when she quotes St. Francis in the parallel sixth chapter of her final rule: "I, little Brother Francis wish to follow the life and poverty of our Most High Lord Jesus Christ and of His Most Holy Mother. . ." It is by sharing this poor life of Jesus and Mary that we come to know the love of the Mother, as at the Porticuncula, as at the "City of the Immaculate."

—Fr. Peter Fehlner, F.I.

In the very beginnings of his printing apostolate he faced financial disaster (page 43) but was rescued by our Lady in what seemed a miracle. Continual "impossible" financial crises would arise but His absolute trust in Mary's all powerful intervention never wavered or failed. He worked long and hard hours. He did all that was humanly possible, but his dreams of world conquests for his Lady Immaculate were realized only through her. What was impossible by ordinary human effort was consistently achieved in his short twenty years of active apostolic labors. The one requirement, besides his rich endowment of natural talents, was his total trust in God and Our Lady - a trust which prompted him to say, "Poverty is our capital."

Even when financial help was rolling into the "City of the Immaculate" in the late thirties there was absolutely no difference in the communities' simple, modest life-style. He made one distinction, "For us, poor clothing, simple food, but for the Immaculata, the best and most advanced machinery."

An example of how Father Kolbe was able to update and reconcile the Franciscan poverty of the 13th Century in a modern setting is shown in the following example: A certain Polish Canon, visiting the City of the Immaculate, stopped before the very latest type of rotary presses available in Europe at that time, and looking at the expensive piece of equipment ironically remarked: "What would Saint Francis, if he were living today, say of these expensive machines?" St. Maximilian responded, "He would roll up his sleeves and turn up the press to its greatest output, and work as these good Brothers are doing in diffusing the glory of God and the Immaculata with these modern means of spreading the Gospel."

"I want to follow the life of poverty of our most high Lord Jesus Christ and of his holy Mother."

St. Francis of Assisi

When he opened his mission in Japan, he and the Brothers at first slept on straw and ate on the floor as they had no tables or chairs. The building was so dilapidated that the ceiling fell in upon the sleeping Brothers. The native Japanese were inspired by Fr. Maximilian and the friars heroic life- style. The Brothers thought little of eating the fare of the poorest in Japan so they could invest more funds into paper and printing equipment. While in Japan his brother, Father Alphonsus, who was guardian of the Polish City, died. His concern for a new superior whom he could trust was centered on two things: "Above all he must have a great love for the Immaculate Virgin . . . and a passion for Franciscan poverty."

In a letter from Japan to his Father Provincial he outlined what he felt were absolutes in any friary that would be a "City of the Immaculate": The aim would be, of course, the same as that of the M.I.; their means would be publications like the Polish Knight; their distinguishing feature, a strict poverty, a reliance on Divine providence through the Immaculata and the greatest possible limitation of creature comforts and personal needs. He would exhort his Brothers, "May our houses be so poor that, if Saint Francis were to come back, he would choose to live in them." Nor was Father Maximilian ashamed of his poverty in the presence of high dignitaries. One of the friars attested to this,

---

> ***"Poverty is a royal virtue: for in the King and Queen it has shone more brilliantly than any other."*** St. Francis of Assisi

---

"If it was meal time, Father Maximilian would always invite any guests to join us at the table. I recall the Cardinal from Krakow, deeply impressed, eating at the same poor table without a tablecloth and drinking milk from a tin cup."

Father Maximilian did not look upon the practice of the vow of poverty as a penance; he loved poverty and was faithful to it to the end. One of the Brothers mentioned that, "I used to come to his room with various business matters and never noticed anything superfluous. Once, when I mentioned that such poverty might generate pride in thinking himself better than others, he just answered me with a brotherly smile." Poverty was a means but never an end in itself.

Of St. Maximilian it can be said that Franciscan poverty and joy were synonymous. Fr. Anselm Kubit, St. Maximilian's one time Father Provincial, said of Kolbe:

> ***"Above all we must have a great love for the Immaculate Virgin... and a passion for Franciscan Poverty."*** St. Maximilian Kolbe

---

"He was actually happiest when the greatest poverty reigned. He said a religious Order must be a school for saints, so the monastery must radiate simplicity, penance and poverty." His dedication and detachment was "catching." Although the Brothers lacked at times the very necessities of life, they worked wholeheartedly in perfect joy.

When Father Maximilian would return from a business trip to Warsaw he would bring back "gifts" for the Brothers. The "gifts" were tools and supplies for the work. They who loved much and worked for a cause far greater than their own comfort and ease found joy in not having. What a contrast to the consumerist society in which we live in today!

In conclusion, Father Maximilian would give us a key to understanding the tremendous accomplishments he achieved in such a short time, and his own progress in personal holiness: "The Immaculate is our goal, and poverty is our capital: these are the two things which the City of the Immaculate may not desert under any circumstances. Without this goal it would cease to be a City of the Immaculate; it would become unfaithful to its task. Without poverty and dependence upon the Providence of God one could not talk of progress, of mounting an offensive." ❑

Many of the witnesses testify that St. Maximilian would hold clandestine spiritual conferences in the concentration camp for his fellow prisoners. These spiritual conferences would plumb the depths of various theological issues: the Catholic doctrines on the Immaculate Conception, the Incarnation and Redemption, the Holy Trinity, and the doctrine of grace. Everyone of the eyewitnesses whom I have interviewed testified that Father Kolbe held the undivided attention of these poor, hopeless, starving, cold prisoners on these deep theological issues. Integral theologian that he was, his exposition of these Catholic doctrines was forceful, understandable, and applicable to their lives.

— Fr. James McCurry, OFM Conv.

Blind Obedience— A Radical Difference

TWO MEN, ONE a Pole, the other a German, grew up in loving Catholic homes; as young boys both devoutly served Mass in their parish church. One was of average intelligence; the other was considered a genius. They were highly motivated, thorough, and conscientious in fulfilling their duties. Both were executed at the fairly early age of 47, when they were at the height of their respective vocations; one a priest, the other a soldier. They both had a high regard for the virtue of obedience, yet that is where a monumental difference arose between the two. To whom and for what reason was each motivated to obedience; an obedience which was unquestioning and total. For St. Maximilian Kolbe, obedience led to the highest tribute accorded to any human, recognition as a saint to be imitated and prayed to. For Rudoph Hoess it led to the gallows and the infamy of a name that will ever be associated with genocide and inhumanity of such magnitude as never before seen in human history.

Kommandant Rudolph Hoess was the head of the infamous death camp of Auschwitz where millions were murdered in the most impersonal and degrading way. He died on the gallows outside the camp, for his execution was not to be construed as an act of vengeance but of justice. Moreover, it was not fitting that he die where so many innocent people were unjustly put to death.

One of the greatest criminals of all time, he was not a psychopath, as Dr. S. Batavia pointed out in his psychological analysis of Kommandant Hoess. He was "a person who didn't show an inclination to crime or sadistic tendencies." He had one fatal flaw, an uncompromising loyalty and commitment to the diabolical ideology of Nazism, which was expressed by and executed through blind obedience. He wasn't born subnormal or morally depraved. According to the doctor, "Hoess was inclined from childhood, thanks to the influence of home environment, to hardly any criticism of events and to easy conformity to all authority. We meet this type of person quite frequently. . . From an early age, he was a man who treated all his duties seriously, performing them conscientiously and fervently. These were usually considered virtues. He was an individual also described as a very strong person with a powerful will."

Unlike the humble Franciscan, who used his superior intelligence for the glory of God, "Hoess reflected little on himself: his mind was set on activity rather than thinking. . .Thus the possibility of critically evaluating of one's goals and one's reactions was eliminated." Unfortunately, Hoess, who at first was a harmless person, through a gradual metamorphosis was changed into the ideal SS man who perfectly performed all of Hitler's orders. He subscribed to the nefarious evil of racial superiority and the goals of the Third Reich - the conquest of the world for Hitler and National Socialism.

This "blind" obedience which makes men tools of Satan is the diametric opposite of St. Maximilian's authentic obedience, and is a danger not only in Auschwitz or the Gulag but everywhere that the modern secularized State claims civil authority over its people independent of the authority of God. Obedience separated from divine authority, even though legitimately exercised, is diabolical and contributes to the culture of death. This is as true of democracies vaunting separation of church and state (consider the abortion holocaust and divorce plague in the USA) who ignore the natural law and the Vicar of Christ as it is of totalitarian dictatorships. In such states, it is ironic that abortion, homosexuality and other evils are not only to be protected by the law, but encouraged - whereas the driver must "buckle up!" It's the law!

It was the law and the racist philosophy of the Nazies that Hoess was obedient to - that, and every command and whim of his superiors, no matter how his conscience reproached him at times. Much too late he recognized the fatal deceit of the devil and the mistaken direction of his life. The following is taken from his last letter to his wife:

"During my long isolated sojourn in prison, I have had ample time and peace to reflect thoroughly on my whole life. . . . I see today very clearly what for me is very hard and bitter, that the whole ideology, and the whole world in which I believed so firmly, was resting upon completely false foundations and certainly had to fall into ruins some day. . . . Likewise, did not my fall from faith in God depend wholly on my false foundations? This was very difficult to overcome. Nevertheless, I have recovered my faith in God."

The inhumanity and total lack of mercy that Hoess as Kommandant of the death camp showed to all who unfortunately fell into his hands, and to whom he caused so much pain and suffering, was after the war absent from the treatment of the imprisoned Hoess by the Polish officers and common guards, some of whom had been inmates in the concentration camps. The contrast was overwhelming, as Hoess pointed out: "They have shown me humane forbearance which deeply abashed me. . . .In spite of everything that happened, yet, they always see in me a human being."

He wrote a very tender and touching letter to his children shortly before he was to die, counseling them and encouraging them to be good to their mother. He also confesses: "The greatest mistake in my life was that whatever came from 'higher authority' I trusted blindly! I did not dare have the least doubts as to the validity of a given order. . .Go through life with an open mind. Don't be one-sided; reflect on the pros and cons of all matters. In all that you undertake, direct yourself not only with your understanding, but particularly pay attention to the voice of your heart."

In reading and contrasting the lives of Hoess and of St. Maximilian, we find both men obedient in a heroic degree. In the case of St. Maximilian, from his writings, which are filled with exhortation to obedience we read: "Dear Brothers, be blindly obedient in every instance, if you wish that God's plans for you are to be fulfilled." And again: "Whatever we perform through obedience is a great thing."

The obedience of one brought Hoess to the ignominious death of a common criminal. The obedience of the other brought

St. Maximilian to the altars as "The Saint for our difficult century."- Pope John Paul II.

The difference of course was in the person whom each one obediently served. That Kolbe's obedience was a rational obedience, Hoess eventually came to understood. The Kommandant had buried his intellect and imagination so he would not have to think of the filthy work in which he was involved.

Kolbe's obedience was ever rational. He saw in legitimate authority God's representative. In obedience he served no mere human being but God Himself. This is clear from just a few quotes from the multitude of his admonitions to the Brothers on obedience: "Not in mortification, not in prayer, not in labor, nor in rest, but in obedience is the essence and merit of holiness," and again, "Obedience and only obedience reveals the will of God to us." It is not an easy task at all times to see God speaking through lawful authority, for as he points out, "We do not obey superiors because they are learned, experienced, prudent, pleasant, amiable, etc." For St. Maximilian we obey, blindly indeed as far as the exercise of obedience does not rest on human calculation. But we obey only if those commanding lawfully represent God because God has chosen them and they exercise God's authority legitimately according to God's standards. Hence, if it happened that the person in authority orders something contrary to the moral law, as was the case with Hoess, the subject must not obey, even at the cost of one's life.

Rudolph Hoess through pride, ambition or fear obeyed the satanic demigod; Adolph Hitler, over God. With the proper subject for his obedience Hoess might have been a saint. He, like all of us, had that potential. Although he will ever go down in history as one of the greatest mass murderers of all times, he is above all an outstanding example of the infinite mercy of God. No matter how hardhearted a person might be, no matter how heinous his crimes, God offers reconciliation to all. And who knows if it wasn't St. Maximilian who tipped the scales of God's justice in favor of Hoess to win his last minute conversion? - *the Editor*

This chapter is based on material (especially the direct quotations) from the book, Kolbe and the Kommandant, Two Worlds in Collision *by Fr. Ladislaus Kluz, O.C.D. The English translation from the Polish is by Sr. M. Angela Santor, SSJ. TOSF., M.A.*

St. Maximilian, Priest and Victim

Friar M. M. De Cruce, F.I.

WHEN ONE SPEAKS of St. Maximilian one spontaneously thinks of his martyrdom in Auschwitz and his unlimited love for the Immaculate. However, it must be underscored that his martyrdom and Marian devotion were lived out in the context of a priestly vocation. "Saint Maximilian, Priest"-this is the official title given him by Holy Mother Church. Popes Paul VI and John Paul II proclaimed Fr. Kolbe to be a luminous "example" and "glory" to the priesthood, a ministerial priest to be numbered among the great priest-saints such as Saints Ignatius of Loyola, Alphonsus M. de Liguori, Louis M. Grignon de Montfort, Vincent de Paul, John M. Vianney, and John Bosco.

St. Maximilian reflected a great deal on the revelatory statement of God to Moses on Mt. Horeb: "I am who am," and that of the Blessed Virgin Mary to St. Bernadette at Lourdes: "I am the Immaculate Conception". It is deeply significant, then, that the last words recorded from Maximilian's lips were those pronounced to the question posed by the Nazi Commandant Fritsch: "Who are you?" His answer too was a self-revelation: "I am a Catholic priest." He identified himself as a priest of Jesus Christ and offered himself as a victim of love.

Priest and victim in the shadow of the tabernacle

St. Maximilian knew well that to be a Catholic priest is to be alter Christus - another Christ. In fact, the week before his ordination he wrote: "The concerns of the Sacred Heart of Jesus are your concerns." Thus he lived out his priesthood ablaze with the very flames of love burning in the divine and priestly Heart of Jesus. He knew no limit and never counted the cost. Bad health, inclement weather, fraternal misunderstandings, foreign cultures and languages, unspeakable dangers, violence, hatred and maltreatment - all these served only to conform him all the more to Jesus, Priest and Victim. "There is no love without sacrifice," he would often say. And so he tirelessly spent himself for "the maximum glory of God" and "the salvation and sanctification of souls".

What sustained his supernatural zeal in his twenty-three years as a priest? It was the Sacred Hearts of Jesus and Mary. As Fr. Jerzy Domanski, O.F.M. Conv. points out, "throughout his life, the priestly spirit, nurtured over the years in the shadow of the tabernacle and kept warm by the Immaculate Heart of Mary, shone brightly" (For the Life of the World, p.32). His incessant union with the eucharistic Heart of Jesus and the Immaculate Heart of Mary enabled him to radiate the Gospel in his life and ministry.

The Holy Mass was the center of the Saint's spirituality. This was evident from his preparation for Mass, his reverence and recollection in celebrating the Sacred Mysteries, and his thanksgiving after Mass (in his retreat before being ordained a deacon he resolved to spend half his day in preparation for Holy Mass and the other half in thanksgiving!). Moreover, he made many spiritual communions throughout the day (every 15 minutes) and was frequently found on his knees in the Chapel making a short or prolonged visit to the Blessed Sacrament.

As a priest he was a man of prayer and sacrifice, that is to say he lived the Sacred Mysteries he celebrated. In all his many activities he never ceased to place prayer in the primary place. "The fruitfulness of work," he once wrote, "solely and exclusively depends on the degree of one's union with God." Furthermore, he made of his life a continual union of sacrificial love with Jesus the Divine Victim. As a result, the end of his life in the concentration camp was but the flowering of a life lived in perennial sacrifice. He became, as it were, an extension of Jesus the great high Priest and royal Paschal Victim; he became an extension of the Holy Sacrifice of the Mass in this world. It was to this end that the Saint offered a Mass during his first year as a priest with the intention pro amore usque ad victimam ("for love unto victimhood") and that he would ask his mother to pray that he might die a martyr.

Kept warm by the Immaculate Heart of Mary

As Jesus was anointed Priest by the Holy Spirit at the very moment of His virginal conception in the womb of Mary, so too, by way of analogy, every priest is anointed such by the Holy Spirit through the maternal mediation of the Immaculate at the moment the Bishop imposes hands on the ordinandi. St. Maximilian actually states this explicitly about his own priesthood in the opening words of his Mass register: "By the mercy of God through the Immaculate... I was ordained a priest of our Lord Jesus Christ."

The Saint had a special love for and understanding of the Immaculate as the Mediatrix of all graces. In the act of consecration he composed for the M.I. as a seminarian he concludes, "... because every grace flows through your hands, from the most sweet Heart of Jesus, to us." Certainly his priesthood was a supreme grace that he received through her maternal mediation.

It is no wonder, then, that as a priest he turned to her Immaculate Heart in everything with an unlimited trust. In a world grown cold, he was able to sustain his priesthood with the warmth of divine charity that dwells in her tender Heart. He did not hesitate to attribute every good that he accomplished to her omnipotent intercession. Among his written resolutions he wrote, "all the fruits of your activities depend on union with Her..." His was a priesthood entirely united and consecrated to the Immaculate. For her he would "live, work, suffer, be consumed and die" as a priest of Jesus Christ.

Zeal for souls

From the Most Sacred Hearts of Jesus and Mary flowed his apostolic zeal. This fervor was fruitful in his many works, whether one considers the two cities of the Immaculate themselves or the many publications they produced. He was an "itinerant" preacher in sermons and conferences, though due to the use of less than one good lung, he preached more through the printed word (the press, and his letters). Of course, his most eloquent sermon was his holy, heroic life. He was also a confessor and effective spiritual director who knew how to encourage souls to Jesus through the Immaculate. And finally he was a leader who guarded and guided his subjects with prudence and order - "Preserve order and order will preserve you," he would say.

St. Maximilian Mary Kolbe was a priest par excellence - a humble and obedient son of the Church who sought to live in union with his Eucharistic Lord in the deep recesses of the Immaculate Heart of Mary. As a priest on earth he said he could only work with "one hand" because he had to clasp his Immaculate Mother with the other; however, as an eternal priest he now labors with "both hands" in Heaven because he is forever secure and abandoned in her heavenly embrace.

Let us conclude with a quote from Pope Paul VI's beatification discourse: "Is not a priest 'another Christ'? And was not Christ the Priest redemptive Victim of the human race? What a glory, what an example for us priests to behold in this new Blessed [Saint Maximilian] a spokesman for our consecration and for our mission!" (Oct. 17, 1971).

Total consecration to the Immaculate Coredemptrix: this is the key to that stupendous conformity to Christ crucified in Francis the deacon, in Maximilian the priest, who sought not to be served, but to serve and give their lives as a ransom for the many (cf. Mk. 10, 45).

On our own we are not only too weak to conquer evil, we are not sure as to how it is to be done. St. Maximilian clarifies: "The conflict with Hell cannot be engaged by men, even the most clever. The Immaculata alone has from God the promise of victory over Satan."

The Suffering Servant

Madeline Pecora Nugent, SFO

"Though he was harshly treated, he submitted and opened not his mouth;

Like a lamb led to the slaughter or a sheep before the shearers, he was silent and opened not his mouth. Oppressed and condemned, he was taken away, and who would have thought any more of his destiny? When he was cut off from the land of the living, and smitten for the sin of his people, a grave was assigned him among the wicked a burial place with evildoers, . . .

Though he had done no wrong nor spoken any falsehood.

But the Lord was pleased to crush him in infirmity.

Because of his affliction he shall see the light in fullness of days; Through, his suffering, my servant shall justify many, and their guilt he shall bear.

Therefore I will give him his portion among the great, and he shall divide the spoils with the mighty, Because he surrendered himself to death and was counted among the wicked;

And he shall take away the sins of many, and win pardon for their offenses." - Isaiah 53: 9, 7-12

The above passage (New American Bible translation) has traditionally been applied to Christ. St. Maximilian would be embarrassed to have it applied to himself and, yet, do we not see him in it? Maximilian:

- Was ridiculed and harshly treated by his own friars as he worked ceaselessly to found his Knights of the Immaculata movement and establish his Cities of the Immaculate.
- Was much more viciously treated by the Nazis who eventually killed him.
- Bore innumerable sufferings without complaint while praising God through them.

- Was taken away to a death camp, forever forgotten (so his captors surmised), cut off from the land of the living because of the sins of the power-hungry. Those suffering with him had done no wrong except in the eyes of their persecutors who deemed certain nationalities and religions to be inferior, unfit to live, an evil idea if ever there was one.
- Was crushed with infirmity from his youth, often so ill that others wondered how he could go on.
- In his patient suffering, he bore witness to God, bringing countless souls to Christ and others into consecrated religious life.
- Surrendered himself to death, to take the place of another.
- Was assigned a crematorium as a grave.
- Because of his life and his surrender to death, he was granted a portion among the saints.
- By his intercessory prayers, wins pardon for the many.

Saint Maximilian Kolbe understood the spiritual dimension of suffering. His understanding began, perhaps, with his boyhood vision in which Our Lady offered him two, one white for purity, the other red for martyrdom. He chose both. From that moment, he may have sensed that both choices would bring suffering.

Maximilian's life is a litany of suffering borne with great joy because he had given his suffering to his Beloved, the Immaculata to save, not just some souls, but ALL souls. From the earliest years when he thought his vocation would not be realized as his parents had no money to send him to the seminary until his death in a starvation bunker, Maximilian did not cease to suffer. He expressed the value of this suffering as early as 1919 when in a conference addressed to clerics, he declared, "All these trials are very useful, necessary, and even indispensable, like the crucible where gold is purified."

Knowing this did not keep him from worry when his plans seemed impossible to realize, his dreams mocked, his hopes shattered. But he immediately laid his anxiety at the feet of the Virgin. "When at times I am tempted to worry, I immediately say to myself: 'Silly one, why do you worry? Is this your work? If all belongs to the Immaculata, will she not attend to it? Then let her lead you!'"

"The Suffering Servant" *Isaiah 53:9*

He spoke little about his physical sufferings which included fevers, headaches, and tuberculosis that left him with a quarter of a good lung. His greatest suffering involved the Virgin. "Nothing causes me more suffering than the mediocrity of souls vowed to the Blessed Virgin. I would give my life a thousand times over to sanctify them." How he mourned for those, especially religious, who had compromised their vow of poverty, who had relinquished their total trust in Our Lord and His Mother! "The supreme abandonment of the agony was the crowning work of Jesus." The suffering of the abandoned Christ was not lost on Maximilian.

His was the high road of self-sacrifice. "We must sacrifice our life to our ideal, not subordinate our ideal to our life. . ." Maximilian knew that sanctity happens only with deep, internal suffering as the human will is conformed to God's. "The real Niepokalanow is our souls. All the rest - even skill - is secondary. Progress is spiritual, or it is not progress at all! Therefore, even though it were necessary to suspend our work, even though all members of the Militia abandoned us, even though we had to be dispersed as leaves swept by the autumn wind, we would say, my Brothers, that we are truly progressing if the ideal of Niepokalanow continues to shine in our souls."

"Here is my formula: v=V. . . . The small v is my will; the capital V is the will of God. When opposed, they cross like this: +, then there is the cross. If you want to cancel out that cross, unite your will with the will of God, who wants you to become saints. It is so simple; the one requisite is to obey!" By following this formula, Maximilian received the graces of the internal peace and fortitude to survive even the pervasive evil of a Nazi death camp.

The end began in September, 1939, when Maximilian and his friars were herded to a prison camp at Amtitz. There on October

---

"When suffering is far away, we feel that we are ready for everything. Now that we have occasion to suffer, let us take advantage of it to gain souls."

St. Maximilian Kolbe

12, his feast day, Maximilian addressed his brothers, "This morning I asked myself what I should give you for my feast. Well, here it is. I want you to belong even more to the Blessed Virgin, each day more profoundly. When suffering is far away, we feel that we are ready for everything. Now that we have occasion to suffer, let us take advantage of it to gain souls. Let us try. Let us try to win as many souls as possible for the cause of the Immaculata."

"Let us make a bargain with the Blessed Virgin. Let us say to her: 'Sweetest Mother, through love I resign myself to remain in this revolting camp, provided the others are permitted to go home. I will remain here to suffer forgotten, despised, alone. I give myself to you to die on this filthy pallet, surrounded by completely insensible and cold hearts. . ." Maximilian could accept the suffering meted to him, could embrace all that Lord and the Immaculata would wish to give him, so that he would save the lives and souls of others. He knew well what to do, for later as the end drew near, he told his friars, "Courage, my children! Our mission is coming to an end. Let us learn how to profit from these last days."

When his friars were released from the camp but dispersed, Maximilian encouraged them by letters. "Let us make no truce in our missionary work. Let us spread its influence in every heart. For that purpose let us offer all our troubles and all our sufferings. Let us desire only that the Immaculata be pleased with us; let us try to make her happy at our expense, whatever the cost. . . How many souls will again find the light, thanks to our dispersion! Let us pray, accepting lovingly all crosses, and loving all our fellowmen with no exception, friends and enemies."

To Maximilian, suffering was not evil because it could be turned to a loving end. "God is love. And as the effect must resemble the cause, all creation lives for love. Not only for the last end, but also for intermediate ends, and in all sound and normal action, love is the principal energy and the principal motive force.

"If good consists in the love of God and in all that springs from love, evil in its substance is negation of love . . . "

Shortly before being sent to the death camp, having suffered beatings that nearly killed him, torturous overwork, starvation, mockery, and the seeming ruination of all his work and accomplishments, St. Maximilian wrote, "The Immaculata, our most loving Mother, has always surrounded us with tenderness and will watch over us always ." How could he say that? Because of what he knew, what he expressed in this, his last letter written to the friars before being sent to Oswiecim, dated May 12, 1941, "Why worry, my sons, since no evil can strike us unless God and the Immaculata know it and allow it?

"Nothing causes me more suffering than the mediocrity of souls vowed to the Blessed Virgin. I would give my life a thousand times over to sanctify them." St. Maximilian Kolbe

---

"Let us be led more and more completely by her, wherever and in whatever may be her good pleasure, so that fulfilling our duty to the utmost, we may through love save ALL souls. . ." Love of God, love of neighbor, borne through every suffering, made every suffering bearable. "Where a soul is perfectly consecrated to the Blessed Virgin, loving her with its whole heart, then it can only be that this perfect love will be reflected on its environment, saving many souls." Suffering to save souls. Was that not the mission of the Suffering Servant of Yahweh? And was it not Maximilian's mission as well? ❑

Above: Fr. Maximilian with three newly ordained priests, two native born Japanese, at the Garden of the Immaculate in Nagasaki.

Father Kolbe was ahead of his times in anticipating the ecumenical movement of Vatican Council II or the call of Pope John Paul II to make this new millenium an age of evangelism.

Missionary Spirit of Saint Maximilian

*Most Reverend Vitale M. Bommarco,**

DURING THE almost eight centuries since the death of St. Francis, many of the Poverello's followers have taken up the missionary paths which he opened. For this reason, the Franciscan Order in all its branches was and still remains the strongest missionary group in the history of the Church.

The fundamental motivation of the missionary action of St. Francis was based on his submergence in the highest degree in the most high God and in Christ incarnated and crucified for us. It was from this love that arose his desire to save all men. St. Maximilian also began from a mystical base, but he added a characteristic of his own: complete surrender to the Immaculata in order better to win souls for Christ the Lord.

To Conquer the World for Christ Through the Immaculata

Consecration to the Immaculata was carried out by Father Kolbe to the highest degree. As a result there arose necessarily the need to communicate this passion to all souls, to conquer the world for Christ through the Immaculata. The Franciscan missionary ideal which began and developed from the little church of St. Mary of the Angels in Assisi, and the constant devotion of the Franciscan Order to the Immaculata, found in this Knight that zeal, that courage, that boldness to dare everything. The genius of St. Francis was brought to life in him for our time.

---

* Archbishop Emeritus Of Gorizia, Italy, Former Minister General of The Friars Minor Conventual.

The Mariology of Father Kolbe is not something sentimental or added on to the work of creation, but it is based on the love which unites God with man and man with God. As St. Francis sang about the love of God in "The Praises of the Most High God," so "Father Kolbe accentuates that God is Love and in calling creatures into existence, He wants from them a response to His love with a love which will be as great as possible. Only one creature gave God an 'equal' (total) response which is the apex of love in all creation. This creature, the most perfect of existing beings, is Mary." (Swieciski 315)

Daring the Unthinkable

The Seraphic Father told his friars: "The Lord will fulfill his designs and will keep his promises." So too Saint Maximilian dared the unthinkable because he considered himself merely an instrument in the hands of the Immaculata, who would bring her plans to completion.

"The action of Mary is a most perfect action of the Holy Spirit," and He, "through the Immaculate Virgin, manifests outwardly his own participation in the work of redemption." Niepokalanow would never have been founded, and there would never have been a Kolbean missionary activity without this Marian theological base that we have scarcely touched upon and which deserves to be studied in depth and better understood.

The missionary action of St. Francis was the witness of his life - the development of fraternity and the spirit of evangelical poverty. We see with admiration and wonder, and with a certain nostalgia, that St. Maximilian had followed faithfully and firmly in the footsteps of St. Francis in the most absolute poverty and in the heroic witness of living the fullness of Franciscan fraternity in his country and in the missions.

Francis was in love with poverty in its highest ascetical and mystical sense. While Kolbe, son of the industrial age, gives to Most High Poverty a working sense: "O truly holy, very holy is our Franciscan poverty, the poverty of Niepokalanow. . . . The Immaculata is the end, and poverty is the capital: these are the two things which Niepokalanow cannot ever abandon under any pretext. . . . Only the limitless fund of Divine Providence can cover the colossal expenses of the battle for the conquest of the entire world for the Immaculata."

Evangelizing by Example of Personal Holiness

Francis went to the Orient with five companions, giving witness to fraternity "by their example of holiness and perfection of religious life." Father Kolbe founded his "City of the Immaculate" not as a great center of activity and industry, but as a fraternity united in unconditional self giving to the Immaculata, through a "total exclusion of any reservation in regard to food, dress, occupation, state (brother or cleric), place (in one's own country or among the enemies of the faith where perhaps certain death awaited them)."

"Our community has a style of life a bit heroic which it ought to be if it truly wishes to acquire its predetermined objective - not only to defend the faith, but to contribute to the salvation of souls, with a fearless attack, not paying any attention to themselves, to win over to the Immaculata one soul after another, one outpost after another."

Francis preached and communicated "the peace of the Lord" to the men of his time, and Father Kolbe always began from this fundamental Franciscan message, to bring peace by capturing the heart of man through love. St. Maximilian sums it up in these inspired words, "Hatred divides, separates, and destroys, while on the contrary love unites, brings peace, and builds. Is it not to be wondered at, then, that only love succeeds in making men perfect? Therefore, only that religion which teaches the love of God and neighbor can perfect men." Wishing to work actively to communicate the love of God to his brothers, Father Kolbe founded a great movement, "The Knights of the Immaculata" (Militia Imrnaculatae) which he describes in this way in one of his articles:

"It is called, of the Immaculata because its members are consecrated without reserve to the Most Holy Immaculate Virgin Mary so that she may work in them and by them and pour out through them on other persons the grace of supernatural light, strength, and happiness. Moreover, it is called Knights because it cannot permit itself to rest but rather intends to conquer, through love, all hearts for the Immaculata and, by means of her, for the divine heart of Jesus and, finally, for our heavenly Father."

Anticipating Modern Evangelizing Activity

The missionary spirit of St. Maximilian, based as it is on the ideals of St. Francis and reinforced by the chivalrous and apostolic attachment to the Immaculata, has produced marvelous results and has indicated some lines of action which anticipate modern evangelizing activity in the Church. In chapter twelve of his Second Rule, Francis indicated three norms for the friars who wished to follow him in his missionary action. Father Kolbe considered all his work missionary and so bound all the friars who consecrated themselves to the same chapter of the Rule:

"Our father, St. Francis, is the model for the missionary; his example, his Rule is highly missionary, and it allows the greatest thrust to be directed to the salvation and the sanctification of souls. The "City" with its vast program of winning the entire world for the Immaculata is subordinate to Chapter XII of the Rule, and, under the threat of losing its reason for existence and the betrayal of its ideal, it cannot change its own finality.

"I also imagine that those who have consecrated themselves without limits to the Immaculata, . . . will ask their Superiors to permit them to bind themselves absolutely with a vow to go, for the sake of the Immaculata, anywhere holy obedience will send them, be it to the most difficult mission and an encounter with certain death. In that way, they would join to the three religious vows this one also, even though the Rule does not expressly oblige them."

The saints can be judged to be dreamers, but it is encouraging to us to view what this man was able to accomplish in only twenty years of activity. But it was nothing compared to what he wanted to do,

"Concerning projects for the future, I have in mind the purpose of the Knights of the Immaculata - that is, the winning of the whole world for the Immaculata - of developing our outpost in the most vigorous possible way so that the Japanese Knight magazine can be delivered as soon as possible to every Japanese home. But at the same time, I am also thinking of beginning the Knight in the Chinese language. But I am also thinking of India, of Annam, of the Syrian 'basin' for the following languages: Arabic, Turkish, Hebrew.

"Nevertheless, I am not thinking of giving up publishing the Knight in English, etc., until the entire world belongs to the

Immaculata. At the same time, however, I hold it indispensable to multiply "Cities of the Immaculata" in Europe . . . in Germany, in France, in Spain, in England, and in the other countries in which our confreres are few or not found at all; and afterwards in other countries as well."

Understanding the Needs and Temper of the Times

Just as St. Francis understood the needs and the movements of his time and knew how to use them, sublimating them to the praise of the Most High God, in love for peace, so too Father Kolbe, living in an industrial age and basing himself on the same principles of St. Francis, knew how to transform work, machines, and men for the glory of God. Anticipating the Ideas of *Evangelii Nuntiandi* of the Second Vatican Council, Saint Maximilian made himself and his followers available to the local hierarchy and placed himself at the service of the local Church. He asked only for the liberty to witness to a heroic life of fraternity and to be able to spread the gospel through the written word.

In the postulatory letter for his beatification by the Bishop of Nagasaki, his Excellency Paul Yagamuchi, we read:

"On April 24, 1930, Father Kolbe arrived unexpectedly at Nagasaki with three friars. This was, without a doubt, an arrival in conformity with a poor missionary of Jesus. The most noteworthy characteristic of his activity certainly was the firmness of his faith, the foundation of his unshakeable confidence, thanks to which he was a man of sacrifice and a missionary filled with great zeal. The work of Father Kolbe was certainly and remains still a wonder in view of its rapid progress in the Japanese world."

His preoccupation with vocations and the formation of native religious is one of Fr. Kolbe's constant concerns and is expressed in various letters. He wrote from Japan to the Niepokalanow community: "Launch an attack of prayer for vocations for Japanese religious brothers because without them there can be no guarantee for the future. And also for vocations to the minor seminary and absolutely for the major seminary. You are numerous; therefore it will be easier for you to implore insistently, beseeching the Immaculata."

Kolbe knew how to find and to train his collaborators because he was not an individualist but worked well with others and was able to arouse their enthusiasm and involve them in his ideals. He never appeared to be a colonizer even if he ardently dreamed of conquering the world; he was a lover who desired to communicate the beauty and riches of his faith through the printed word and the media of social communication, which are free forms of dialogue. And he truly held a dialogue with everyone, especially with the pagans. The Japanese magazine, the Kishi, was addressed not only to Catholics but to pagans, to Protestants, and to other non-Catholics.

In the beginning the readers received it with curiosity, then with unusual appreciation to such an extent that a good number of them received the grace of holy baptism. Patiently ingrafting the Church of Christ among the pagans "without abusing the baptismal water" - this was the original method of Father Kolbe, who trusted in God totally through the Immaculata, but at the same time did not spare himself and did everything which was in his power.

Young Churches Not Only Object but Subject of Church's Mission

The Conciliar Decree Ad Gentes speaks extensively of the missionary activity of individual Churches and urges that the young Churches be not simply the object but also the subject of mission. Father Kolbe anticipated this decree in practice because the Polish Niepokalanow substantially helped with manpower and materials the birth of the Japanese "City" which, on the other hand, contributed to the enrichment of the missionary spirit in all of Poland. His Excellency John Wosinski, Auxiliary Bishop of Plotsk in Poland, in an article dedicated to the missionary contribution of Father Kolbe, writes:

". . .what is taken up in the Conciliar Decree, Ad Gentes, was verified, in as much as the young missionary Churches reanimate by their presence the older Churches from which they receive help. In fact, the Japanese Niepokalanow greatly enlivened and made the Polish "City of the Immaculate" more missionary, whether throughout Poland or beyond its borders through the ranks of the Knights of the Immaculata. . . . We see here Father Maximilian not only as a missionary but as one fully dedicated to organizing help for the missions and missionaries and as an apostle who wished to make all of us in Poland missionaries."

The same Bishop summarizes his analysis of the missionary characteristic of Father Kolbe in this way:

"He is for us a splendid example of the complete Christian according to our time - one who left nothing untried to exploit the 'signs of the times' and the possibility of the moment. For this reason, he is so rich in his personality and so difficult to fully understand. How much spiritual energy was contained in his frail body! How much spiritual good was accomplished in his short life!

"This total Franciscan, religious, priest, martyr, is a magnificent example whom the Immaculata raised up as the apostolic model, the ideal missionary of our times!" ❑

The Late Cardinal Wyszynski, Primate of Poland, confronted the Communists and was greatly revered by his fellow Poles.

"Father Maximilian is a kind of an individual that the world cannot easily dismiss. His life is one that cannot be filed away in archives. . . . Even in the framework of religious life he must have risen above the established order of things and maybe his religious contemporaries also wanted to place him in a line, but Father Maximilian said: 'I form a new line.' And he placed the Franciscan religious family in that line. And this was good because this was a particularly great grace in those times for the Franciscan religious family. And therefore this person, who towers above us all, will not permit himself, as they say, to be easily classified. He will always and for a long time tower above all of us by a head. . . ." — *Cardinal Wyszynski,*

The original chapel still stands, built by the Brothers when they first moved into the field donated by Prince John Drucki-Lubecki. The statue of the Immaculata - the first resident of the Niepokalanow - welcomes visitors.

Pope Paul VI is presented with a painting of St. Maximilian at his beatification by the Franciscans of Niepokalanow. Cardinals Krol (the American from Philadelphia), Wyszynski, and Wojtyla (the future John Paul II) were present.

PART V:
IMPACT ON SOCIETY

Renewal of Religious Life By Means of the Militia Immaculatae

Kolbe's Gift to the Jews

Religious Communities Inspired and Founded on His life and Ideals

Sisters Minor of Mary Immaculate (SMM)
The Franciscans of the Immaculate
The Father Kolbe Missionaries of the Immaculata
Marytown in the United States

Patron of the Pro-Life Movement

Fr. Kolbe, Mass Communications Expert

St. Maximilian's Vision of Catholic Drama Realized

"Who Would Dare Suppose?"

Fr. Maximilian and two other friars receive the vows of newly professed friars in the late 30's.

There was no shortage of vocations in Poland in 1939. The above is a community picture of the "City of the Immaculata" at the height of its development when Kolbe was alive. See him in the center of picture and to his right the General of the Conventual Franciscans, Fr. Bede Hess.

Renewal of Religious Life by Means of the Militia Immaculatae

Fr. George Domanski, O.F.M.Conv.

THE FIRST MEMBERS of the M.I. were Religious, confreres of St. Maximilian Kolbe, who by means of the M.I. wanted to bring about a new springtime to the Franciscan Order. However, Fr. Maximilian wrote a religious in 1936,

"It is necessary that the Immaculata become as soon as possible the Queen of all - of persons and of associations, and of each individual. Whoever obstinately does not wish to subject himself to her reign will perish. Whoever instead recognizes her as Queen and strives, as a Knight, to win the world for her will live, prosper and grow more and more spiritually. This will be true of every soul, every institution and every community."

St. Maximilian, a man with a great ideal and a talent for organization, did not found a new Order as some think. With anguish, he saw sluggishness and indifference in his own and in other Orders in a greater or lesser degree. He was aware of the excuse that every Order drifts away from its founder's ideals, and the older an Order grows, the weaker it becomes. Father Maximilian vigorously opposed this defeatist view since the spirit is not subject to the material laws of aging. "Only the drifting away from the ideal," he writes, "and the failure to keep pace with the changing conditions of the times causes a weakening of life and vigor, and the stunting of growth."

Father Kolbe intended implementing renewal of his Order through the Knights of the Immaculata movement. This took place first of all in the friaries that he founded - Niepokalanow in Poland and *Mugenzai no Sono* in Japan. His City of the Immaculate, founded in 1927, in a little more than a decade had 762 members, and was involved in many apostolates. *Mugenzai no Sono*, established in 1931, became a province of the Order in October, 1969 with the majority of its members native Japanese.

Fr. Anselm Kubit, the Superior of the Polish province in 1933, wrote that Father Kolbe "created such a great spirit of mortification, simplicity, Franciscan joy and zeal for his ideal, that life in Niepokalanow, with hundreds of Religious, was similar to that of Rivo Torto, and the Portiuncula in the time of St. Francis."

The essential element of Religious renewal which the founder of the M.I. gave his followers by word and example is the unlimited consecration of one's self and one's community to the Immaculata. For a renewal of the Order, Father Kolbe argued, it is not enough to have the wisest rules even if these are enforced by the most rigorous sanctions. To accomplish renewal - as in every instance of growth in holiness - supernatural grace is necessary, the grace of sanctification. And since the Mediatrix of every Grace, by the will of Jesus, is the Immaculata, it is therefore necessary that the renewal of an Order be accomplished through her intercession.

"The nearer a Religious comes to her," Father Kolbe wrote to his Minister Provincial, Father Kubit, "the more abundantly he will live according to the spirit. And the most perfect form of drawing near to her is the total consecration. Therefore, consecration to the Immaculata not only of the individual friars, friaries and provinces, but the whole Order as such, will regenerate the whole Order." One must not fear that such a consecration would be a kind of deviation, from the ideal of its Founder. On the contrary, such a consecration is the full acceptance of the Marian tradition that exists in greater or lesser degree in every Order in the Church. Moreover, it favors wonderfully the preservation and development of its original spirit.

When the objection was made that he had changed the character of the Franciscan Order by means of the M.I., he responded: "That this path is somewhat different from the early days of the Order is possible; but I deny that this is not what it should be." And he explained: "All things do not develop at once and arrive at perfection immediately, but with the passage of time. We cannot therefore expect that our predecessors in ages past would have had as well-developed an idea of the cause of the Immaculata as we have today, after the definition of the dogma of the Immaculate Conception.

"For us it is not legitimate to be content with the degree of development attained in ages past. Moreover, in the history of the Order we also find negligence. The Order has not responded to the graces the way it should have, hence has not achieved the acme of perfection. One can say the same of other Religious Congregations as well." It was written well of the Knights of the Immaculata in Switzerland around the year 1950:

"The M. I. is not a pious union, although juridically it is known as such, nor a Third Order, nor an organization. Whoever thinks of the M.I. in this fashion wounds it and kills it. The M.I., as Father Maximilian saw it, is a movement, a soul, a spirit. Its fundamental need and condition sine qua non, is the consecration to the Immaculata, total consecration without limits and without conditions; it is total dependence on the Immaculata. The soul of the M. I. can and must enter into every Catholic entity in order to give it more force and apostolic dynamism, and supernatural effectiveness to achieve the purpose given it by Divine Providence.

"There is not an Order, there is no work of the lay apostolate, no association that would not profit by appropriating for itself the spirit of the M. I., i.e. using the inexhaustible treasures that flow from consecration to the Immaculata to achieve its ends. The men and women Religious who live this consecration do not weaken their bond with their Orders, but on the contrary they strengthen this bond. The Marian consecration perfects the proper vocation of each person. The M.I. is a soul looking for a body in order to give it the fullness of life and the greatest possible development."

Religious life is total consecration to God in the most perfect manner, and as such it also serves one's neighbor in the most efficacious manner by means of the apostolic, charitable, contemplative activity proper to each Order. The ideal of such life, as for every Christian life, is the Immaculata. The M.I. enkindles unceasing love for the Immaculata in souls, as its founder writes, "In order that they might become one sole entity with her, become identified with her: in order that she herself live, love and work in them and through them. As she belongs to Jesus, to God, likewise every soul by means of her and in her will become the property of

Jesus, of God; that is, in a manner much more perfect than they would without her." The Immaculata prepares in souls that are consecrated to her a throne for Divine Love, for the Heart of Jesus, where they love Jesus with the Heart of the Immaculata, that is, according to her example and with her help.

Saint Maximilian asserts: "When by means of the total offering of oneself we become like herself, then also all our Religious life becomes hers." The purpose of the Franciscan Order - and other Orders - is a life conformed to the Gospel and the preaching of the Gospel to the world; that is the imitation of the Lord Jesus in the hidden life and in activity. When we consecrate ourselves totally to the Immaculata, then we will preach the Gospel in the most effective way, since she will preach by means of us; and we will live most perfectly according to the Gospel, since she will live it by means of us. "This is the most secure and easiest manner to achieve perfection in every respect and to perfect others," reasons Father Kolbe.

The principle means for achieving the greatest possible love in the Order is the observance of the Evangelical counsels: obedience, poverty and chastity! The unlimited consecration of oneself to the Immaculata renders easy the perfect understanding and consequent observance of the vows.

Our Obedience Is Hers Through Consecration

The Immaculata, as the Handmaid of the Lord, always said "fiat," and never, "I will not serve," and thus she is the most perfect example of obedience. Consecrating our selves totally to the Immaculata, we make our own her actions in the service of God; our rapport in regard to Religious rules and the superiors whom God has placed over us will be motivated in the light of the Immaculata, and we will draw strength from her fullness of grace. With the unlimited consecration of ourselves to the Immaculata, our obedience not only becomes more complete and more easy, but also more supernatural, because in the will of our superiors, if not contrary to the laws of God and of the Church, we see the will of the Immaculata.

Father Kolbe points out: "She directs the intellect, in order that in Religious obedience one sees her will. She directs the will, in order that the subject will not love anything outside of what she wills and by means of her, of what Jesus Christ wills." Obedience puts us at the disposition of the divine intelligence and divine prudence. Actually, divine grace and the protection of the Immaculata are prepared for the Religious in those places where they are stationed by obedience and not elsewhere. This does not mean that one must not have any initiative in the Religious life. Father Kolbe encouraged this initiative greatly, but according to him the final person to judge the projects of the Religious and to decide regarding them is their superior.

Our Poverty - Her Other-worldliness

Consecrated to the Immaculata, we better observe the vow of Religious poverty, because we live according to her spirit. Father Kolbe speaks of "our poverty - her other-worldliness." We consider everything - our goods and our time as the property of the Immaculata, which must serve only for her cause. Moreover, trusting only in Divine Providence by means of the Immaculata, we will find the effective means we need for the apostolate. Father Kolbe writes,

"I think that for all times and in all places the words of Christ continues to hold true: 'Seek first of all the Kingdom of God and his justice and all the rest will be given to you besides.' "

He considered Franciscan poverty to be the inexhaustible cash box of Divine Providence. But from this cash box the Religious can take for themselves (with the permission of the superiors, of course) only that which is necessary, while the rest must be consecrated to the cause of the Immaculata. "The offerings which people give for the cause of the Immaculata," our saint writes, "must serve exclusively for that cause, and whatever one takes away for his own comfort beyond real necessity, would constitute a theft of the offerings given for the sanctification of souls." Father Kolbe following these principles was able to develop an enormous apostolic action by means of the press.

Our Chastity - Her Chastity

When we consecrate ourselves totally to the Immaculata, then "our chastity becomes similar to her virginity" ("our chastity - her virginity") : from her we take our example and at the same time the necessary help that she does not refuse to those who are her possession and property. We arrive thus at such a state as almost irradiating her immaculateness. The vow of chastity favors not only our growth in holiness, but also the apostolate. "Whoever takes the vow of chastity," St. Maximilian teaches, "renounces the love of creatures, of a family, in order to become the mother of many souls." Moreover, consecrated without restriction to the Immaculata, we render ourselves ready for every sacrifice. "Our body is hers, in order that it might be exposed voluntarily to suffering and to fatigue for her."

The total consecration to the Immaculata also strengthens the common life, making every friary or convent like the family of Nazareth. There is in such a community "one sole family, whose father is God, whose mother is the Immaculata, and whose eldest brother is the divine Prisoner in the Eucharist; and all the others are, not merely companions, but brothers who love one another reciprocally, as little brothers."

The convents or friaries consecrated to the Immaculata will radiate to outsiders this family spirit; they will radiate Christian love, in order to change all humanity into one family, in which the law of Christian love will reign. There are always crosses in Religious communities that come from the weaknesses of its members. However, we who are consecrated to the Immaculata see in these crosses the opportunity for our own growth in holiness and for the benefit of the apostolate. For this reason we bear them with patience, indeed with joy, drawing strength from the Immaculate Heart of Mary.

Saint Maximilian, contemplating the life of Mary and seeking the most efficacious means to achieve the purpose of the M.I., introduces harmony between the contemplative life and the active life. He accentuates the primacy of the interior life, but he does this not only to defend the Religious from the dangers connected with over apostolic activity in the world but also to multiply a hundred-fold the effects of this activity. Mindful of the words of Christ: "without me you can do nothing" (Jo. 1 5, 5), he affirmed that:

"The fruit of our work does not depend on cleverness, strength, money, even though these things are gifts of God and also useful for apostolic activity; but only and solely on the degree of our union with God. If this is lacking or becomes sluggish, all other contributing factors will not help at all. Rather, if such union with God is strong, we will find all things possible and without difficulty."

The M. I., which wants to use all legitimate means for the cause of the Immaculata, gives the first place - even in the time of maximum exterior expansion - to prayer and to mortification as to the most efficacious means for the conversion and the sanctification of souls. Many Religious, not only in the Franciscan Order, have appropriated the Kolbean ideal of the M.I. In the Polish Niepokalanow hundreds of Sisters have consecrated themselves to the Immaculata according to the example of St. Maximilian.

In Japan in 1949 a Religious Congregation was born called the Franciscan Sisters of the Knights of the Immaculata, who live the third degree* of the M. I. with great zeal. Many contemplative Religious follow in the foot-steps of Saint Maximilian. Kolbe's total consecration also has a great attraction to idealistic youth. A Montfort Father pointed out that, "St. Maximilian Kolbe was called to exercise among the souls of the 20th Century that zeal which St. Louis de Montfort exercised at the beginning of the 17th Century." Thus Saint Maximilian has been and will be a powerful patron and secure guide for the Religious renewal anticipated by Vatican Council II and which is becoming realized in the 21st century. ❑

> ***"The greatest saints come from the cloister, but from these same cloisters come the worst damned souls, the greatest love or the greatest ruin. It cannot be otherwise. Whoever does not earnestly work on himself wanders from the road of perfection. Religious life is a continual warfare. Even if we should have spent long years in the Religious life, we still have to struggle."***
>
> St. Maximilian Kolbe

* Considered the "heroic degree" of total consecration, in which a consecrant is actually ready and willing to do anything and go anywhere at the command of his commandress, the Immaculata.

St. Maximilian, victim of love, receives the crown of martyrdom promised him by Our Lady when he was a small boy. This mosaic is found in Marytown's Kolbe chapel.

Kolbe's Gift to the Jews

Roy Schoeman

AS A JEW, ALBEIT one who has received the grace to recognize the Catholic Church as the fulfillment of the promise God made to the Jews, and as the son of German-Jewish holocaust refugees, I find it particularly offensive that St. Maximilian Kolbe - who did so much to aid the Jews - is the object of calumnies accusing him of anti-Semitism. I would like to take this opportunity to address this unfounded libel.

The accusations against Kolbe seem to fall into two categories- that he held to an "anti-Semitic" personal theology, and that anti-Semitic writings were published in his *Knight of the Immaculata magazine.* Addressing the first category first, a Catholic cannot be accused of being an "anti-Semite" just for adhering to the revealed truths of the Catholic faith. Catholics know as an incontrovertible fact that Jesus was, in fact, the long-awaited Messiah promised to the Jews, and was in His person the fulfillment of the promise of the Old Covenant. Therefore, Jews who do not accept Him are in error, although not necessarily through their own personal fault, and the tenets of the religion to which they adhere - the necessity of adhering to the Mosaic covenant, and the awaiting of the (first-coming of) the Messiah - are no longer valid. This is not to say that there is no merit in their fidelity to the one true God and to the divinely revealed faith to which they remain loyal. Nonetheless, either the Catholic faith is true or it isn't. If the Catholic faith is true, then there is something fundamentally flawed in the theology of a Jew who rejects Jesus as the Messiah of Judaism. Kolbe should not be accused of being an anti-Semite simply for believing in the fullness of Catholic doctrine!

Then there is the issue of Kolbe's attitude towards Jews who actively engaged in what he saw as destructive social movements. There is no doubt that he considered that the Jews who were actively promoting Communism and Freemasonry were working for the forces of evil. Again, Kolbe cannot be accused of anti-Semitism for being strongly morally opposed to what they were doing. And when he made reference to these individuals, it is true that his description at times mentioned the fact that they were Jewish. Although this may appear distasteful to us, it does not reflect anti-Semitism on Kolbe's part. It was merely an accurate description of the individuals and events being described, and if there was a particularly visible presence of Jews involved in the emergence of Communism, is that not more a matter of shame for us Jews, than a cause for "shooting the messenger of bad tidings"?

And yet, rather than admitting the fault and perhaps expressing the sort of corporate contrition which the Holy Father John Paul II recently did with respect to sins committed by his fellow Catholics, the chairman of the American Section of the World Jewish Congress in the middle of the 20th century, Rabbi Israel Goldstein of New York City, named Leon Trotsky - who played a key role in afflicting the world with the horror of atheistic communism - as one of the "Ten Greatest Jews of the Last Fifty Years." On which side is there religious chauvinism? And Kolbe cannot be faulted if he felt that it was not entirely irrelevant that many of the key players in the Communist revolution were Jewish. For having discarded the possibility of the Messiah-hood of Jesus Christ, their rightful desire for a betterment for mankind's condition - a "messianic" impulse which might be particularly pronounced among Jews given their God-given role to pray for the coming of the Messiah - had to search for other outlets, sometimes tragically falling on ones diametrically opposed to all that was truly good for the future of man.

It is also true that Kolbe mistakenly put credence in the anti-Semitic libel of the so-called Protocols of the Elders of Zion - a fictional anti-Semitic work which had recently appeared, purporting to be a secret insiders' account of a plot among a group of Jews to take over the world. Although Kolbe fell for the scurrilous anti-Semitic hoax, so did almost the entire non-Jewish world at the time. And in the era of world-shaking conspiracies in which Kolbe lived - that of Freemasonry, which had brought about the French revolution and tried to destroy the Christian faith causing tens of thousands of martyrdoms in the process, and that of Communism, which brought about the Bolshevik revolution and untold millions of deaths - was it absurd for him to put credence in yet another "secret-society" based conspiracy behind world events?

As to the claim that anti-Semitic writings were published in Kolbe's *Knight of the Immaculata*, much of the furor stems from an article in an April 1982 issue of the anti-Catholic Austrian periodical, Wiener Tagebuch. That article makes reference to an issue of the *Knight* which was produced while Kolbe was in Asia. Kolbe therefore could not have had any prior knowledge of it nor any part in approving it. It might well have been the very issue which prompted the following reprimand from Kolbe: (July 12, 1935 letter from Father Kolbe in Nagasaki to Father Marion, acting editor of the *Knight* in Poland):

> *"When speaking of the Jews, I would be very careful not to arouse by accident nor add to the hatred for them, which some readers already entertain, for many people are already ill-disposed in their regard, or are even actually hostile towards them. . . . our main purpose is, as always, the conversion and sanctification of souls, winning them over to the Immaculate through love for all souls, including those of Jews..." (The Kolbe Reader, Fr. Romb Editor, p.124)*

That Kolbe felt a special love and concern for the Jews, and for their conversion, is reflected by the fact that he chose to celebrate his very first Mass at the "St. Michael" altar in the church of San Andrea della Fratte in Rome - the very spot where the Blessed Virgin Mary appeared to the agnostic Jew Alphonse Ratisbonne, resulting in his instantaneous conversion. Ratisbonne went on to become a priest, and started a religious community in the Holy Land to pray for the Jewish people to come to know the Messiah for whom they had waited so long - Jesus. (This miraculous conversion is recounted in more detail in the book *Marian Shrines in France*, published by the Franciscans of the Immaculate.)

The fact that Kolbe looked after the temporal needs of Jews as well is documented elsewhere in this book. Many stirring accounts are also narrated in Patricia Reese's excellent biography of Kolbe, *A Man for Others.* While head of the City of the Immaculate friary in Poland, Kolbe fed, clothed and sheltered thousands of Jews who had nowhere else to turn - often at the expense of adequate resources for his own friars. And in Auschwitz he gave love and hope, and much of his meager rations, to Jewish as well as non-Jewish fellow prisoners.

But as important as it is to relieve the suffering of our brothers while on earth, it pales in insignificance in comparison to assuring their eternal salvation. And Kolbe never stopped for a moment - either before or after his internment in Auschwitz - to pray, suffer and work for the salvation of Jews as well as atheists and fellow-Christians. And by being present at Auschwitz - a fate which Kolbe willingly took on, declining at least one opportunity to avoid it - and voluntarily taking on his own execution, Kolbe perhaps performed the greatest service to the Jews in the history of the world. Through his own identification with the suffering Christ, and his presence and his prayers and his love for his fellow-prisoners, he was perhaps able to serve as an intermediary in uniting the suffering of his fellow-prisoners who did not know Christ with those of our Savior and Redeemer, and thereby ensure that their sufferings and deaths too would have redemptive value, for themselves, for their co-religionists, and for the world. ❑

He Anticipated Space Travel

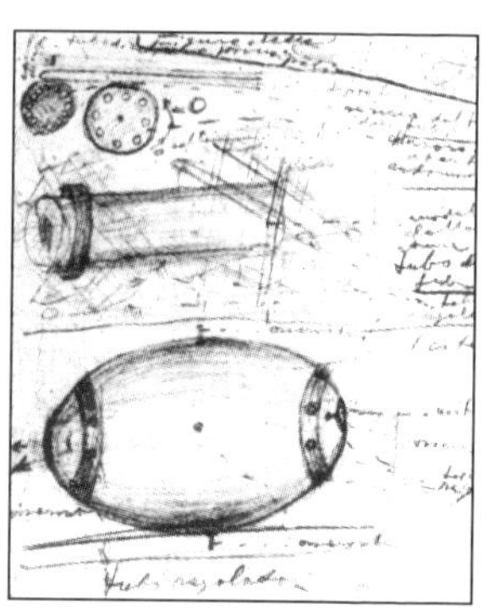

Many times, St. Maximilian shared one of his pet projects with his friend, his belief that "flight to the moon is possible" and he expected to see it in his lifetime. "At the beginning of the 20th century there were only a few men who were seriously considering man landing on the moon... At the time, Fr. Maximilian's views appeared to me as a fantasy," Fr. Bronislaus admits. Yet, Kolbe, the mathematician and amateur astronomer, had been entertaining this possibility since he was a young boy. While he was a student in Rome, he was so convinced of space travel that he designed a space vehicle, propelled by rockets which would have the necessary thrust to escape the earth's gravitation. A noted physicist professor of his checked out Kolbe's calculation and said it was all quite realizable.

Religious Communities Inspired and Founded on the Ideals by St. Maximilian

THE FATHER KOLBE MISSIONARIES OF THE IMMACULATA

This Kolbean Institute was founded in Bologna, Italy, during the Marian Year, 1954, by Fr. Luigi M. Faccenda, a Conventual Franciscan confrere and disciple of St. Maximilian. On March 25, 1992, the Institute received the approval of Pope John Paul II as a Secular Institute of pontifical right. Following the example of the Mother of the Lord, the Fr. Kolbe Missionaries are laywomen consecrated to God by the perpetual vows of chastity, poverty and obedience. They are salt and leaven in the world, bringing souls to Christ. They may live alone, in family or in community.

The Institute's specific charism is the Marian and missionary spirituality that springs forth from witnessing to Christ Crucified and from the spiritual legacy of St. Maximilian Kolbe. Each day is a "gift from the Redeemer," which the Missionaries entrust totally to Mary. They strive to live in her their spousal union with God and collaborate in her maternal mission which is to lead all people to her Son. In this way they rediscover their dignity and joy as children of God in His Family, the Church.

Every person is an object of God's love, and the Missionaries wish to share the gift of Mary's presence as Mother, sister and model. They collaborate in the spreading of the Gospel above all by seeking to give witness in every place and aspect of society through various initiatives, such as the use of the mass media, especially periodicals and books.

Associated members, lay people, and clerics (Fr. Kolbe Volunteers of the Immaculata) strive for evangelical perfection by sharing in the Marian missionary spirituality and mission of the Institute. The Fr. Kolbe Missionaries are in Italy, the United States, Argentina, Bolivia, Brazil, Luxembourg and Poland. They collaborate with the Conventual Franciscan Friars in a Center of Spirituality near Auschwitz in order to offer to all the message of love and hope of the martyr of charity, St. Maximilian. They recently established in Brazil a men's branch of the Fr. Kolbe Missionaries of the Immaculata.

SISTERS MINOR OF MARY IMMACULATE (SMMI)

The Sisters Minor of Mary Immaculate were founded by Mother Mary Elizabeth Patrizi in Rome on August 14, 1983 at Casa Kolbe, where St. Maximilian founded the *Militia Immaculatae* movement. The Institute was canonically erected in the diocese of Rome as a public association of the faithful on August 15, 1985 by Cardinal Ugo Polatti. Pope John Paul II approved the first Statutes on December 8, 1989. On June 18, 1993, Cardinal Camillo Ruini erected the SMMI as a religious Institute of Diocesan rite and approved their Constitutions. At this time it was officially entrusted to the Order of the Friars Minor Conventual.

Besides being members of the great Franciscan family, the institute draws much from the Carmelite spirituality, making room for a new charism in the Church. The Constitutions of the Sisters Minor recognize St. Maximilian Kolbe and St. Thérèse of the Child Jesus as their spiritual Founders.

As Franciscans, the SMMI lay great stress on poverty, fraternity, and joy, the fruit of their contemplative life. They strive to imitate St. Maximilian's heroic gift of self through total consecration to Mary Immaculate - to be used in the Immaculate's maternal hands, as docile instruments for the salvation and sanctification of souls. As daughters of St. Thérèse, they wish to be a holocaust of love in a mystical, spousal union with God in a spiritual maternity within the Church, through intense prayer and generous penance.

The Sisters work in close collaboration with diverse branches of the Franciscans - the Conventuals, Capuchins, and Minors. They work with youth, the aged, and with the *Militia Immaculatae* (M.I.), at universities, youth centers, parishes, nurseries, and at the Marian shrine of Tre Fontane. Through a fourth vow, they unite themselves to Mary to be ever available as instruments in her hands for the salvation of all mankind.

THE FRANCISCANS OF THE IMMACULATE

This Institute embraces both men and women religious.

Living in friaries and convents near each other they are united in ideals, spirit and the apostolate. The Friars and Sisters observe the same Rule of St. Francis, a community life patterned after St. Maximilian Kolbe's "Cities of the Immaculate". Their community life independent of each other, as Friars and Sisters of the Immaculate, may be summarized in a few words as a life of prayer, poverty and penance in the context of total consecration to Mary Immaculate.

From their daily community schedule, it is apparent that everything flows from the prayer life of the friars and sisters. Nothing is allowed to take precedence over prayer, both private and communal. The Sacrifice of the Mass is central, followed by the divine office and at least an hour of mental prayer. Eucharistic Adoration, Our Lady's Rosary and other community vocal prayers make up a contemplative life that is conducive to furthering spiritual progress.

The goal of this "Order of Penance," as St. Francis's Order is known, is to be formed by Mary into another poor, humble, Christ Crucified even as were St. Francis and St. Maximilian. The Friars and Sisters model their lives on the primitive observance as lived by the early friars at St. Mary of the Angels in Assisi.

It is preeminently a Missionary Order (see missionary article on page 163). Following the example of both Francis and Maximilian all its members, in view of their Marian vow of total consecration to Mary, are committed to go anywhere at any time to further the kingdom of Christ through Mary Immaculate. Since they are instruments in the hands of the Immaculate, she is free to use them as she best sees fit for the conversion and sanctification of all peoples and nations. Since it is Mary operating through the Friars and Sisters - through their total obedience, radical poverty and complete emptying of self - the greatest amount of good will be accomplished by her who is the Mediatrix of all Graces. The Institute's International headquarters is in Italy. It has missions in the Philippines, Benin, Nigeria (Africa), Russia, Australia, Brazil and the U.S.A.

The Franciscans of the Immaculate, founded by Frs. Stefano M. Manelli and Gabrielle M. Pellettieri, has been given Pontifical Status (Right) by Pope John Paul II.

MARYTOWN IN THE UNITED STATES

Considered the third "City of the Immaculate," Marytown U.S.A. was founded on the feast of Our Lady of Sorrows, September 15, 1948 by Fr. Dominic Szymanski, OFM Conv. who had met St. Maximilian several times. Its first home was a small caddy house on the property of the minor seminary of the Conventual Franciscans of St. Bonaventure Province. With six aspirants to religious life and no funds, Marytown got off to a very modest start. If the founder had not the support of Fr. Cyril Kita, OFM Conv., Father Provincial at the time, Fr. Dominic's dream would never have materialized. Fr. Cyril was a classmate of St. Maximilian in Rome and supported the Marytown initiative wholeheartedly.

Out of such a small "mustard seed," inspired and nurtured by Fr. Dominic's unlimited trust in Our Lady and much suffering, came today's nationally known friary with its many apostolates. Foremost among these is the National Center of the *Militia Immaculatae* movement, which recently was designated by the Bishop's Conference of the United States as the National Shrine of St. Maximilian Kolbe. The official organ of the shrine is the IMMACULATA magazine, which was first edited and printed by the Brothers. The first issue of May 1950 carried articles about St. Maximilian and the M.I. as well as about Eucharistic Adoration, which Fr. Dominic introduced at Marytown. A year later he joined Fr. Maximilian and other knights in the heavenly "City of the Immaculate."

Although today the Brothers are no longer as involved in the editing and printing of the magazine as in the past, the ideals of St. Maximilian and Fr. Dominic live on in the collaborative efforts of the Franciscan Friars and lay people, many of whom are consecrants of Our Lady Immaculate. The measure of success of Marytown's youth work, gift/book store, retreats, and publications, IMMACULATA in particular, are all secondary to the heart and soul of Marytown which is its very beautiful Chapel where Jesus in His Eucharistic presence is solemnly exposed day and night. Fr. Maximilian, who dreamed of some day having perpetual adoration at the original City of the Immaculate, would be immensely pleased and perhaps even "envious" if that were possible in heaven. ❑

Knights At the Foot of the Cross

"Perhaps the hour has struck when the M.I. should start thinking about organizing groups that would pray and offer up sufferings for the M.I. We would benefit much if, for instance, nuns and especially the contemplatives, would offer up some of their sufferings or hours of adoration before the Blessed Sacrament for the M.I. The sick too could win many souls through their sufferings. Maybe it's time to organize such groups." -St. Maximilian Kolbe

IN THE MIDST OF establishing two Cities of the Immaculate, one in Poland, the other in Japan, both within less than three years of each other, and while suffering continuously from ill health, Fr. Maximilian wrote the above to his Superior from Japan in 1931. He had much personal suffering and knew how fruitful suffering could be if united with that of the suffering and passion of Our Savior. (see page 157). However, he never got around to establishing a group of M.I. members who would generously offer up their suffering to help support the growth and fruitfulness of the Militia Immaculatae. That came later by two Franciscan Friars in the U.S.A.

In 1983 Fr. James McCurrry OFM Conv., when he was National Director of the M.I. in the States, had the inspiration and passed on the challenge of heading such an initiative to Franciscan Brother, Paschal Kolodziej. It was fitting as both friars are from the same Conventual Franciscan Province of St. Anthony as Fr. Lawrence Cyman. Fr. Cyman, you may recall, (page 44) helped Fr. Kolbe purchase his first press, which enabled him to inaugurate his great printing venture (see page 201) in the late twenties.

The "Knights at the Foot of the Cross" (KFC's), as Fr. James called this unique apostolic movement, was officially inaugurated on May 31, 1993, the feast of the Visitation, when fifteen elderly Franciscans of the same province made their consecration as Knights at the foot of the cross. In less than ten years it has grown to 1,300 KFC's in the United States.

There is so much suffering in our country and throughout the world! And for the most part it is wasted suffering. As if that were not enough, men add to the suffering that God permits in His loving Providence, extra suffering by anticipating suffering that may never come. God will not tempt man beyond his means, which includes suffering. But enduring suffering, especially mental suffering so common in our society today, requires faith, and the gift of Faith comes primarily through grace and grace is obtained by humble, persevering prayer.

Kolbe capped off a life of suffering at the horrible death camp of Auschwitz. The brutality, inhumanity, diabolic hatred, and torture inflicted on prisoners there is hard to even imagine. Is it any wonder many prisoners threw themselves onto the electric fences surrounding the camp? One such prisoner in a fit of despair attempted suicide. He was stopped and given fifty lashes. St. Maximilian heard about it and talked to him, calming him down to the extent that he never attempted to take his life again.

This same prisoner told how the Saint would gather prisoners together during their free time to give them talks on spiritual topics. Of course this was forbidden under penalty of death, but as Maximilian pointed out, "I don't fear death; I fear sin." According to the same fellow prisoner, Kolbe not only showed bravery at all times, but communicated a certain bravery to those around him.

The spiritual dimension of suffering, such as portrayed in this story, is touched upon in the *Vanguard*, a quarterly Newsletter that Brother mails from Marytown. There is also a 48 page "Knights at the Foot of the Cross Prayer booklet," which has, besides prayers, the major feasts of Our Lady, a short biography of St. Maximilian and a history of the Militia Immaculate. It is a great aid for shutins. Brother Paschal has many other ideas for expanding this great work. He can be reached for enrollment and information packets on the KFCs at Marytown, 1600 West Park Ave. Libertyville, IL 60048.

St. Maximilian Kolbe:

Patron of the Pro-Life Movement

PROPOSING A CANONIZED Saint, Maximilian Kolbe, as a special patron for the pro-life movement may seem un-ecumenical. Wouldn't he, being a Catholic Saint, be another impediment in uniting in a joint effort Protestant and Catholic pro-lifers? It need not be so.

St. Maximilian is a universal Saint for all times and in particular these times. He has captured the imagination and admiration of all people by his heroic sacrifice of giving up his life for a fellow prisoner in a Nazi concentration camp. He thus witnessed to the value of human life. His inspiring life and ideals are not going to disunite it any more than it already is. It may be just the opposite.

There never was, nor will there be, a common goal and united effort the way things now stand with the pro-life movement. One reason is that the pro-abortion juggernaut has been successful in setting the terms upon which the battle is being fought. In a secularized culture, which has separated God from the daily affairs of man, it is altogether too easy to fall into the prevalent mentality, "It's a law of the land, therefore it must be moral," or, "It is the will of the majority of people, therefore it must be the right way to go." In a pluralistic society which spawns religious indifferentism under the misconception of being "tolerant" or "non-judgmental" how does one, for example, surmount the problem of those who do not see the logical connection between contraception and abortion, between the secular and the spiritual, between a matter of principle and material advantage.

Contrary to the Church's clear teaching on pro-life issues, the majority of Catholics vote consistently for pro-abortion candidates.

It all comes down to a lack of commitment, subscribing to the erroneous standards of the world, "if it feels right for me it must be alright." The pro-life David pitted against the monstrous anti-life Goliath, backed by the mass media and the federal government, has to do something much more radical to what is already being done and proven unsuccessful. More education, more counseling, more lobbying, more boycotting, more political action, is but a holding operation and will never effectively address the fundamental problem.

The culture of death has to be changed to a culture favorable to life. It cannot be done without acknowledging God's place in such an essential role as life. God speaks of Himself as the "Way, the Truth and the LIFE." He will not be ignored indefinitely in this fundamental issue. Dr. Charles Rice of the Notre Dame University, School of Law puts his finger on the main flaw in the crusade for life:

"Legalized abortion and euthanasia are essentially symptoms of a loss of faith in God. They are religious issues."

This brings up what should be the ultimate goal of the pro-life forces. It is not only to save bodies from the abortionist's knife, but souls as well, including the souls of the perpetrators and cooperators of the crime as well as its victims. The late John Cardinal O'Connor of New York, a great pro-life champion once said:

"I am not sure all of us appreciate why we are in pro-life activities. This is not merely an act of trying to save lives, as important as that is. The pro-life movement is an apostolate to save souls. . . to bring about a metanoia, a complete change of heart, a gradual awareness of why we are here on earth and what we are destined for in eternity."

It is a battle of words and how they can be used to misrepresent and manipulate the truth and fragment the pro-life forces. An example: The enemy make it appear that abortion is strictly a Catholic religious issue. Although it should be, it obviously isn't. According to the election results, the standard response from Catholic pro-lifers is, "Abortion is not a religious issue." Unwittingly, by fighting the war of words on the turf of the pro-aborts, they may make a point that it is not strictly a Catholic moral issue, but a universal right of all human beings, and as such, every one has the obligation to fight this evil. Thus, the enemy misleads and confuses Catholics into saying it is not a religious issue, which of course, it is in the final analysis.

A recent presidential election exit poll conducted by Voter News Service, showed that among voters, the greater the religious affiliation, the greater were the number who voted for Bush. Sad to relate Catholics gave the edge of their votes nationally to Gore, 50-47, while Protestants voted for Bush, who incidentally is not 100% pro-life. One wonders how Catholic voters could back a man who has a consistent record of being openly pro-abortion, even supporting infanticide. Obviously they are not voting for Gore on principal but rather motivated by self-interest. When one considers that over 80 percent of young Catholic couples, voting age, use some form of artificial birth control which the Church teaches is seriously sinful, it is no surprise. This shows how the breakdown of morality in the initial stage of procreation leads to abortion - the back up for failed "birth control." Fr. Paul Marx, the founder of "Human Life International" shows statistically that wherever contraception is introduced to prevent unwanted pregnancies, abortions increase dramatically.

In his encyclical *Humanae Vitae* (1968), Pope Paul VI warned the Catholic world of the many inherent evils which would follow from the acceptance of artificial contraception. Few paid any attention to this prophetic document and as a result we see its rotten fruit in the sexual revolution - skyrocketing premarital sex, widespread homosexuality followed by an AIDS epidemic, broken marriages, one parent families, etc. The Church has not failed its erring children. Individual Catholics have failed to subscribe to the Church's hard teachings. To defend the right to life effectively one does not look upon new life, created in the image and likeness of God, as something to be avoided at all cost - even to the extent of playing God. Frustrating God's plan of human sexuality by denying one of its essential two-fold ends - procreation and a physical expression of uniting love - is basically selfish and an implicit denial of God's loving Providence.

Coupled with the sexual "freedom" afforded by the pill to "liberated women," (having sex without having to bear its aftermath- unwanted children) we have almost universal classroom sex education programs. These programs, like pouring gasoline on the already raging fires of unrestrained passion, are corrupting our youth and preparing the way for further breakup of marriages and the family. This destruction of Christian moral values didn't just happen, suddenly or accidentally; it was far too well organized. St. Maximilian Kolbe explains:

"Such implacable hatred for the Church and the ambassadors of Christ on earth is not in the power of individual persons, but of a systematic activity stemming in the final analysis from Freemasonry (see pages 38 and 233). In particular, it aims to destroy the Catholic religion. Their deceits have spread over the whole world, in different guises, but with the same goal: religious indifferentism and weakening of moral forces, according to their basic principle: We will conquer the Catholic Church not with argument, but rather from within through moral corruption."

Maximilian Kolbe cut across the pragmatism and selfishness of our times in his total selflessness. He offers a radical solution that deals with the essential problem and the ultimate answer to the culture of death. In a number of ways Kolbe, the victim of the Nazi Holocaust, also identifies with the innocent victims of the abortion Holocaust. In his day he stood against the anti-life, genocide philosophy of the Nazis bringing hope in the most hopeless imaginable places - a virtual hell on earth - the Nazi death camps. He gave up his life for a total stranger, an innocent man condemned to die a slow agonizing death by starvation and dehydration. On October 10, 1982, Pope John Paul II canonized him. In his homily the Holy Father pointed out:

"Father Maximilian Kolbe, . . . defended in that place of death an innocent man's right to life. He defended his [Gajowniczek's] right to life, declaring that he was ready to go to death in that man's place, because he was the father of a family and his life was precious to his dear ones. Father Maximilian Mary Kolbe thus reaffirmed the Creator's exclusive right over innocent human life."

He placed himself before the executioner, a victim, to save another man's life even as some heroic pro-lifers do in our day by placing their bodies between the abortionists and the innocent babies slated to die. These "Lambs" face imprisonment for "breaking the law," which is no law at all since it contradicts God's law, "Thou shalt not kill." It is worth noting the similarity of our Saint's death to the increasing number of victims of involuntary euthanasia. The martyr of charity was condemned to die by starvation and dehydration, similar to Nancy Cruzan and others who were given the "exit" treatment. In Kolbe's case he was not dying fast enough, so he was killed by an injection of poison. This seems, in today's society, to be a common way of dispatching the elderly and infirmed who are considered to be an extra "burden" on individual families and the national economy.

St. Maximilian's reaction to the anti-life movement of our day would assuredly be no compromise under any circumstance. In 1938 a campaign against abortion was conducted through columns in the Knight magazine. There is no such thing as exceptional cases when it comes to outright killing of the innocent. Abortion is killing a defenseless innocent human being. Euthanasia, is not mercy killing. It is the killing of innocent humans, period! The Saint would settle for nothing short of an absolute no to deliberate killing of the innocent. His heroic life and death is in sharp contrast to the mentality of the worldly-wise. His total honesty, total commitment and total dependence on God is what the pro-life cause needs more of today.

Giving up his life for a total stranger was not a sudden, irrational impulse done on the spur of the moment. It naturally followed from a life of total self-giving, motivated and sustained by an on-going daily living out of his total consecration. His model and inspiration for this total consecration was Mary Immaculate. Her perfect response as a creature to the Infinite love of God, her total sinlessness and conformity of her will to God's Will was an ideal he ever strove to imitate. In this spiritual warfare anything short of total consecration, total commitment to the cause, would be incomprehensible and inconsistent in the mind St. Maximilian Kolbe. Such a sense of total commitment by pro-lifers is an absolute, which will pull the movement out of the doldrums it finds itself in today.

Understandably, in this spiritual warfare the secular humanists, especially those in the mass media prompted by Satan the "father of lies" and the "murderer from the beginning" (Jn 8: 44), are intent on preventing Catholics from understanding the real nature of the battle. As Kolbe saw it, the battle ultimately goes back to the creation of the world and the fall of our first parents. God set up an enmity between the Woman of Genesis, Mary, and the Serpent. The dehumanizing, despiritualizing goals and methods of the anti-life forces are truly diabolical - Mary and the devil are ever opposed to each other. The anti-life secularists hate Mary because she represents what is most noble and virtuous in womanhood and virginity. It is the world against Mary Immaculate. Literature put out by Planned Parenthood mocks the Blessed Mother, confessing as do the demons, their anti-Marian character, while for the most part the pro-lifers haven't quite grasped this reality in the same way.

There are many indications that the final battle between the Blessed Virgin and the devil, between good and evil, between the pro-life and anti-life forces, between truth and falsehood is reaching its final stage.

One doesn't have to consult a poll to find out that Catholics who are most faithful to the Church's teachings are devotees of Mary and are the most committed pro-life militants. As such they will be attacked by the enemies of life and truth. These attack the Church in a subtle way by accusing two holy church men, both champions of Mary, of being anti-Semitic. Distorting the truth and totally ignoring the facts that both Pope Pius XII and Maximilian Kolbe were just the opposite of anti-Semitic. It has been thoroughly documented that Pope Pius XII was responsible for saving tens of thousands of Jewish lives. The accusation leveled on St. Maximilian of being anti-Semitic is refuted on page 181.

When St. Maximilian opened his successful reform movement within the Franciscan Order, he emphasized the poverty of St. Francis of Assisi which brought about a reform of Religious life and the Church in the 13th century. St. Maximilian wisely and effectively adapted "Sister Poverty" to life of religious in the 20th century. The materialism of these times, especially in an affluent country like the United States, can have a debilitating effect on the pro-life apostolate. On the other hand, the fact that the pro-abortion people have huge financial backing from the government and large foundations shouldn't discourage the small "widow's mite" of the pro-life people. It is to their advantage and befits those who are on the side of God. Here again Kolbe is a good model for the pro-life people to imitate (see page 191). You can't buy victory in this battle, which is ultimately spiritual. As Christ points out: "You can't serve both God and mammon."

In St. Maximilian's life amazing victories attended above all his total consecration to Mary Immaculate - the all powerful Mother of God. The whole focal point of the Saint's life and his efforts of conquering the world for the Sacred Heart of Jesus, centered on the Queen and Mother of Jesus and of the Church. Kolbe's total uncompromising consecrationimplies tapping into the infinite power of prayer, especially the Rosary and Eucharistic Adoration.

"Truly I say to you, if you ask anything of the Father in my name, He will give it to you."

Sacrifice (faithful fulfilling of the duties of ones state in life) is vitally necessary. Christ made it clear, "You are either for me or against me." There is no middle ground, no room for compromise when it comes to human life and the eternal salvation of souls. The goal of the right to life of all human beings is the salvation of everyone, including the abortionist and even the so called "pro-choice" politicians.

Every radical pro-lifer who gives him or herself over, body, soul, intellect and will to Mary to be used as an instrument in her battle against the demon of impurity, and enemy of life, brings the ultimate triumph of good over evil that much closer. Jesus showed the way to victory by the way of the Cross - to lay down one's life. Bishop Sheen used to say that the communists believed in the spirit of revolution, whereas we Christians believe in the revolution of the spirit. There has to be a violent change of heart in the ranks of pro-lifers.

The newly beatified children of Fatima, Jacenta Marto (7) and her brother Francisco (9) show us by their example that there can be no talk of victory without penance. St. Maximilian, a follower of the "Little Way of Spiritual Childhood" (see ad for our book St.Thérèse, Doctor of the Little Way on page 251) offered up in a spirit of penance the suffering he patiently bore throughout his life, uniting it with Christ's suffering for the ultimate triumph unto eternal life. He extended Christ's victory on Calvary into modern times through his sacrificial death. What made it all possible was

Mary Immaculate. As the Mediatrix of all graces, she has the graces and promise of victory from her Divine Son. The connection between total consecration to Mary Immaculate and the pro-life movement runs deep and is vitally essential. The sooner the pro-life forces realize this the sooner will the sound of Victory be heard around the world.

- BFM

His Pro-life Witness Motivated by Total Consecration

When St. Maximilian was ordered by his religious superior to return to Poland as the Second World War was gearing up, he wrote: "I have dreamed of being able to leave my bones beneath the foundation of the Japanese Niepokalanow, but the Immaculata has other plans, and holy obedience obliges me to tread another path." Clearly, it was God's Will and Heaven's design that Kolbe's bones be mixed with the ashes of the countless, nameless Holocaust victims. His pro-life witness was the fruition of his total consecration.

- Helen M. Valois

Random thoughts, based on St. Maximilian — Model and Defender of Human Life

The pro-life forces have everything going for them. "With God, we are the majority," as the saying goes. The offensive must be taken over by those who champion the life of the innocents as opposed to those who for selfish reasons subscribe to the secular humanists philosophy focused on self, ignoring God and His moral imperative, "Thou shalt not kill."

* * * * * * *

The Holocaust, yesterday and today, is essentially an attack on the spiritual side of man. Springing from an atheistic neo-paganism which sees men as mere animals, and lowers the beautiful gift of sex as something he has no control over, and so rationalizes the sin of the contraception and abortion as no sin at all. Thus, man is deprived of the supreme dignity in his sharing in the same humanity of the Son of God and His Mother Mary, the perfection of mankind. Is it any wonder that the Pro-choice people have no love for either virginity or motherhood as epitomized in Mary Immaculate?

* * * * * * *

If we wish to convert those involved in advancing the culture of death we must devote ourselves to prayer; praying the Rosary and spending time in prayer before the Blessed Sacrament. All our efforts to change the laws of this country, elect pro-life people to government positions, close down abortion clinics, talk women out of aborting their babies, will only be successful if accompanied by prayer and a significant amount of it. So let us imitate the example of St. Maximilian by serving Our Lady with all our heart and promoting total consecration to her as the most powerful weapon against Satan. And may we devote ourselves to sacrificing some time on a regular basis to the Rosary and prayer before the Blessed Sacrament. With these two means, we can bring unity to the pro-life movement and ultimately change our culture throughout the world from a culture of death to a culture of life.

As loyal and dedicated servants for Our Lady, the truth will never be compromised, we will defend the dignity of every human life from conception to natural death without exception, and we will have the strength, joy and zeal to carry out Our Lady's mission for us under the most difficult circumstances. St. Maximilian found all his strength in Mary to accomplish his many great deeds and to endure terrible suffering throughout his life. He persevered to the end as the servant of Mary and her knight, and she rewarded him with the glorious crown of martyrdom. In following his example of total surrender to Our Lady, we defenders of life will also be able to persevere to the end.

* * * * * * *

Sacrificing a definite amount of time during the week or even each day to be with Our Lord in adoration is a great opportunity to meditate on the sufferings of Our Lord's passion and Our Lady's compassion beneath the cross. According to St. Alphonsus Ligouri, meditation is the key to holiness and without it it is practically impossible to be a saint. Meditation before the Blessed Sacrament will make us more holy and allow us to be more effective and zealous in the cause of life.

* * * * * * *

Pro-life people must be very precious to Mary and be ever under her mantle. They have the great consolation of her motherly love in their arduous, unappreciated labors. She assuredly sustains them and as Mediatrix of All Graces gives them the necessary help they need to persevere under the many trials and setbacks they face. As the mother of a family, the Church, Our Lady will ever unit the pro-lifers in their fight against their common enemy, if they but seek her help.

* * * * * * *

What are the weapons that can do real damage to the anti-life movement? St. Maximilian spelled them out in his writings, and wielded them expertly in his life and death. There is prayer and sacrifice. There is the Miraculous Medal. This "bullet" against Satan needs to be incorporated more in the pro-life efforts.

— Helen M. Valois and arranged by the Editor

Fr. Kolbe — Mass Communications Expert

THIS CHAPTER IS ABOUT one of the most successful mass communication ventures of the Catholic Church in modern times. It occurred in Poland during the height of the depression in the thirties. No one can deny the great impact the printed word has in shaping public opinion and even in defining the goals of free governments and their means for reaching them. In the hands of totalitarian governments it is a most potent weapon for keeping people in servitude. We see this in the seventy odd years Communism dominated Russia. St. Maximilian was acutely aware of how effectively the devil uses the press to undermine and destroy the Church. In 1919, shortly after he was ordained a priest, he gave a talk on Catholic action to a group of Militia members in Cracow, Poland. In this talk he dwelt in much detail on the fact that the Masons and certain internationalists - for the most part atheists - had taken over the whole mass communication field in Central Europe and England. In spite of the fact that most of these countries were predominantly Catholic, they consistently attacked the Catholic Church.

Kolbe quotes the folk-writer Wetzel: "Look around you today's world. Who has changed it most in the last decades? Who sows unbelief among the people? Who takes away their hope of heaven and causes the people to seek happiness strictly in worldly things and their abuse? Who silenced the voice of conscience in their hearts? Who broke the laws of the land. Who disturbed the public order to such an extent that crimes of the greatest variety are committed more and more frequently? All these consequences are the work, the action of the daily press which is antagonistic to the Church."

If such were the case in 1922, how much more so today? Kolbe had even predicted as much when he said, "Modern times are dominated by Satan and will be more so in the future. . . ." Let us look at the state of the press and mass media in the United States today.

To appreciate the secularism, anti-God, anti-Christian bias dominating the press, TV, radio, records, etc., one must look at the mentality of those behind the big networks and the entertainment elite. In an interview with 240 journalists, and broadcasters of the most influential newspapers, magazines and news departments of major broadcasting networks, the research team of Lichter and Rothman found that 85% of them seldom or never attend worship services. Only 12% of those in television, entertainment, and the news media are Catholic. Thus the need of a Catholic presence is overwhelming. In the press and TV coverage of the news, 90% say women have the right to abortion, and 97% TV personnel take a "pro-choice" stance.

In a book on the subject, Watching America: What Television Tells Us About Our Lives, by the same research team, we read that 66% of the TV entertainment people feel they should "play a major role in promoting social reform"; 80% do not regard homosexual relations as morally wrong and 51% do not regard adultery as wrong. Obviously these people are intent in shaping society according to a secular humanism "religion" contrary to that which any believing Christian holds as true and good.

In the face of this tremendous takeover of the mass media and entertainment fields by the secular humanists, one might be tempted to take a defeatist attitude. The religion of secular humanism, another name for Masonry, has spawned religious indifferentism and moral corruption through the press and all of the mass media channels of communication for decades. What would Kolbe's reaction be?

"In the face of such strong attacks by the enemies of the Church of God, are we to remain inactive? Is that all we can do- complain and cry? No! Everyone of us has a holy obligation to build a trench and personally hurl back the assaults of the enemy!"

In 1922 he began a very unpretentious magazine titled the *Knight of the Immaculata.* In a note from the editor, he stated,

"Because of lack of funds, we cannot guarantee our readers regular delivery of the review." Once he had a large debt he could not pay. Praying before a statue of our Lady he noticed at her feet a sealed envelope. It contained the exact sum he needed to pay his bill and to continue his publication. At another time he was tempted in giving up the whole enterprise when an American friar visiting Poland was so impressed with his great dedication and humility that he gave him sufficient funds to buy his first press, which he and other Brothers ran by hand. It took sixty thousand turns of a wheel to print 5,000 copies of his review. They worked late into the night, their hands often bloody from bruises and blisters. After Father Kolbe took his turn he would retire to his room to work still later into the night editing the magazine.

From such a small, painful beginning, Father Maximilian built one of the most advanced religious printing plants in Europe by the end of the thirties. He was constantly supplementing his printing presses with new machines. The huge monastic complex, the "City of the Immaculate" had three rotary presses, one of which could print, bind and stitch a 144 page booklet. We must not forget that this was over sixty years ago in a country just emerging from an agrarian economy, and during the depression years of the late thirties.

The late Fr. Marion Wojcik, O.F.M. Conv, who edited the daily newspaper just before World War II writes, "Contrary to critics, who sought to deprecate the religious level of the City's publications. . . this Marian outpost was one of the causes of a strong religious revival in Poland after both the First and Second World Wars.

"Most Catholic periodicals in Poland at the time, because of their high scientific and literary level, did not reach the broad masses and thus had little influence on them. On the other hand, all the publications of the 'City,' from the *Knight* to the Little Journal were designed to reach the masses. They were read both by shepherd in the foothills of the Carpathian mountains and by university professor. Their directness and honest reporting appealed to both laborer and scholar."

Fr. Marion sums up the press of the "City:"

"The friars' printing establishment raised the religious consciousness of the broad masses of the Polish people, popularized the papal encyclicals and the pastoral letters of the Polish Bishops, roused the consciousness of duties toward the faith, charity and missions, gave answers to questions and objections of nonbelievers. The life of the Church was presented in a popular and attractive way. Above all the Franciscan's publications aroused confidence and love toward the Immaculate, Mediatrix of All Graces."

It would seem that the last line of this quote gives the key to St. Maximilian's great success as mass communications expert. He was thoroughly Catholic, subscribing to all that the Church teaches, including Mary's universal mediation. He did not talk over the heads of his readers. In his uncompromising presentation of the truth and unflinching loyalty to the Holy Father and the magisterium he aroused confidence and love towards Holy Mother, the Church. ❑

The large rotary press which the friars used to print their newspaper. At the height of production just prior to World War II, the Franciscans used the most modern presses to spread the word of God with over a dozen different publications.

St. Maximilian's Vision of Catholic Drama Realized

ST. MAXIMILIAN BELIEVED that all modern inventions and all means of mass communications should be marshaled to praise and worship God and win souls. He spoke of movies as an ideal media to be used in the apostolate. He was fully aware, even in the early days of the 20th century, of how movies were beginning to be used by the enemy as a corrupting influence on society. Rather than just bemoan the fact, he spoke of positive action to counteract the bad with the good, the true for the false and the beautiful for the ugly. He didn't live long enough to develop his dream of using drama to supplement his effective use of the printed word in the apostolate.

If St. Maximilian were alive today, he would surely be pleased by what is being done by a Catholic actor, Leonardo Defilippis, in using drama to evangelize. He has made St. Maximilian and other well known Saints live again in the minds and hearts of thousands through the monologues he has presented across the country, and even in Rome for the World Youth Day, 2000.

It all began some twenty years ago when, with great trust in the Blessed Mother, he started Saint Luke Productions, a professional Catholic drama group. Defilippis has many talents for the production and acting of one-man dramas, for the most part on the lives of the Saints and the Gospels. As a Catholic layman in a profession in which one hardly expects to find exemplary faith and total commitment to a religious ideal, Leonardo has succeeded where others have failed. His love of the Church and infectious apostolic zeal, however, were not always so.

He had spent six years acting in the Oregon Shakespeare festival, and admits, "I learned a great deal about acting, which I

Actor Leonardo Defillipis portrays Saint Maximilian Kolbe.

look upon as a providential preparation for my work today, but it was also a period of great culture shock. The deterioration of moral life in society was reflected particularly in the theatrical world." Helping an actress friend break a heroin addiction, he came to realize that he had to rely on God's help. "I started to pray again and read the Scriptures. I soon returned to the practice of the Catholic Faith of my youth."

From its beginnings twenty years ago, Saint Luke Productions cut across a culture so secularized and indifferent to human life that Pope John Paul II spoke of it as a "culture of death." Leonardo developed his first dramatic one-man show based on the first six chapters of the Gospel of St. Luke. This monologue and its sequel went over so well that he wrote and dramatized a production on St. Francis of Assisi, which he played to packed houses across the country. A television version was made, which won several awards.

About this time, a friend, Tony Ryan, the marketing director of Ignatius Press, interested him in doing a program on the newly canonized St. Maximilian Kolbe. Working closely with Fr. Peter Fehlner, a Franciscan priest and authority on the life and theology of the Saint, he produced an accurate and dramatic script. The Franciscans of Marytown, in Libertyville, Illinois, helped to subsidize the production of the play, which had its first showing at the Paramount Theatre in Denver for the World Youth Day in 1993.

With an imaginative and simple set, for easy transportation, and assisted by a sound and light technician, Leonardo went on the road. He has traversed the country many times since and has produced several video tapes which, along with his live presentations, have done much good in acquainting people with the Gospels of St. Luke and St. John, as well as St. Maximilian, St. John of the Cross, St. Francis of Assisi, St. Thérèse of Lisieux and the Confessions of St. Augustine.

The video on St. Maximilian has been aired countless times both in this country and abroad, winning numerous awards and wide acclaim. Still, the video doesn't quite compare to the one-man live play in which Defilippis, on stage, switches roles from Maximilian to a Nazi S.S. officer, Satan, Kolbe's superior, and the voice of a narrator. Throughout the action, one is reminded of Kolbe's great love of Mary Immaculate, by a haunting melody, "Who are you O Immaculate?" His wife Patti supplied the voice of Kolbe's mother.

From the beginning of his apostolic venture, Patti, who is an actress, has done much of the behind the scenes work, script writing, directing, etc. Besides her moral support, she is the mother of seven children, which she looks upon as a special blessing. In today's Church, husband and wife apostolic teams are not that uncommon, but the Defilippis couple goes one step further. They offer the technicians, actors and actresses who work with them the opportunity to grow in the Faith, as an extended "family." It is quite common to see the staff praying together on the set before and after their day's work. The enthusiasm and dedication of the couple help to explain how and why they have attracted so many young people to their work over the years. One of their actresses found her vocation to the religious life while working for them.

The first to join their "family" was Callie Cribbs, who had suffered burn out as an executive in a large corporation. She joined the Defilippises in their first office, located in the basement of their house, as a "part-time" employee. She has been a full-time employee ever since, bringing organizational skill, which has helped immeasurably in the growth of the apostolate. In the secularized world which surrounds them, this growing drama community,

Through St. Luke Productions, Leonardo intends to evangelize the culture and in particular that aspect of culture that has been taken over by the devil and his cohorts. He has involved and will do so even more in the future, young actors and actresses in this creative work. In his own words, "I believe that the involvement of young people is a central focus of the ministry of Saint Luke productions."

based as it is on prayer and sacrifice, and directed ultimately to spiritual growth, is stirring up a hurricane of fresh air.

The latest, and possibly most significant development at Saint Luke Communications is the beginnings of a film studio, Luke Films Inc. Its first full-length feature film is on St. Thérèse of Lisieux. The film developed out of a one-woman drama, Thérèse: Story of a Soul, performed by 19 year-old Maggie Mahrt. At this time it became clear that Saint Luke Productions was providing many young people with various talents an opportunity to use them in a wholesome atmosphere. It is a Heaven-sent answer to the prayer of concerned parents who have sons and daughters pursuing careers in drama.

Leonardo had at first decided to put the popular presentation of St. Thérèse on video. One thing led to another and he ended up planning his first full-length movie. Incidentally, the musical score was written by a Carmelite nun, Sr. Marie Therese Sokol, OCD, of the Seattle Carmelite Monastery. The dream of Defilippis of "forming a team of talented young artists, working together to produce a beautiful film that gives glory to God, is happening. . . I thank God for drawing all these dedicated people together to learn so much about the art of film making. We are building for the future here."

Leonardo's twenty years in producing theatre and video drama of high quality with deep spiritual messages will be shared with others, especially youth, in an important media, which has been too often misused and abused by the evil one. In his own words, he is hoping, through the generous support of others, "To expand this ministry, to include young actors and other artists who will create new videos, films and live dramas that glorify God with their loyalty to the Truths of Jesus Christ." His intent of evangelizing our culture through drama can be done, but not without much prayer and sacrifice. Let's hope that he receives the support he needs to expand this worthy apostolate and to do, as Mother Theresa wrote him, "something beautiful for the Lord."

For further information about this growing apostolate and an attractive Newsletter which has the schedule for the upcoming dramatizations throughout the country, as well as their video tapes contact: Saint Luke Productions, P.O. Box 761, Beaverton, OR 97075 (503) 641-1255.

"Who Would Dare Suppose?"

St. Maximilian Mary Kolbe, OFM Conv.

Who would dare to suppose, that you, O God Unending, Eternal One, loved me from all time, and even more than all time, since it is from the very moment that you are God - hence you loved me and love me always? . . . Even though I did not yet exist, You already loved me and precisely because You loved me, O Loving God, you brought me forth from nothingness into being. For me you created the heavens strewn with stars, for me the earth, seas, mountains, rivers and so many, many beautiful things on the face of this earth. . . .

But this was not enough: in order to show me close-up, how tenderly you love me, you came down from heaven with the purest of delight to this sullied and tear-stained earth, lived your life amidst poverty, pain and sorrow - until at last, despised and derided, you willed to be painfully strung up on the shamed gallows between two thieves... It is through such a terrible and highly sacrificial means that you redeemed me, O God of Love! . . .

Who would dare to suppose?

You did not however stop at this, but seeing that nineteen centuries would pass by, since these proofs of Your love poured themselves forth and that only then would I appear on this earth you even took that into account! [For] Your heart did not permit that I would be nourished only by the remembrance of Your great love. So You chose to remain on this lowly earth in the Most Holy and Wonderful Sacrament of the Altar and now come to me and unite Yourself with me - fully, because under the form of food. . . And now Your Blood flows in my blood, Your soul, O Incarnate God, permeates my soul, nourishes it and fortifies it.

O great wonder! Who would dare to suppose?

And what more could You have given me, O God, in giving me Yourself to have as my very own? . . . Your Heart burning with love for me directed You to grant me one more gift: yes, still one more gift! . . .You told us to become your children, if we wish to enter the Kingdom of heaven. And you know that a child needs a mother: You yourself established this rule of love. And so Your goodness and mercy creates for us a Mother - the personal embodiment of Your graciousness and Your boundless love - and from beneath the cross on Golgotha you give Her to us and us to Her ... And you are resolved, O God Who Loves us, that She should be for us a powerful Mediatrix of all Your graces and our Advocate - You will deny Her nothing, just as She is incapable of denying anything to anyone.

And so now, who can permit themselves to be condemned? Who cannot secure their heavenly reward? Perhaps that senseless, stubborn hater of his own self; who freely and consciously does not wish to be saved . . . and even from the best of Mother's flees and despises her mediation. . . Let us gaze into our own souls: is it not true that each time we have totally surrendered ourselves to the Mother of God and our Mother - the Immaculata - each time we have felt God's peace enter our hearts? . . . Is it not true, that when temptation struck us, and we have not in hope failed to flee to Mary, as children to a mother, and hold ourselves in Her embrace - that truly our will always found sure support, [and so] did not succumb?

Was this not the case? Whoever has yet to experience this, let him take a chance! Let him see, let himself be convinced, how powerful and how good is the Mother of God and our Mother. Yes and Our Mother ... our very own Mom

Truly, who would dare to suppose, if it were not the heart of faith and the clarity of our daily experience?

(Delivered at Niepokalanow, sometime before July 1929)
Translated from Polish by Fr. John P. Grigus, OFM Conv.

PART VI: THE PAPACY ON THE SAINT

"Apostle of the Cult of Mary" excerpts from the homily of Pope Paul VI at the Beatification

"Kolbe's Response to the Culture of Death" - Homily of Pope John Paul II at the Canonization Mass

"Love of Mary Central in Kolbe's Spiritual Life," Pope John Paul II's homily on December 8, 1982

St. Maximilian is "among the great Saints and clairvoyant minds that have understood, venerated and sung the mysteries of Mary." — Pope Paul VI

Right: The painting of the new Bl. Maximilian in the Window of Glory in St. Peter's. Below: During the beatification of Kolbe, the Second Synod of Bishops was still in session. Three hundred Bishops and 52 Cardinals were present at the ceremony. The pope set the new Blessed before this august assembly as a perfect modern day exemplar of the priesthood.

Pope Paul VI Speaks of Kolbe as . . .

An Apostle of the Cult of Mary

AT THE BEATIFICATION MASS, in which Pope Paul VI officiated and gave the homily on the new Blessed, he asked: "What does it mean to beatify one such as Maximilian Kolbe? It means that the Church recognizes in him an exceptional figure, a man in whom God's grace and his soul met in such a way as to produce a marvellous life. . . to the extent of reaching that extraordinary image of moral and spiritual greatness that we call holiness. . . ."

He went on to point out that besides recognizing that the Blessed is in heaven, the Church places the Blessed before us for imitation, even as St. Paul addressed the Christians of his time:

"I urge you then to be imitators of me, as I am of Christ...."

"Who is Maximilian Kolbe?" The Pope then gave a short summary of his life and added:

"Maximilian Kolbe was an apostle of the cult of the Blessed Virgin, seen in her first original privilege, as she defined herself at Lourdes: 'I am the Immaculate Conception.' It is impossible to separate the name, the activity and the mission of the Blessed Kolbe from that of Mary Immaculate. It was he who instituted the Militia of Mary Immaculate, here in Rome, even before he was ordained a priest on October 16, 1917....

"It is well known how the humble and meek Franciscan, with incredible audacity and extraordinary organizational genius, developed the initiative and made devotion to the Mother of Christ, contemplated as clothed with the sun (cfr. Apocalypse 12, 1) the focal point of his spirituality, his apostolate, his theology. Let no hesitation restrain our admiration, our adherence to this message that the new Blessed leaves to us as a heritage and as an example, as if we too were mistrustful of such a Marian exultation, on the grounds that two other theological and spiritual movements, prevalent in religious thought and life today, the christological and the ecclesiological movements, were in competition with the mariological one. There is no competition. Christ, in Kolbe's thought, holds not only the first place, but the only place necessary and sufficient, absolutely speaking, in the economy of salvation; nor is love of the Church and of her mission forgotten in the doctrinal conception or the apostolic aim of the new Blessed. On the contrary, it is precisely from her subordinated complementariness, with regard to Christ's cosmological, anthropological and soteriological plan, that the Blessed Virgin derives her every prerogative and greatness.

"Well we know it. And Kolbe, like the whole of Catholic doctrine, liturgy and spirituality, sees Mary inserted in the divine plan, as the 'fixed term of eternal counsel,' the fullness of grace, the seat of Wisdom, the predestined Mother of Christ, the queen of the messianic kingdom (Luke 1, 33), and at the same time the Lord's handmaid, the one chosen to offer the Incarnation of the Word her irreplaceable cooperation, as the Mother of the Man-God, our Savior. 'Mary is the One through whom men reach Jesus, and the One through whom Jesus reaches men' (L. Bouyer, Le trane de la Sagesse, p.69).

"Therefore our Blessed is not to be reproved, nor the Church with him, for enthusiasm for the cult of the Blessed Virgin. It will never equal the merit, nor the advantage of such a cult, precisely because of the mystery of communion that unites Mary with Christ, and which finds in the New Testament a fascinating documentation. The result will never be a 'mariolatry,' just as the sun will never be darkened by the moon; nor will the mission of salvation specifically entrusted to the ministry of the Church ever be distorted, if the latter honors in Mary an exceptional Daughter and a spiritual Mother.

"The characteristic aspect, if you like, but in itself not original, of the Blessed Kolbe's devotion, of his 'hyperdulia' to Mary, is the importance he attributes to it with regard to the present needs of the Church, the efficacy of her prophecy about the glory of the Lord and the vindication of the humble, the power of her intercession, the splendor of her exemplariness, the presence of her maternal charity. The Council confirmed us in these certainties, and now from heaven Father Kolbe is teaching us and helping us to meditate upon them and live them.

"This Marian aspect of the new Blessed qualifies him and classifies him among the great saints and seers who have understood, venerated and sung the mystery of Mary. . . ."

Excerpted from the homily of Pope Paul VI given at the beatification Mass of Father Maximilian Kolbe taken from the complete text as it appeared in the English edition of L'OSSERVATORE ROMANO, October 28, 1971.

Pope John Paul II's Canonization Homily

"Greater love has no man than this, that a man lay down his life for his friends"(Jn.15:13)

FROM TODAY on, the Church desires to address as "Saint" a man who was granted the grace of carrying out these words of the Redeemer in an absolutely literal manner. For towards the end of July 1941, when the camp commander ordered the prisoners destined to die of starvation to fall in line, this man- Maximilian Maria Kolbe-spontaneously came forward and declared himself ready to go to death in the place of one of them. His offer was accepted and, after more than two weeks of torment by starvation, Father Maximilian's life was ended with a lethal injection on August 14, 1941.

All this happened in the concentration camp at Auschwitz where during the last war some four million people were put to death, including the Servant of God, Edith Stein [the Carmelite nun, Sr. Teresa Benedicta of the Cross who was canonized in 1998]. Disobedience to God - the Creator of life who said, "Thou shalt not kill"- was to cause in that place of an immense holocaust of so many innocent persons. And so our age has thus been horribly stigmatized by the slaughter of the innocent. Fr. Maximilian Kolbe, himself a prisoner, defended in that place of death an innocent man's right to life, declaring that he was ready to go to death in the place of the condemned, because he was a father of a family and his dear ones needed him. Fr. Maximilian Maria Kolbe thus reaffirmed the Creator's exclusive right over innocent human life. He bore witness to Christ and to love. For the Apostle John writes: "By this we know love, that He laid down his life for us. And we ought to lay down our lives for the brethren" (1 Jn 3:16).

The Church has venerated Father Maximilian as "Blessed" since 1971. By laying down his life for a brother, he became like Christ. Gathered today before the Basilica of St. Peter in Rome, we wish to express the special value which the death by martyrdom of Fr. Maximilian Kolbe has in the eyes of God. "Precious in the sight of the Lord is the death of his saints." These are the words we have repeated in today's responsorial psalm. It is truly precious and inestimable! Through the death which Christ underwent on the Cross, the redemption of the world was achieved, for this death has the value of supreme love. Through the death of Fr. Maximilian Kolbe, a shining sign of this love was renewed in our century which is so seriously and in so many ways threatened by sin and death.

In this canonization liturgy there seems to appear before us that "martyr of love" of Oswiecim (as Paul VI called him), saying: "O Lord, I am thy servant. I am thy servant, the son of thy handmaid. Thou has loosed my bonds" (Ps 115 (116):16). And as though gathering together in one sacrifice the whole of his life, he - a priest and a spiritual son of St. Francis - seems to say: "What shall I render to the Lord for his goodness to me? I will lift up the cup of salvation and call on the name of the Lord" (Ps. 115 (116):12).

These are words of gratitude. Death undergone out of love - in the place of one's brother - is a heroic act of man. It is an act through which, together with the one already beatified, we glorify God. For from God comes the grace of such heroism, of this martyrdom. Therefore let us today glorify God's great work in man. Before all of us gathered here, Fr. Maximilian Kolbe lifts up his "cup of salvation." In it is contained the sacrifice of his whole life, sealed with a martyr's death "for a brother."

Maximilian prepared for this definitive sacrifice by following Christ from the first years of his life in Poland. From these years comes the mysterious vision of two crowns-one white and one red. From these our saint does not choose. He accepts both. From the years of his youth, in fact, Maximilian was filled with a great love of Christ and the desire for martyrdom.

This love and this desire accompanied him along the path of his Franciscan and priestly vocation, for which he prepared himself both in Poland and in Rome. This love and this desire followed him through all the places of his priestly and Franciscan service in

Poland and in his missionary service in Japan.

The inspiration of his whole life was the Immaculata. To her he entrusted his love for Christ and his desire for martyrdom. In the mystery of the Immaculate Conception was revealed before the eyes of his soul that marvelous and supernatural world of God's grace offered to man. The faith and works of the whole life of Father Maximilian show that he thought of his cooperation with divine grace as a warfare under the banner of the Immaculate Conception. This Marian characteristic is particularly expressive in the life and holiness of Father Kolbe. His whole apostolate, both in his homeland and in the missions, was similarly marked with this sign. In Poland and in Japan the centers of this apostolate were the special cities of the Immaculata- Niepokalanow in Poland and *Mugenzai no Sono* in Japan.

What happened in the starvation bunker in the concentration camp at Auschwitz on August 14, 1941? The reply is given in today's liturgy. "God tested" Maximilian Maria "and found him worthy of himself" (Wis 3:5). God tested him "like gold in the furnace and like a sacrificial burnt offering he accepted him" (Wis 3:6). Even if "in the sight of men he was punished," yet "his hope is full of immortality." For "the souls of the righteous are in the hands of God and no torment will ever touch them." And when - humanly speaking - torment and death came to them, when "in the eyes of men they seemed to have died. . .when their departure from us was thought to be an affliction . . . they are in peace." They experience life and glory "in the hands of God" (Wis 3:1-4).

This life is the fruit of death like Christ's death. Glory is the sharing of his Resurrection.

So what happened in the starvation bunker on August 14, 1941? There were fulfilled the words spoken by Christ to the Apostles that they "should go and bear fruit and that their fruit should abide" (Jn. 15:16). In a marvelous way the fruit of the tragic death of Maximilian Kolbe endures in the Church and the world!

Men saw what happened in the camp at Auschwitz. And even if to their eyes it must have seemed that a companion of their torment had "died," even if humanly speaking they could consider "his departure" as "a disaster," nevertheless in their minds this was not simply "death."

Maximilian did not die but "gave his life. . . for his brother." In that death, terrible from the human point of view, there was the whole definitive greatness of the human act and of the human choice. He spontaneously offered himself up to death out of love. And in this human death of his there was the clear witness borne to Christ: the witness borne in Christ to the dignity of man, to the sanctity of his life, and to the saving power of death in which the power of love is made manifest.

Precisely for this reason the death of Maximilian Kolbe became a sign of victory. This was victory won over all systematic contempt and hatred of man and for what is divine in man - a victory like that won by our Lord Jesus Christ on Calvary.

"You are my friends if you do what I command you" (Jn 15:14).

The Church accepts this sign of victory - won through the power of Christ's redemption -with reverence and gratitude. She seeks to discern its eloquence with all humility and love. As ever when the Church proclaims the holiness of her sons and daughters, as also in the present case, she seeks to act with all due exactness and responsibility, searching into all the aspects of the life and death of the Servant of God. Yet at the same time the Church must be careful, as she reads the sign of holiness given by God in His earthly Servant, not to allow its full eloquence and definitive meaning to go unnoticed.

And so, in judging the cause of St. Maximilian Kolbe even after his Beatification, it was necessary to take into consideration the many voices of the People of God - especially of our Brothers in the episcopate of both Poland and Germany - who asked that Maximilian Kolbe be proclaimed as a martyr saint.

Before the eloquence of the life and death of Bl.. Maximilian, it is impossible not to recognize what seems to constitute the main and essential element of the sign given by God to the Church and the world in his death. Does not this death - faced spontaneously, for love of man - constitute a particular fulfillment of the words of Christ?

Does not this death make Maximilian particularly like unto Christ - the Model of all Martyrs - who gives his own life on the Cross for his brethren?

Does not this death possess a particular and penetrating eloquence for our age? And so, in virtue of my apostolic authority, I have decreed that Maximilian Maria Kolbe - who after his Beatification was venerated as a Confessor - shall henceforward be venerated also as a Martyr!

"Precious in the eyes of the Lord is the death of his faithful ones!" Amen.

Members of the College of Cardinals and other hierarchical leaders flanked the altar on which the Mass of Canonization was celebrated. Pilgrims from all over the world filled St. Peter's square.

Presenting the offertory gifts from the Conventual Franciscans of North America are Bro. Raphael Ruffelo (center) and Fr. James McCurry. At that time Brother was Superior of Mayrtown and Father James was the National Director of the Militia Immaculatae in North America.

Pope John Paul II venerating the spot in the death bunker where St. Maximilian Kolbe was martyred. Whenever he is in the vicinity of Auschwitz, Poland he pays tribute to Kolbe and the many millions who died in the death Camp.

Above: The procession of priests for the distribution of Holy Communion at the Mass of Canonization. Below: A pilgrimage group from the United States waves to the photographer in St. Peter's Square, prior to the canonization ceremony.

'Hail, Full of Grace, the Lord is with Thee" (Lk 1, 28)

Pope John Paul II points out -
Love of Mary Central in Kolbe's Spiritual Life

AS THESE WORDS of greeting of the Angel re-echo sweetly in our soul, I wish with the spiritual eye of St. Maximilian Mary Kolbe to turn my glance, together with you, dear Brothers and Sisters, to the mystery of the Immaculate Conception of the Blessed Virgin Mary. St. Maximilian bound all the works of his life and his very vocation to the Immaculate. . . Love of the Immaculate, in fact, was the center of his spiritual life, the fruitful principle animating his apostolic activity. The sublime model, who is the Immaculate, enlightened and guided his entire existence on the pathways of this world and made of his heroic death in the Auschwitz death camp a splendid Christian and sacradotal witness. With the intuition of the Saint and the subtlety of the theologian, Maximilian Kolbe pondered with extraordinary acumen the mystery of the Immaculate Conception of Mary in the light of Sacred Scripture, the Magisterium and Liturgy of the Church, finding therein wondrous lessons for life. He has appeared in our times as prophet and apostle of a new "Marian era," destined to shread splendor throughout the world on Jesus Christ and His Gospel.

This mission which he promoted with such ardor and dedication "classifies him", as Pope Paul VI affirmed in the homily for his beatification, "among the great Saints and discerning spirits who have understood, venerated and sung the mystery of Mary" (Insegnamenti di Paolo VI, IX, 1971, p. 909). Though aware of the inexhaustible depths of the mystery of the Immaculate Conception, for which "human language is simply inadequate to describe her who has become Mother of God" (Gli Scritti di Massimiliano

Kolbe, eroe di Oswiecjm e Beato della Chiesa, 3 vols. Florence, Citta di Vita, 1975, III, p. 690), nonetheless his greatest sorrow was that the Immaculate was not sufficiently known and loved after the example of Jesus Christ and as the Tradition of the Church and example of the Saints teach. In loving Mary, in fact, we honor God who has raised her to the dignity of Mother of his very own Son made Man and we unite ourselves to Jesus Christ who has loved her precisely as His Mother. We will never love her as much as He loved her:

> *"Jesus was the first to honor her as His very Mother and we must imitate Him also in this. We will never, as much as we try, love her with a love equal to that with which Jesus loved her" (Ibid. II, p. 351). Love for Mary, says St. Maximilian, is the simplest and easiest way to sanctify ourselves, in realizing our Christian vocation. The love of which he speaks is not a certain superficial sentimentalism, but a generous commitment, a donation of the whole person, as he himself demonstrated with his life of gospel fidelity concluded by his heroic death.*

The attention of St. Maximilian Kolbe was constantly focused on the Immaculate Conception of Mary so as to mine the wondrous riches embedded in that Name which she herself revealed and which constitutes the explanation of what today's Gospel teaches us in the words of the Angel Gabriel: "Hail, Full of Grace, the Lord is with Thee" (Lk 1, 28). Referring to the apparitions of Lourdes, which for him were a stimulus and incentive to understand better the sources of Revelation, St. Maximilian observes:

> *"To St Bernadette, who had asked her many times, the Virgin replied: 'I am the Immaculate Conception.' In these words she made clear that she was not merely conceived without sin, but that she is the very 'Immaculate Conception', just as it is one thing to be a white object and another to be whiteness itself, to be something perfect and to be perfection itself" (Ibid., III, p. 516). Immaculate Conception is the Name which reveals with exactitude who Mary is: not asserting merely a quality, but delineating precisely her Person. Mary is radically holy in the totality of Her existence, from its very beginning.*

Such transcendent supernatural greatness was granted Mary in view of Jesus Christ. It is in Him and through Him that God made her participate in the fullness of grace: Mary is Immaculate because she is to be the Mother of God and she becomes Mother of God because she is Immaculate, so Maximilian Kolbe neatly recapitulates. The Immaculate Conception of Mary uniquely and sublimely reveals the absolute centrality and universal salvific role of Jesus Christ. "From the divine Maternity flow all the graces conceded to the Most Holy Virgin Mary and the first of these is the Immaculate Conception" (Ibid. III, p. 475). For this reason Mary is not simply in the same condition as Eve before the fall, but was enriched with an incomparable fullness of grace because she is the Mother of Christ. Her Immaculate Conception was the beginning of a prodigious, uninterrupted growth in her supernatural life.

The mystery of Mary's holiness must be contemplated in the context of the divine economy of salvation in order to be venerated in balanced fashion and not appear as a kind of privilege which divorces her from the Church which is the Body of Christ. Father Maximilian was especially careful to link the Immaculate Conception of Mary and her role in the plan of salvation to the mystery of the Trinity, in particular to the person of the Holy Spirit. With geniality and depth of insight he developed various aspects of the title "Spouse of the Holy Spirit," aspects well known to the patristic and theological tradition and suggested by the New Testament:

> *"The Holy Spirit shall come upon thee, and the power of the Most High shall overshadow thee; and therefore the Holy One to be born shall be called Son of God" (Lk 1, 35). It is an analogy St. Maximilian Kolbe insists, which enables one to perceive the ineffable, intimate and fecund union between the Holy Spirit and Mary. "The Holy Spirit made his own dwelling in Mary from the first moment of her existence, took such absolute possession of her and so impregnated her very being that the name Spouse of the Holy Spirit expresses but a faint shadow, pallid and imperfect, of the reality of that union" (Ibid. III, p. 515).*

Studying with ecstatic admiration the divine plan of salvation, whose origin is the Father who freely willed to communicate to creatures the divine life of Jesus Christ revealed wondrously in Mary Immaculate, Father Kolbe, enthralled and enraptured, exclaims: "Everywhere is love" (Ibid. III, p. 690). The gratuitous love of God is the answer to all doubt. "God is love", says St. John (I Jn 4, 8). All that exists is the reflex of the free love of God, and so every creature, in some way, reflects its infinite splendor. In particular, love is the center and vertex of the human person, made in the image and likeness of God. Mary Immaculate, the highest and most perfect of human persons, eminently reproduces the image of God and therefore is made able to love God with incomparable intensity as the Immaculate, without deviations or hesitation. She is the unique Handmaid of the Lord (cf. Lk 1, 38) who with her free and personal Fiat responds to the love of God doing always what he asks.

Like that of every other creature hers is not an autonomous response, but is a grace and gift of God. In that response is involved all her freedom, the freedom of the Immaculate. "In the union of the Holy Spirit with Mary love unites not only these two Persons, but the first love is all the love of the Most Holy Trinity, while the second, that of Mary, is all the love of creation and so in that union Heaven is united to earth, the whole of uncreated Love with the whole of created love. . . This is the vertex of love" (Ibid. III p. 758).

The circularity of love, whose origin is the Father and which in the response of Mary returns to its source, is a characteristic and fundamental aspect of the mariology of Father Kolbe. This is a principle at the base of his Christian anthropology, of his vision of history and of the spiritual life of every man. Mary Immaculate is archetype and fullness of every creaturely love. Her limpid and most intense love for God encloses in its perfection that fragile and defective love of all other creatures. Mary's response is that of all mankind.

None of this obscures, nor does it lessen the absolute centrality of Jesus Christ in the order of salvation, but illuminates and vigorously proclaims it, because Mary receives all her greatness from Him. As the history of the Church teaches, the role of Mary is that of making resplendent her own Son, of leading all to Him and helping all to accept Him.

The continuous deepening, theologically, of the Mystery of Mary became for Maximilian Kolbe the font and motive of unconditional dedication and extraordinary dynamism. He truly knew how to incorporate the truth into life, above all because he had attained like all the Saints the acquaintance of Mary not only in reflection guided by faith, but especially in prayer: "Who is unable to bend his knees and implore of Mary in humble prayer the grace to know who She really is has no hope of learning anything much about her" (Ibid. III, 474).

And now, gathered in this splendid Basilica for the Eucharist in honor of the Immaculate Conception and heeding that final exhortation of the heroic son of Poland and herald of Marian devotion, we bend our knees before Her Icon and we insistently repeat with that ardor and filial piety so distinctive of St. Maximilian the words of the Angel: "Hail, Full of Grace, the Lord is with Thee". Amen.

Homily of Pope John Paul II during the Holy Mass in the Basilica of St. Mary Major, Dec. 8, 1982, the year of the canonization of St. Maximilian Kolbe (Translated from the Italian L'Osservatore Romano, Dec. 9-19, 1982).

Our Lady of the Blessed Sacrament Chapel at Marytown, Libertyville, Illinois. The interior and exterior view of the Chapel, where the friars have Perpetual Eucharistic Adoration — something St. Maximilian dreamed of having someday at the "City of the Immaculate."

St. Maximilian, Franciscan, indicated by the Franciscan coat of arms, priest with surplice and stole, Mass communication expert, with his two main publications, the KNIGHT, one in Polish, the other in Japanese.

PART VII: APPENDIX

Important Biographic Dates

1894 January 8: Raymond is born at Zdunska Wola, the second son of Julius and Marianne (Dabrowska) Kolbe, baptized the same day and given the name of Raymond.

1902 June 29: Raymond receives his First Holy Communion at St. Matthew Church, Pabianice.

1907 August 18: During a parish mission given by a Franciscan Fr. Peregrine Haczela, OFM Conv., Raymond and has brother Francis decide to enter the seminary of the Conventual Franciscans in Lwow.

1910 September 4: Raymond receives the Franciscan habit and the name, Maximilian, at the novitiate in Lwow.

1911 September 5: Friar Maximilian profcsscs his first, "simplc" vows at the novitiate in the hands of the Father Provincial, Fr. Peregrine Haczela.

1912 November: Friar Maximilian is sent to the Order's international seminary in Rome, and begins his study of philosophy at the Jesuit Gregorian University.

1913 Marianne Kolbe enters and lives as a tertiary Oblate in the Felician Sisters' Motherhouse in Krakow, where she died in 1946, aged 76.

1914 Julius Kolbe joins the Polish Army to fight for the liberation of Poland from Russian rule during World War I, is captured by the Russians and is executed as a traitor due to his Russian citizenship. November 1, Friar Maximilian professes his final, "solemn" vows of poverty, chastity and obedience in the Order's seminary in Rome.

1915 October 22: Friar Maximilian earns his doctorate in philosophy from the Gregorian University and begins his study of theology in the Pontifical Faculty of St. Bonaventure.

1917 January 20: Fr. Rector related the story of the miraculous conversion of the Jew, Alphonse Ratisbonne. Friar Maximilian resolves to establish a Marian movement, using the Medal of the Immaculate Conception (commonly known as the Miraculous Medal) as a insignia means for evangelization in his movement.

1917 October 16: Friar Maximilian establishes the Militia of the Immaculate with six other student friars of the Order's seminary. The same year, during a ball game, Friar Maximilian suffers his first hemorrhage, indicating tuberculosis.

1918 April 28: Friar Maximilian is ordained a priest by Cardinal Basil Pompilii, in the Church of Sant' Andrea della Valle in Rome. The same year, April 29: Fr. Maximilian celebrates his first Mass in the Church of Sant' Andrea delle Fratte at the very altar where Our Lady appeared to Alphonse Ratisbonne in 1842.

1919 April 4: Fr. Dominic Tavani, Vicar General of the Order, blesses and confirms the M.I. in writing. July 22: Fr. Maximilian obtains his doctorate in theology and is assigned to teach at the Order's seminary in Krakow. On August 10: Fr Maximilian leaves Krakow for treatment of tuberculosis in the Tatra Mountain village of Zakopane and carries on a fruitful apostolate, converting a number of patients.

He is discharged on April 28, 1921.

1922 January 2: The M.I. is approved in Rome as a "Pious Union" by Cardinal Basil Pompilii, Vicar General of the Archdiocese of Rome. January: The first issue of the Knight of the Immaculate is printed with a press run of 5,000 copies. October 20: Fr. Maximilian is transferred to the friary of Grodno, where he continues as editor, with the help of two brothers.

1926 September 18: He returns to Zakopane for treatment and remains until April 13, 1927. Pope Pius Xl sends his personal blessing to the movement of Kolbe's, the Militia Immaculatae, and grants indulgences to the M.I. which is canonically erected in the International Seraphic College in Rome.

1927 Fr. Maximilian makes arrangement with Fr. Ciborowski, the pastor of Adamowice, and agent of Prince Drucki-Lubecki, to examine the possibility of obtaining land from the prince for a new friary and publishing house near Warsaw. August 6: Fr. Maximilian blesses the statue of the Immaculate on the grounds of the future friary at Teresin, near Warsaw, and building begins soon after. November 21: Fr. Maximilian and his brothers move their printing machines from Grodno to the new location. It is now known as the "City of the Immaculate" (Niepokalanow).

December 7: The Minister Provincial, Fr. Cornelius Czupryk, blesses the new foundation, which consists of two priests and eighteen professed brothers. Fr. Maximilian is named the first guardian (superior).

1929 June 2: The Minister Provincial gives permission for the establishment of a minor seminary in Niepokalanow, which opens three months later.

1930 February 26: After a preparatory pilgrimage to European shrines, Fr. Maximilian, with four Brothers, sets out for Japan to found another "City of the Immaculate."

April 24,they arrive in Nagasaki, where Bishop Hayasaka permits them to publish a magazine on the condition that Fr. Kolbe teach philosophy and theology at his seminary.

May 24: One month after their arrival the first issue of the Japanese Knight, Seibo no Kishi, is published with a press run of 10,000 copies. The friars rent a house near the cathedral.

June and July, Fr. Maximilian returns to Poland to attend the Provincial Chapter.

July 24, he is appointed superior of the Japanese mission and his brother, Alphonse, appointed the guardian (superior) of Niepokalanow.

December 3: Fr. Alphonse Kolbe, the superior of the "City" and blood brother of Fr. Maximilian, dies in a Warsaw hospital.

1931 March 4: Fr. Maximilian purchases land for a new friary in the poor district of Nagasaki-Hongochi at the base of Mt. Hikosan.

May 16, the friars move to the new facility, which is named *Mugenzai no Sono* (Garden of the Immaculate).

1932 May to July: Fr. Maximilian goes to India, to arrange for another "City."

1933 April to May: He returns to Poland for the Provincial Chapter after a stopover of three weeks in Rome.

July 17-20, he attends the Provincial Chapter in Krakow, during which his ex-provincial and good friend, Fr. Cornelius, is named superior of the Japanese mission. August, they return to Japan.

1936 April 16: A minor seminary is opened in the Japanese "Garden of the Immaculate."

May and June: Fr. Maximilian leaves Japan for good, returning for the Provincial Chapter in Poland where he is appointed guardian of Niepokalanow on July 16. The following December 8, at the urging of Fr. Maximilian the Conventual Franciscan Order is consecrated to Mary Immaculate.

1937 January and February: He travels to Italy to reorganize the M.I. there and help celebrate the twentieth anniversary of his Militia Immaculatae (M.I.).

1938 February: He publishes the first issue of the Miles Immaculatae, (Knight of the Immaculate) a quarterly in Latin to propagate the M.I. among the clergy.

December 8: The Friars inaugurate their radio station with a sermon by Fr. Maximilian.

1939 May 22: He travels to Lithuania for a possible City of the Immaculate there.

September 1: Poland is invaded by Nazi Germany and the 772 professed and candidates of the "City" are allowed to leave for their own safety.

September 19: Fr. Maximilian is arrested for the first time with thirty-five brothers.

December 8, Fr. Maximilian and the friars are set free and return the next day to Niepokalanow.

1940 November 21: After several requests Fr. Maximilian is allowed to publish one issue of the Knight of the Immaculate with a press run of 120,000 copies, dated December, 1940.

1941 February 17: He is arrested on and taken to the Pawiak Prison in Warsaw by the Gestapo where he is cruelly treated.

May 28: Fr. Maximilian is transported in a trainload of prisoners to Oswiecim (Auschwitz).

July 28 - August 1: During this five-day period Fritsch, the Commandant, sentences ten prisoners from Block 14 to death by starvation in retaliation for an escaped prisoner from their block. Fr. Maximilian's offers to die in place of one of the condemned, Francis Gajowniczek. The ten condemned are placed in the underground bunker of Block 13.

August 14: Fr. Maximilian is killed by an injection of lethal acid in his arm, which he lifts up to his murderer.

August 15: His body is cremated and his ashes scattered as he predicted.

1960 The apostolic process begins in Padua, Italy and continues for three years.

1971 June 14: The two miracles attributed to Ven. Maximilian are confirmed by Pope Paul VI.

October 17: Pope Paul VI proclaims the Confessor, "Blessed" at Peter's in Rome.

1982 October 10: Pope John Paul II, before a large crowd in St. Peter's square, declares the Blessed, Saint Maximilian Maria Kolbe, a martyr of charity. ❑

Niepokalanow with a large ornate Basilica of the Immaculate Conception predominating the scene. It was built shortly after the end of World War II. It is one of the most popular pilgrim shrines in all of Poland. The friars still carry on with the printing apostolate and publish the *Knight* magazine which St. Maximilian founded in 1922 (see page 53).

Why Was Saint Maximilian Opposed to Freemasonry?

By Bro. Charles Madden OFM Conv.

When Saint Maximilian founded his Militia of the Immaculata (MI) he specifically included the conversion of Freemasons in the daily prayer to be recited by MI members. In his writings he also referred to the Freemasons as the "head of the serpent" which Mary's heel would crush. Why? What is Freemasonry all about? Often people consider it to be merely a fraternity, many of whose members are Protestants, that performs humanitarian works, and indeed this is true to a great extent.

However, in reality Freemasonry is a form of religion, which in both belief and practice promotes religious indifference in the guise of religious tolerance while at its very core is against both Christianity and Judaism. Although there isn't space to go into the history and origins of Freemasonry, let it be said that elements of it trace back to the medieval stonemason guilds, the suppressed Knights Templar of the early 1300's, and occultic elements having yearnings of returning back to the so-called "ancient wisdom" of the pagan polytheistic religions of Persia, Egypt, Greece, etc. These same pagan nations persecuted the Jews for their belief in monotheism, i.e., the belief in the One True God.

In 1717 the form of Freemasonry which exists today was formed by four lodges in England. They established themselves in a more public and less secret manner. This new more public form of Freemasonry rapidly spread from Protestant England to the European continent, including Catholic nations such as Spain, France, and Italy. The Continental lodges quickly showed themselves to be anti-Christian with an especially anti-Catholic twist. That emphasis was not so apparent in England as there were so few Catholics there. This has led to the mistaken belief common today that somehow English Freemasonry---and by extension American Freemasonry since it came from England---was fundamentally different from European Freemasonry.

About twenty years later, in 1738, Pope Clement XII issued the first of the Catholic Church's many condemnations of Freemasonry. His successors right up to the present time have done likewise. In the same decade the Protestant governments in Holland and Sweden, and the city of Geneva, Switzerland banned Freemasonry.

One of the best expositions on the dangers of Freemasonry is to be found in the encyclical Humanum Genus issued by Pope Leo XIII in 1884. Here are some of the salient points of that encyclical:

1) The lodges of Freemasonry are secret societies whose members hold mysteries which were hidden even from many of their own members.

2) All members take severe blood oaths swearing that whatever they know now or learn in the future will never be revealed to non-members and swear always to obey their leaders. These blood oaths bind under penalty of mutilation and death.

3) Their ultimate purpose is "...the utter overthrow of that whole religious and political order of the world which the Christian teaching has produced, and the substitution of a new state of things in accordance with their ideas, of which the foundations and laws shall be drawn from mere 'Naturalism.'" (Pope Leo goes on to define Naturalism as a system of belief that makes human nature and human reason supreme in all things and denies that anything has been revealed or taught by God, or that there is any teaching authority established by God.)

4) Freemasonry intends that "...the office and authority of the Church may become of no account in the civil state; and for this same reason they declare to the people and contend that Church and State ought to be altogether disunited. By this means they reject from the laws and the

commonwealth the wholesome influence of the Catholic religion."

5) Freemasonry not only wants to hinder the work of the Church and destroy the papacy but also intends to undermine all religion "...that a regard for religion should be held as an indifferent matter, and that all religions are alike. This manner of reasoning is calculated to bring about the ruin of all forms of religion." This in turn would undermine belief in the existence of God, negate Christian morality based on the Ten Commandments, lead to the denial of the consequences of Original Sin, and finally would lead to considering what was once portrayed as sin as no longer evil but even good.

6) Freemasonry promotes laws undermining the sanctity of marriage and encouraging the total secularization of education which, in turn, leads to the undermining of all lawful government authority.

7) Freemasonry also promotes, in various guises, a revival of the ancient Mid-East polytheistic pagan religions and their so-called "ancient wisdom."

8) In the political sphere they would cooperate with Socialists and Communists in their attempts to overthrow established governments everywhere.

That was Pope Leo XIII's analysis. Now let us see what Freemasons say about themselves. They still say that they are members of a secret society and still conceal their mysteries -- even from many of their own members -- and also still bind themselves by blood oaths. The quotes below are taken from the book Morals and Dogma by Albert Pike, the most renowned Mason of nineteenth century America. It was he who lifted Freemasonry in America from the doldrums in the aftermath of the anti-Masonic crusade of Protestant ministers in the 1830's. His book is still one of the most respected of Masonic authorities and can be found in most Masonic lodge libraries. Pike wrote the following:

1) "Masonry, like all Religions, all the Mysteries, Hermeticism, and Alchemy, conceals its secrets from all except the Adepts and Sages, or the Elect, and uses false

explanations and misinterpretations of its symbols to mislead those who deserve only to be misled; to conceal the Truth, which it calls Light, from them, and to draw them away from it. Truth is not for those who are unworthy or unable to receive it, or would pervert it. So God himself incapacitates many men, by color blindness, to distinguish colors, and leads the masses away from the highest Truth, giving them power to attain only so much of it as it is profitable for them to know. Every age has a religion suited to its capacity." (p. 104).

2) "Secrecy is indispensable in a Mason of whatever Degree. It is the first and almost the only lesson taught to the Entered Apprentice." (p. 109).

3) "The Blue Degrees [the first three Degrees, which most members never go beyond -- Ed.] are but the outer court or portico of the Temple. Part of the symbols are displayed there to the Initiate, but he is intentionally misled by false interpretations. It is not intended that he shall understand them; but it is intended that he shall imagine he understands them. Their true explication is reserved for the Adepts, the Princes of Masonry...It is well enough for the mass of those called Masons, to imagine that all is contained in the Blue Degrees." (p. 819).

A man entering the very first degree of Freemasonry is assured that nothing he swears to in his first degree oath will conflict with his religious or personal beliefs, yet he is immediately led, phrase by phrase, through a terrible blood oath never to reveal the secrets of the lodge, "...binding myself under no less penalty than that of having my throat cut from ear to ear, my tongue torn out by its roots, and buried in the sands of the sea...." This is a real oath sworn while one's hand is on the Bible or Torah, etc. (Some claim that this oath is not meant seriously, but one should never swear on the Bible, which is calling on God to witness to the truth of what we say, if we do not mean it! The oath, meant or not, is a blasphemous use of the Bible). It should be noted that in the old pagan religions blood oaths were also used to conceal secrets and rituals.

Pope Leo XIII, as mentioned above, warned that not only did Masonry seek to undermine all forms of religion and morality but also that it would abet communist and socialist revolutionaries. This came true within thirty years of his death in 1903. Most of the nations of Europe at that time were under the influence of Masonic governments. Then after World War I Communism, Fascism, and Nazism ran rampant through Europe. Nazism, for example, was an occult religion seeking to restore pre-Christian paganism to Germany. Another example of the political aspect was the exposure in 1981 of the Masonic P2 Lodge plot against the Italian government. In Italy, unlike America, magistrates undertake investigations of crimes. It is clear from the report issued by the investigating magistrate that this plot was a sustained effort by the P2 Lodge to control the Italian government.

What is the Catholic Church's position on Freemasonry today? In the 1960's and 1970's confusion arose concerning Freemasonry due to the lifting of some Church penalties and a

Freemasonry - a Paragon of Tolerance? ? ?

In our country, over a long period of time, Freemasonry has had a devastating influence in reinterpreting the U.S. Constitution such as to remove systematically or to restrict religion (particularly Christianity) and religious influence in many institutions of our society. For three decades, 1940-1970, the U.S. Supreme Court was dominated by Freemasons, and it was during this period that so many court decisions inimical to religion were written.

One of the great ironies of this period is that many laws and practices directed against black Americans were struck down by a Supreme Court, most of whose members belonged to Freemasonry, which explicitly excludes blacks! Separate and unequal is the watchword for Freemasonry. While there is the Prince Hall system of Masonry for blacks, it is not considered authentic. Freemasonry's support for the Ku Klux Klan is almost forgotten today, yet these two racist and anti-Catholic secret societies worked hand-in-glove for years.

- Bro. Charles Madden, OFM Conv.

misguided form of ecumenism in some quarters. This resulted in some Catholics joining the Masons with the approval of their pastors. However, when the new Code of Canon Law was issued in 1983, the Holy See clarified the canon on secret societies, in which the Masons are no longer mentioned by name, by stating clearly that membership in the Masons is forbidden to all Catholics everywhere, and that to do so is a serious sin which automatically denies Holy Communion to anyone who joins the lodge. This clarification was ordered at the direction of Pope John Paul II. Local ordinaries may not make exception to this rule. In 1985 the U.S. Bishops also declared that Freemasonry is irreconcilable with Catholicism.

It is important to note also that many Protestant denominations, despite the presence of many Protestants within Masonry, have condemned membership in the lodge. Lutherans, American and Scottish Presbyterians, Quakers, Mennonites, some Baptists, the Church of England, the Assemblies of God, and others as well have taken this stance.

Another aspect of Freemasonry is its close affinity with the New Age movement. The book New Age Youth and Masonry, written in 1972 by Lynn Perkins, clearly makes the links between the two movements. Structurally they are poles apart. Masonry is highly, rigidly structured while the New Age movement seems to have no organization to it. One can safely say that the New Age movement is in some ways an outgrowth of Freemasonry. What are some of the elements common to both movements? Both seek "Light". When all is said and done that "Light" turns out to be Lucifer. Both deny the existence of divinely revealed religion. Both denigrate Sacred Scripture by denying its inerrancy and its divine inspiration, and consider the Scriptures as merely a collection of ancient sacred books written by men. Both deny the divinity of Jesus Christ and His role as Savior and Redeemer, and that He ever established a Church. Both promote hidden "ancient wisdom" which can be gleaned from the ancient pagan religions of the East. Both promote astrology and reincarnation. Both have elements of Gnosticism with its elitist mentality and the lure of secret knowledge and wisdom (which not everyone should be privy to) at the core of their beliefs. Ultimately both movements can lead into the worship of Lucifer, although the vast majority of members of both movements do not realize this.

Let us look at two of these elements common to both movements. Belief in reincarnation is quite popular today. It is an integral part of the New Age movement and it is clearly important to Freemasonry. J.D. Buck, who was a 32-degree Mason, and a still well respected Masonic author from the 1920's, wrote the following in his book Symbolism of Freemasonry or Mystic Masonry and the Greater Mysteries of Antiquity in 1925. Referring to those who help the poor: "Reincarnation being true, these servants of humanity are laying by a store of good karma, which is literally, 'treasure in heaven', and which must inevitably secure for them still broader opportunities and greater power for good in another life; and best of all, they are unfolding the higher spiritual perceptions."

Another quote from the same author on Salvation and on Christ states: "Every soul must 'work out its own salvation' and 'take the Kingdom of Heaven by force'. Salvation by faith and the vicarious atonement were not taught, as now interpreted, by Jesus, nor are these doctrines taught in the exoteric Scriptures. They are later and ignorant perversions of the original doctrines. In the early Church, as in the Secret Doctrine, there was not one Christ for the whole world, but a potential Christ in every man. Theologians first made a fetish of the Impersonal, Omnipresent Divinity; and then tore the Christos from the hearts of all humanity in order to deify Jesus; that they might have a God-man peculiarly their own!" You will find similar thinking in the New Age movement.

Manly Hall, a 33rd degree Mason, in the 1976 edition of his book, The Lost Keys of Freemasonry, makes it plain that in Masonry's belief system Jesus Christ is not divine. He says, "The true disciple of ancient Masonry has given up forever the worship of personalities...". He explains: "As a Mason his religion must be universal: Christ, Buddha or Mohammed, the names mean little, for he recognizes only the light and not the bearer. He worships at every shrine, bows before every altar, whether in temple, mosque or cathedral, realizing with his truer understanding the oneness of all spiritual truth..." Hall says further, "No true Mason can be narrow, for his Lodge is the divine expression of all broadness. There is no place for little minds in a great work." This is his way of saying that all religions are alike. This attitude is one of religious indifference, not religious tolerance, as Pope Leo XIII pointed out over 100 years ago.

What about Freemasonry and Judaism? There are those who use the participation of some Jews in Freemasonry as an excuse to indulge in anti-Semitism. Judaism, like Christianity, believes in only one God, therefore on that basis alone, Judaism is incompatible with Freemasonry. Like Christians, Jews have seen elements and symbols of their faith used by Masonry for its own purposes. Masonry seeks to recover and revive the "wisdom" allegedly found in the ancient polytheistic religions of the East, whose adherents ruthlessly persecuted the Jews of old for worshipping the one True God. It is no mere coincidence, therefore, that the modern day pagan occultists of Nazism also persecuted the Jews.

Another aspect of Freemasonry is the connection between it and the worship of Lucifer. In a letter written to French Masons in 1889 on the occasion of the 100th anniversary of the French Revolution, Albert Pike wrote the following: "That which we must say to the crowd is -- We worship a God, but it is the God that one adores without superstition.

"To you, Sovereign Grand Inspectors General, we say this, that you may repeat it to the Brethren of the 32nd, 31st, and 30th degrees---The Masonic Religion should be, by all of us initiates of the higher degrees, maintained in the purity of the Luciferian Doctrine.

"If Lucifer were not God, would Adonay (The God of the Christians) whose deeds prove his cruelty, perfidy and hatred of man, barbarism, and repulsion for science, would Adonay and his priests calumniate him?

"Yes, Lucifer is God, and unfortunately Adonay is also God." Pike concludes with this statement, "...the true and pure philosophical religion is the belief in Lucifer, the equal of Adonay; but Lucifer, God of Light and God of Good is struggling for humanity against Adonay, the God of Darkness and Evil."

An interesting correlation with this is the experience of Cardinal Edouard Gagnon when he was the canonist for the late Cardinal Leger of Canada. In a 1991 interview he said, "I often had to lodge requests with the Apostolic Penitentiary in Rome for excommunication orders to be lifted in the cases of people who had stolen the Sacred Host on Masonry's orders. They had been well paid for the task and some regretted their action, asking the Church to pardon them." Then in response to the interviewer's remark that this was more typical of a satanic sect, Cardinal Gagnon said, "No, some forms of Masonry also celebrate black masses. The episode I have just related took place in Canada where Masonry is not believed to be anti-religious."

One final point; in the ritual for raising Masons to the Knights Kadosh 30th degree there is a platform on which rests three skulls, one of which is surmounted by a Pope's triple crown. Immediately after taking the first of four oaths the candidate, following the example and instruction of the Thrice Puissant Grand Master, stabs the skull crowned with the Pope's crown and cries out, "Down with imposture, down with crime."

It is important to realize that in the ritual of this degree the word "imposture" always refers to the Pope's role as Vicar of Christ! Later on in the ceremony the candidate is told, "This represents the Tiara of the cruel and cowardly Pontiff, who sacrificed to his ambition the illustrious order of those Knights Templar of whom we are the true successors. A crown of gold and precious stones ill befits the humble head of one who pretends to be successor, the Vicar, of Jesus of Nazareth. It is therefore the crown of an imposter, and it is in the name of him who said 'neither be ye called masters', that we trample it under our feet." Following this instruction the papal tiara is thrown to the floor and all present trample it under foot while shouting "Down with imposture!" The candidate having thus "discarded all stupid and vulgar prejudices" is knighted Kadosh by the Grand Master.

Is there any doubt, therefore, why Saint Maximilian wanted the conversion of the Freemasons so earnestly, and why he referred to Freemasonry as "the head of the serpent?" ❑

The Militia Immaculatae Movement in Kolbe's Own Words

The Militia Immaculatae, (M.I.) or sometimes (M.I.M.) Mission of the Immaculate Mediatrix,as written by St. Maximilian in the Original Charter:

"She shall crush your head" (Gen. 3, 15). "You alone (Mary) have crushed all heresies in the whole world" (Office of the B.V.M.).

I. Purpose of the Knights: Pursue the conversion of every person living in sin, heresy, schism, and especially Freemasonry; and the growth in holiness of all persons, under the protection of the B.V.M. Immaculate. (See Kolbe's *Total Consecration* on p. 247)

II. Conditions of Membership:

1. Make a voluntary and total consecration of oneself to the B.V.M. Immaculata as an instrument in her most holy hands.
2. Carry or wear the "Miraculous Medal."
3. Have one's name placed on the register of the Pious Union at the Primary Center or at some canonically erected Affiliated Center.

III. Means of the Apostolate :

1. Once a day if possible, pray to the Immaculata with the ejaculation : "O Mary, conceived without sin, pray for us who have recourse to you, and for all who do not have recourse to you especially for the Freemasons."
2. Use all the legitimate means that one's particular state in life, condition and varying opportunities make possible, the choice of which is left to the zeal and prudence of each member; and especially, propagate the "Miraculous Medal."

On the day one makes his/her Act of Total Consecration *to the Immaculata, it is expected that they use the official* Consecration *composed by St. Maximilian Kolbe as found on page 247.*

The Difference between Kolbean Consecration and De Montfort's

One of the most common questions of those familiar with St. Maximilian's form of total consecration and St. Louis De Montfort's consecration as found in his famous treatise True Devotion to Mary is, "What is the difference between the two?"

ACCORDING TO St. Maximilian himself, there is little difference between the two in the essential point, that is in the giving of oneself totally to the Blessed Mother. When St. Maximilian first came across De Montfort's work in the early twenties, he remarked that this was exactly what the Militia Immaculatae was all about. The two sainted mariologists both were maximists. They never felt that the last word and last honor had been given to the Mother of God and Mother of the Church. Though they lived two centuries apart from each other, they understood that to love Mary as she deserved to be honored and loved was nothing more than what she predicted in her Magnificat. "All generations shall call me blessed."

The following are some of the accidental differences:

St. De Montfort made much of giving over to Mary all the merits of one's good works and prayers to be used as Our Lady saw fit, while St. Maximilian intended by his consecration to not only give her the merits that one gains but to give one's very self to her, to be used as an instrument or tool in her hands for the salvation and sanctification of souls. The French Saint spoke of slavery to express the totality of one's consecration to Mary (see slavery concept in St. Paul in Philippians 2:7.). Besides being completely and ever available to Our Lady as an instrument, Kolbe also spoke of Knighthood and militancy which would indicate a more active role of the consecrant. However, there is no contradiction between a tool, moved only by Our Lady, and a Knight, which is far from passivity. Maximilian held that none of these titles by themselves adequately express all that total consecration means.

De Montfort's preparation for the act of total consecration is quite well worked out and extensive, amounting to 30 days preparation. Whereas, Kolbe would leave the preparation itself to the discretion and inspiration of the person wishing to consecrate himself according to his formula of consecration which he composed for the Militia Immaculatae (M.I.) in Rome in 1917 (see page 242). One could say that Saint Louis's consecration was more directed at a select few, whom the Holy Spirit would inspire to heroism similar to the heroic degree of the consecration in Kolbe's movement.

It would seem that both the times and the national characteristics had something to do with the way the two Marian Saints looked upon the preparation for the consecration. France in the 17th century was plagued by the heresy of Jansenism, which was an over rigorous interpretation of the justice of God at the expense of His mercy and love. Saint Louis never fell into the error of Jansen, of a vengeful God who was far from being a compassionate Father.

The Sacred Heart devotion was gaining popularity at the time, through the apparitions of the Sacred Heart to St. Margaret Mary. St. Louis De Montfort centered his devotion to Mary ultimately on the Heart of Jesus, and the establishing of His Reign of love through the Queen of All Hearts. Nonetheless 17th century France needed a more rigorous understanding of mariology and perhaps a more extensive preparation to avoid Jansenism.

The Polish people in Kolbe's day had a tender devotion to their Queen and Mother. St. Maximilian moreover had a special devotion to their National Madonna, Our Lady of Czestochowa. His mystical experience of the two crowns (see page 17) as a small boy also inclined him to love this tender, understanding mother who was the dispenser of God's mercy. As a result he opened up the consecration to anyone who would entrust himself to her maternal care, allowing her full freedom to take over one's spiritual life and deepen the consecration as time went on. Regardless of their different concepts leading up to consecration, both St. Louis and St. Maximilian agreed that the shortest, easiest and surest way to establishing the Kingship of the Sacred Heart was through Mary.

The mariology of St. Louis De Montfort zeroes in on Mary's maternal role in the plan of salvation by showing how she is ever mediating graces to her children as their spiritual Mother. His spirituality has its roots in the French school of total consecration to Mary of the previous century. As a Franciscan, St. Maximilian's spirituality is naturally based on the Franciscan school with its centuries-long defense and promotion of the truth of Mary's Immaculate Conception. The definition of Mary's Immaculate Conception in 1854 by Pope Bl. Pius IX, and Lourdes, 1858 where Mary identified herself as "the Immaculate Conception," had a profound influence on St. Maximilian's consecration and mariology. These events were not available to De Montfort in the 17th century.

Both made much of the action of the Holy Spirit in the sanctification of souls. Kolbe carried the identification of Mary as "Spouse of the Holy Spirit" by St. Francis of Assisi, to its logical conclusion, that she was the Mediatrix of all Graces. Maximilian, the mystic, explained through much prayer and suffering, the intimate relationship between the created Immaculate Conception (Mary) to the Uncreated Immaculate Conception (the Holy Spirit). These insights of the Franciscan are not to be understood as putting down De Montfort, but point out how these events and others in the 19th century made consecration to Mary that much more an imperative in the 20th century to win converts and make progress in the spiritual life.

Both saints were integral mariologists; theory was not sterile but was fruitful to an amazing degree. It was exemplified in their personal lives through the heroic practice of the theological virtues that ultimately led the Church to recognize their holiness by raising them to the altars. They had an impact on millions of souls who were evangelized and sanctified through their efforts, while they were alive, and even more so after their death.

Consider the influence the little book on True Devotion to Mary, by St. Louis De Montfort, had on a certain Polish young man, who devoured its contents thoroughly during the Second World War. It contributed greatly to his outstanding devotion to Mary and in no small measure to his desire to become a priest, which led to his consecration as a bishop and finally election as the

Bishop of Rome - we refer to Pope John Paul II. Think of the world-wide impact this Pope has had on society in so many ways - the influence he has had in furthering devotion to the Blessed Mother - the promotion of the De Montfort spiritual classic which has inspired many other souls to follow his example by making the act of total consecration to Mary.

The Legion of Mary, considered by many as the most fruitful international lay movement in the Church today, founded by Frank Duff in Dublin, Ireland in 1921, is spiritually based on True Devotion to Mary. According to the Legion Handbook, the total consecration which members are expected to make is the driving force behind its world-wide success in evangelization. As the name implies, it is both Marian and militant, requiring uncompromising commitment and much sacrifice. As the Legionaries are expected to follow the Handbook to the letter, there is not much room for private interpretation. Many regard this discipline of not allowing any tampering or private interpretation of the Handbook as one of the main reasons why Legion of Mary has held together so well and accomplished so much over the years in so many different nations and cultures.

On the other hand, the Militia Immaculatae which St. Maximilian Kolbe founded in Rome in 1917, as a movement, is not as structured as the Legion, nor is it easily attacked and suppressed, as was the case of the Legion of Mary in China in the fifties. How do you suppress a movement, or spiritual entity? Kolbe ever looked upon the M.I. as a Marian spirit looking for a "body" to give new life. Thus, this Marian spirit of the M.I., in Kolbe's mind, could give new life and vigor to any and all existing religious communities, societies and other entities within the Church. This does not mean that the Militia does not need organization or group action, as found in the Second degree of the M.I.

Kolbe had a great talent for organization and encouraged group activity among his first-degree consecrants. He left wide latitude concerning the purpose (working in pro-life, youth, pro-family, home schoolers, etc.) of the group. This allowed M.I. Circles greater freedom in writing up their statutes, which had to be approved by the central headquarters of the M.I. Periodically they had to give reports on their activities. In this looser structure, Kolbe followed the Franciscan spirit which tends to emphasize the spirit more than structure or organization, which at times can become an end in itself, and thus stifle the spirit.

The similar goal of the Legion of Mary and the Militia Immaculatae is brought out in the fact that both founders of these two Marian apostolates, Frank Duff and Maximilian Kolbe, ultimately focused their zeal for souls upon establishing the reign of the Sacred Heart of Jesus through Mary. In 1933 St. Maximilian summed up the fiery zeal generated by total consecration of the Militia Immaculatae, which also applies to the Legion as:

"We have to win the universe and each individual soul now and in the future, down to the end of time for the Immaculate, and by her for the Sacred Heart of Jesus." -BFM

Solemn Act of Consecration of St. Maximilian

O Immaculate, Queen of heaven and earth, Refuge of sinners and our most loving Mother, God has willed to entrust the entire order of mercy to You, I, an unworthy sinner, cast myself at Your feet, humbly imploring You to take me with all that I am and have, wholly to Yourself as Your possession and property. Please make of me, of all my powers of soul and body, of my whole life, death, and eternity, whatever pleases You. If it pleases You, use all that I am and have without reserve, wholly to accomplish what has been said of You: "She will crush your head", and "You alone have destroyed all heresies in the whole world." Let me be a fit instrument in Your immaculate and most merciful hands for introducing and increasing Your glory to the maximum in all the many strayed and indifferent souls, and thus help extend as far as possible the blessed Kingdom of the Most Sacred Heart of Jesus. For, wherever You enter, You obtain the grace of conversion and sanctification, since it is through Your hands that all graces come to us from the Most Sacred Heart of Jesus.

V. Allow me to praise You, O most holy Virgin.
R. Give me strength against Your enemies.

Our Contributors

In Order of Their Appearance in the Book

Fr. James McCurry, OFM Conv. The former National Director of the Knights of the Immaculate Movement, is one of the most knowledgeable authorities on Kolbean spirituality and his life. He is a member of the Mariological Society of America of which he served once as President. He is presently Superior and Novice Master at the Friary in Granby, MA.

Dr.Mark Miravalle, S.T.D. He graciously wrote the Preface of our book perhaps due to our mutual commitment to further the definition of Mary Mediatrix, Coredemptrix and Advocate. He is professor of mariology and theology at the Franciscan University of Steubenville. He is the founder and President of the Catholic movement Vox Populi Mariae Mediatrici.

Bro. Francis Mary Kalvelage, FI Editor and author of various chapters without a "by" line in the book. He has been a Franciscan Friar for over fifty years, practically all of which were at Marytown, (presently located in Mundelein, IL). He edited Immaculata magazine for over 25 years.

Fr. Peter Damian Fehlner, FI, S.T.D. Is the Regional Superior of the Franciscans of the Immaculate in North America, author, lecturer (for over forty years professor of dogmatic and Franciscan Theology), guest speaker. He gave a series on Mariology on Mother Angelica's EWTN network.

Joseph P. Czarnecki Author of the book Lost Traces: The Lost Art of Auschwitz, published by Macmillan Publishing Co. The chapter in this book titled Teddy, the Boxer's Encounter with a Saint was excerpted from the chapter "Heroes" from the original book by Czarnecki.

Fr. M. M. De Cruce, FI The newly ordained priest of the Franciscans of the Immaculate is a graduate of the University of Steubenville with a degree in theology. He is presently assigned as a translator in Italy, where he is continuing advanced studies.

Madeline Pecora Nugent, SFO A regular contributor to our books, Madeline is the author of several books of her own, the latest on St. Clare, is to be available soon through the Daughters of St. Paul. She is the Secretary of the International Catholic Association, the Brothers and Sisters of Penance.

Archbishop Vital Bommarco, OFM Conv. The former Minister General and Supreme Moderator of the Militia Immaculatae was very supportive of anything pertaining to total consecration and St. Maximilian. The former Archbishop of Gouzia in Italy, he is now retired.

Fr. George Domanski, OFM Conv. The former International Director of the Militia Immaculatae, superior of the City of the Immaculate in Poland and editor of the Knight in Polish is probably the most knowledgeable person alive today on anything pertaining to the MI and St. Maximilian.

Roy Schoeman is a Jew who found the Messiah and the Church through Christ's Mother Mary. A graduate of M.I.T. and of the Harvard Business School, where he also taught, he is a regular contributor to our books.

Helen M. Valois Writer and young Mother, is a graduate of the University of Steubenville. Helen has been involved in the pro-life apostolate for a number of years and at the same time has promoted St. Maximilian Kolbe as patron as the Pro-life movement.

Fr. John Grigus, OFM Conv. Retreat Master, lecturer and spiritual director, he has been a member of the Marytown community for four years, during that time he has reorganized and directed its Perpetual Adoration program.

Bro. Charles Madden, OFM Conv. Is the author of the book, Freemasonry, Mankind's Hidden Enemy, which gives a short incisive examination of Masonry, and of the current official Catholic stand against the cult. He is a member of the Franciscans at Marytown and writes regularly for *Immaculata*.

Academy of the Immaculate Books Instruct, Inspire, Evangelize for the New Millennium

All Generations Shall Call Me Blessed *by Stefano Manelli, F.I.* A scholarly, easy to read book tracing Mary's role in the Old Testament through prophecies, figures, and symbols to Mary's presence in the New Testament. A concise exposition which shows clearly Mary's place in the economy of Salvation. (List 19.95)

Totus Tuus *by Msgr. Arthur Burton Calkins* provides a thorough examination of the Holy Father's thoughts on total consecration or entrustment to Our Lady based on the historic, theological and scriptural evidence. Vital in clearing away some misunderstandings about entrustment and consecration. (List 14.95)

Jesus Our Eucharistic Love *by Fr. Stefano Manelli, F.I.* A treasure of Eucharistic devotional writings and examples from the Saints showing their stirring Eucharistic love and devotion. A valuable aid for reading meditatively before the Blessed Sacrament. (List 5.00)

Virgo Facta Ecclesia *by Franciscan Friars of the Immaculate* is made up of two parts: the first a biography on St. Francis of Assisi and the second part on the Marian character of the Franciscan Order based on its long Marian tradition, from St. Francis to St. Maximilian Kolbe. (List 5.00)

Not Made by Hands *by Thomas Sennott* An excellent resource book covering the two most controversial images in existence: the Holy Image of Our Lady of Guadalupe on the tilma of Juan Diego and the Sacred Image of the Crucified on the Shroud of Turin, giving scientific evidence for their authenticity and exposing the fraudulent carbon 14 test. (List 7.95)

For the Life of the World *by Jerzy Domanski, O.F.M. Conv.* The former international director of the Knights of the Immaculata and Guardian of the City of the Immaculate in Poland examines Fr. Kolbe's Eucharistic, spiritual life as a priest and adorer of the Eucharist, all in the context of his love of the Immaculate. (List 5.00)

Padre Pio of Pietrelcina *by Fr, Stefano Manelli, F.I.* This 144 page popular life of Padre Pio is packed with details about his life, spirituality, and charisms, by one who knew the Padre intimately.

The author turned to Padre Pio for guidance in establishing a new Community, the Franciscans of the Immaculate. (List 4.50)

Come Follow Me *by Fr. Stefano Manelli, F.I.* A book directed to any young person contemplating a Religious vocation. Informative, with many inspiring illustrations and words from the lives and writings of the Saints on the challenging vocation of total dedication in the following of Christ and His Immaculate Mother through the three vows of religion. (List 4.00)

Mary at the Foot of the Cross *Acts of the International Symposium on Mary, Coredemeer, Mediatrix and Advocate.* This over 400 page book on a week-long symposium held last year at Ratcliffe College in England, has a whole array of outstanding Mariologists from many parts of the world. To name a few: Bishop Paul Hnilica, Fr. Bertrand De Margerie, S.J., Dr. Mark Miravalle, Fr. Stefano Manelli, F.I., Fr. Aidan Nichols, O.P. , Msgr. Arthur Calkin, and Fr. Peter Fehlner, F.I. who was the moderator.

Do You Know Our Lady *by Rev. Mother Francesca Perillo, F.I.* This handy treatise (125 pages) covers the many rich references to Mary, as prefigured in the Old Testament women and prophecies and as found in the New Testament from the Annunciation to Pentecost. Mary's role is seen ever beside her Divine Son, and the author shows how scripture supports Mary's role as Mediatrix of all Graces. Though it can be read with profit by scripture scholars, it is an easy read for everyone. Every Marian devotee should have a copy for quick reference.

SAINTS AND MARIAN SHRINE SERIES

Edited by Bro. Francis Mary, F.I

A Handbook on Guadalupe This well researched book on Guadalupe contains 40 topical chapters by leading experts on Guadalupe with new insights and the latest scientific findings. A number of chapters deal with Our Lady's role as the patroness of the pro-life movement. Well illustrated (List 12.50)

St. Thérèse: Doctor of the Little Way A compendium of 32 chapters covering many unique facets about the latest Doctor of the Church by 23 authors including Fr. John Hardon, SJ, Msgr. Vernon Johnson, Sister Marie of the Trinity, OCD, Stephanè Piat. This different approach to St. Thérèse is well illustrated. (List 12.50)

Marian Shrines of France The four major Marian shrines and apparitions of France during the 19th century: Our Lady at Rue du Bac, Paris (Miraculous Medal), La Salette, Lourdes and Pontmain shows how in the 19th century — Our Lady was checkmating our secular, Godless 20th century, introducing the present Age of Mary. Well illustrated with many color pictures. (List 12.50)

Padre Pio - The Wonder Worker The latest on this popular saint of our times including the two inspirational homilies given by Pope John Paul II during the beatification celebration in Rome. The first part of the book is a short biography. The second is on his spirituality, charisms, apostolate of the confessional, and his great works of charity. (List 12.50)

Marian Shrines of Italy Another in the series of "Marian Saints and Shrines," with 36 pages of colorful illustrations on over thirty of the 1500 Marian shrines in Italy. The book covers that topic with an underlying theme of the intimate and vital relationship between Mary and the Church. This is especially apparent in Catholic Italy, where the center of the Catholic Faith is found. (List 13.50)

Special rates are available with 10% to 50% discount depending on the number of books, plus postage. For ordering books and further information on rates to book stores, schools and parishes: Academy of the Immaculate, POB 667, Valatie NY, 12184, phone/FAX (518) 758-1594. E-mail Mimike@pipeline.com. Quotations on bulk rates shipped directly by the box from the printery, contact: Friars of the Immaculate, P.O. Box 3003, New Bedford, MA 02741, (508) 984-1856, FAX (508) 996-8296, E-mail: ffi@marymediatrix.com.

Further information on St. Maximilian Kolbe, and his Marian Movement may be obtained at the following addresses:

The National Ctr. of the MI
Conventual Franciscans (Marytown)
1600 West Park Ave.
Libertyville, IL 60049

Franciscans of the Immaculate
Our Lady's Chapel
600 Pleasant Street/POB 3003
New Bedford, MA 02741

Fr. Kolbe Missionaries of the Immaculata
531 E. Merced Ave.
West Covina, CA 91790

Sisters Minor of Mary Immaculate
15 Eld Street,
New Haven, CT 06511.

Communities founded upon the ideals and the life of St. Maximilian Kolbe see page 185.

Printed by Park Press, Inc. Waite Park, MN 56387